Lecture Notes in Computer Science   8535

Commenced Publication in 1973
Founding and Former Series Editors:
Gerhard Goos, Juris Hartmanis, and Jan van Leeuwen

FoLLI Publications on Logic, Language and Information

Subline of Lectures Notes in Computer Science

Subline Editors-in-Chief

Valentin Goranko, *Technical University, Lynbgy, Denmark*
Michael Moortgat, *Utrecht University, The Netherlands*

Subline Area Editors

Nick Bezhanishvili, *University of Amsterdam, The Netherlands*
Anuj Dawar, *University of Cambridge, UK*
Philippe de Groote, *Inria-Lorraine, Nancy, France*
Gerhard Jäger, *University of Tübingen, Germany*
Fenrong Liu, *Tsinghua University, Beijing, China*
Eric Pacuit, *University of Maryland, USA*
Ruy de Queiroz, *Universidade Federal de Pernambuco, Brazil*
Ram Ramanujam, *Institute of Mathematical Sciences, Chennai, India*

Nicholas Asher   Sergei Soloviev (Eds.)

Logical Aspects of Computational Linguistics

8th International Conference, LACL 2014
Toulouse, France, June 18-20, 2014
Proceedings

Volume Editors

Nicholas Asher
Sergei Soloviev
IRIT
118 route de Narbonne
31062 Toulouse, France
E-mail:{asher, soloviev}@irit.fr

ISSN 0302-9743   e-ISSN 1611-3349
ISBN 978-3-662-43741-4   e-ISBN 978-3-662-43742-1
DOI 10.1007/978-3-662-43742-1
Springer Heidelberg New York Dordrecht London

Library of Congress Control Number: 2014940056

LNCS Sublibrary: SL 1 – Theoretical Computer Science and General Issues

Typesetting: Camera-ready by author, data conversion by Scientific Publishing Services, Chennai, India

Printed on acid-free paper

Springer is part of Springer Science+Business Media (www.springer.com)

Preface

We are pleased to provide the proceedings of the 8th International conference on Logical Aspects of Computational Linguistics, LACL, which was held in Toulouse, France, from June 18 to June 20, 2014. LACL aims to be a forum for the exchange of ideas involving all aspects of formal logic within computational linguistics, from syntactic parsing to formal semantics to discourse interpretation. This year papers dealt mainly with syntactic and semantic themes.

We had 26 submissions from which we accepted 13 high quality papers for oral presentation. Each paper received three reviews (sometimes more) provided by the Program Committee consisting of 29 colleagues listed below.

LACL 2014 included three invited talks by: Zhaohui Luo (Royal Holloway, University of London), Michael Moortgat (Universiteit Utrecht, UiL OTS), and Reinhard Muskens (Tilburg University).

We would like to thank all those who submitted papers for consideration at LACL, the three invited speakers and all conference participants. We want to thank our international team of reviewers, who often gave extensive comments to authors. We hope very much that these comments will be of use to those who submitted papers in their future research.

We are also grateful to our institutional sponsors and supporters: the Association for Logic, Language and Information (FoLLI), CNRS, IRIT, INP and Université Paul Sabatier de Toulouse.

We would also like to express our gratitude to the Organizing Committee and all the people whose efforts made this meeting possible.

April 2014   Nicholas Asher
                                                                Sergei Soloviev

Organization

Organizing Committee

Nicholas Asher	IRIT/CNRS, France (Co-chair)
Denis Béchet	LINA/CNRS, France
Joseph Boudou	IRIT, Toulouse
Sylvain Pogodalla	LORIA/Inria, France
Jean-Philippe Prost	LIRMM/CNRS, University of Montpellier, France
Sergei Soloviev	IRIT/Paul Sabatier University, France (Co-chair)

Program Committee

Nicholas Asher	IRIT/CNRS, France (Co-chair)
Chris Barker	NYU, USA
Denis Béchet	LINA/CNRS, France
Raffaella Bernardi	University of Trento, Italy
Wojciech Buszkowski	Poznan University, Poland
Philippe de Groote	LORIA/Inria, France
Markus Egg	Humboldt Universität Berlin, Germany
Nissim Francez	Tehchnion, Israel
Mohan Ganesalingam	University of Cambridge, UK
Makoto Kanazawa	NII, Japan
Greg Kobele	University of Chicago, USA
Marcus Kracht	University of Bielefeld, Germany
Hans Leiss	Universität München, Germany
Zhaohui Luo	Royal Holloway University of London, UK
Uwe Mönnich	Universität Tübingen, Germany
Michael Moortgat	Universiteit Utrecht, UiL OTS, The Netherlands
Richard Moot	LaBRI/CNRS, France
Glyn Morrill	Universitat Politècnica de Catalunya, Spain
Reinhard Muskens	Tilburg University, The Netherlands
Sylvain Pogodalla	LORIA/Inria, France
Carl Pollard	The Ohio State University, USA
Jean-Philippe Prost	LIRMM/CNRS, University of Montpellier, France

Christian Retoré	LaBRI/CNRS, France
Sylvain Salvati	Inria, France
Matthew Stone	Rutgers, USA
Sergei Soloviev	IRIT, France (Co-chair)
Edward Stabler	University of California at Los Angeles, USA
Mark Steedman	University of Edinburgh, UK
Isabelle Tellier	Université Paris 3, France

Abstracts of Invited Talks

Formal Semantics in Modern Type Theories: Is It Model-Theoretic, Proof-Theoretic, or Both?

Zhaohui Luo

Royal Holloway, University of London

Abstract. In this talk, we contend that, for NLs, the divide between model-theoretic semantics and proof-theoretic semantics has not been well-understood. In particular, the formal semantics based on modern type theories (MTTs) may be seen as both model-theoretic and proof-theoretic. To be more precise, it may be seen both ways in the sense that the NL semantics can first be represented in an MTT in a model-theoretic way and then the semantic representations can be understood inferentially in a proof-theoretic way. Considered in this way, MTTs arguably have unique advantages when employed for formal semantics.

Continuations and Derivational Ambiguity

Michael Moortgat

Universiteit Utrecht, UiL OTS

In categorial grammar, compositional interpretation is implemented along the lines of Montague's 'Universal Grammar' program, taking the form of a structure-preserving mapping (a homomorphism) relating a source logic to a target logic. The homomorphism requirement implies that for an expression to be associated with multiple 'readings', there must be derivational ambiguity at the source end of the compositional mapping.

In this talk, I study the kind of derivational ambiguity that arises in some recent continuation-based categorial approaches. In Bastenhof (2013) and Moortgat and Moot (2013), the source derivations for compositional interpretation are focused proofs of a polarized sequent calculus or its graphical alternative; different notions of derivational ambiguity result from the choices one can make in fixing the polarity of atomic formulas. I compare this approach to the handling of continuations in terms of the combinatory and multimodal sequent calculi one finds in Barker and Shan (2014).

References

[1] Barker, C., Shan, C.-C.: Continuations and Natural Language. Oxford Studies in Theoretical Linguistics, vol. 53. Oxford University Press (2014)
[2] Bastenhof, A.: Categorial Symmetry. PhD thesis, Utrecht University (2013)
[3] Moortgat, M., Moot, R.: Proof nets for the Lambek-Grishin calculus. In: Heunen, C., Sadrzadeh, M., Grefenstette, E. (eds.) Quantum Physics and Linguistics, pp. 283–320. Oxford University Press (2013)

Combining Frame Semantics and Phrasal Semantics: A Proposal

Reinhard Muskens

Tilburg University

Abstract. Frame theory in the sense of Barsalou and others has very interesting things to say about various cognitive functions such as perception, categorisation, proprioception, and introspection. In fact, frames are supposed to implement, in Barsalou's words, 'a fully functional conceptual system'. Applying the theory to word meaning, as Löbner, Petersen & Osswald, and others have done, is highly attractive, as this results in a form of lexical semantics that is well embedded in a more general theory of cognitive functions. But while frames in general can convincingly represent content words and even certain simple sentences, it is, pace Barsalou, much less clear that they can also deal with logical notions, such as negation, disjunction and (generalised) quantification. In this talk I will therefore propose a two-level system, in which a base component of meaning given by frames is extended with a phrasal semantics in Montague's way. I will borrow certain insights from Frank Veltman's Data Semantics and will let incompatibility of frames be a central notion, more central in fact than negation, which will be explained in its terms. Frames will play a double role, as carriers of lexical meaning, but also as standing proxy for possible worlds or situations. Since frames offer a lot more structure than is usually provided for in phrasal semantics, more operations become available to the compositional system and we shall consider some of these.

Table of Contents

Regular Articles

Invited Speaker

Building PMCFG Parsers as Datalog Program Transformations

Arthur Ball, Pierre Bourreau[2], Émeric Kien, and Sylvain Salvati[1]

[1] INRIA-LaBRI - 351, Cours de la Libration - 33405 Talence Cedex (France)
salvati@labri.fr
[2] CNRS - Lattice - UMR8094 - 1, rue Maurice Arnoux - 92120 Montrouge (France)
pierre.bourreau@gmail.com

Abstract. Kanazawa [6,7] proposes to view recognition algorithms for Multiple Context-Free Grammars (MCFGs) as Datalog program transformations. He illustrates this view by transforming a Datalog program implementing CYK recognizers for MCFGs into programs that implement prefix-correct recognizers for MCFGs. We enhance his results in three different directions: (i) we present an extension of Datalog so as to build parsers instead of recognizers; (ii) we adapt his program transformations to extended Datalog programs that construct prefix-correct parsers for Parallel Multiple Context-Free Grammars (PMCFGs); (iii) we propose another program transformation for extended Datalog programs that produces left-corner parsers for PMCFGs.

1 Introduction

Multiple Context-Free Grammars (MCFGs) [16] are extensions of Context-Free Grammars (CFGs) that derive tuple of strings. They were introduced so as to overcome the limitation of CFGs in modeling natural language [17]. Parallel MCFGs (PMCFGs) enrich MCFGs with a copying power that turns out to be useful when modeling copying phenomena that do not fall into the scope of MCFGs such as in Old Georgian [13], or Yoruba [9]. Moreover, PMCFGs encompass a fragment of the Grammatical Framework [10].

In the tradition of using logic programming to parsing [3,15], Kanazawa [6,7] proposes a very elegant construction of prefix-correct recognizers for MCFGs based on Datalog program transformations. His transformation is an adaptation of the now well-established magic set rewriting program transformation [19]. In this respect, the work of Kanazawa can be seen as a concrete application of parsing schemata transformation [18] adapted to MCFGs.

The aim of this paper is to show that Kanazawa's approach brings a fresh and powerful look to parsing in general. For this we first propose a rather simple extension of Datalog that allows programs to produce a parse forest while recognizing an input. This allows us to extend the scope of Kanazawa's method from recognition to parsing. Afterwards, we propose two methods for compiling PMCFGs to extended Datalog programs. We then adapt Kanazawa's program transformation so as to obtain programs that perform prefix-correct parsing

N. Asher and S. Soloviev (Eds.): LACL 2014, LNCS 8535, pp. 1–13, 2014.
© Springer-Verlag Berlin Heidelberg 2014

of PMCFGs. Finally, we give another transformation that produces programs that perform left-corner parsing. A prefix-correct parsing algorithm for PM-CFGs has been proposed by Angelov [1], while a left-corner algorithm has been proposed by Ljunglöf [12]. Here, our construction allows one to combine both prefix-correctness and left-corner optimization.

The paper is structured as follows. Section 2 introduces standard algebraic notions and PMCFGs; it also gives a succinct presentation of Kanazawa's work on MCFG recognizers. Section 3 introduces an extended version of Datalog which we use to adapt Kanazawa's recognizers into parsers. Section 4 is dedicated to show how to deal with string copies so that Kanazawa's technique can be extended to PMCFGs; this leads to the construction of a CYK-like parser. In section 5, we give a transformation based on magic set rewriting that constructs a prefix-correct parser for PMCFGs. Finally, we give a program transformation that constructs left-corner parser in section 6.

2   Datalog Recognizers for MCFGs

2.1   Preliminaries

We take for granted the usual notions of alphabet, words on a given alphabet, length $|w|$ of a word w and number of occurrences of a letter a in a word w (written $|w|_a$).

We recall the definition of a multi-sorted alphabet $\mathcal{T}$ as a tuple (T, S, ρ) where T is a finite set of letters, S a finite set of sorts, and $\rho : T \to S^+$ is the sorting function. The sets $(\mathcal{T}_s)_{s \in S}$ of terms of a given sort are the smallest sets so that if r is in T, $\rho(r) = s_1 \ldots s_n s$ and $t_1, \ldots, t_n$ are respectively in $\mathcal{T}_{s_1}, \ldots, \mathcal{T}_{s_n}$, then $r(t_1, \ldots, t_n)$ is in $\mathcal{T}_s$. A ranked alphabet is a multi-sorted alphabet whose set of sorts is a singleton $\{\omega\}$. We write $\mathcal{T}^{(n)} = \{r \in T \mid \rho(r) = \omega^{n+1}\}$ the set of symbols of rank n. As it is usual, for a given set of sorted variables $\mathcal{X}$, we write $\mathcal{T}(\mathcal{X})$ for the set of tree contexts defined on the multi-sorted alphabet $\mathcal{T}$. A substitution σ is a mapping from $\mathcal{X}$ to the term built on $\mathcal{T}$ that respects sorts. We write $t \cdot \sigma$ for the term resulting from substituting every variable x in t with $\sigma(x)$.

2.2   MCFGs and PMCFGs

PMCFGs were introduced in [16] as a grammatical formalism which can be informally defined as context-free grammars of tuples of strings with copy and deletion. Formally, a PMCFG is a tuple $G = (\Sigma, \Omega, S, P)$ where Σ is the alphabet of *terminals*, Ω is the ranked alphabet of *non-terminals*, $S \in \Omega^{(1)}$, and P is a finite set of rules of the form:

$$A_0(w_1, \ldots, w_{p_0}) \leftarrow A_1(y_{1,1}, \ldots, y_{1,p_1}), \ldots, A_m(y_{m,1}, \ldots, y_{m,p_m}) \tag{1}$$

where:

- A_i is in $\Omega^{(p_i)}$, for every $0 \leq i \leq m$;

- for every $1 \leq i \leq p_0$, w_i belongs to $(\Sigma \cup \{y_{i,j} \mid 1 \leq i \leq m \wedge 1 \leq j \leq p_i\})^*$;
- and the variables $y_{i,j}$ $(1 \leq i \leq m, 1 \leq j \leq p_i)$ are pairwise distinct.

If for every $1 \leq i \leq m$, and every $1 \leq j \leq p_i$, $y_{i,j}$ has exactly one occurrence in $w_1 \ldots w_{p_0}$, G is called a multiple context-free grammar (MCFG).

Given $A_0 \in \Omega$, $\mathcal{L}(G, A_0)$ is the set of tuples of strings generated from A_0 in G and defined as the smallest set such that if there is a rule such as (1) in P, and if $(w_{1,1}, \ldots, w_{1,p_1})$, ..., $(w_{m,1}, \ldots, x_{m,p_m})$ are respectively in $\mathcal{L}(G, A_1)$, ..., $\mathcal{L}(G, A_m)$, then $(w'_1, \ldots, w'_n)$ is in $\mathcal{L}(G, A_0)$, where w'_k results from substituting w_{ij} for y_{ij} (for $1 \leq i \leq m$ and $1 \leq j \leq p_i$) in w_k, for every $1 \leq k \leq p_0$. The language $\mathcal{L}(G)$ generated by G is $\mathcal{L}(G, S)$.

When a tuple $(w_1, \ldots, w_n)$ is in $\mathcal{L}(G, A)$, we witness its membership with successive applications of rules of G presented as a tree structure. Such witnesses are named *rule trees* and are similar to the usual *derivation trees* used in the context of Context-Free Grammars. A rule tree can be seen as the term of a multi-sorted alphabet whose sorts are the non-terminals of the grammar, and a rule like (1) is seen as a symbol of sort $A_1 \ldots A_m A_0$.

Example 1. Consider $G = (\Sigma, \Omega, S, P)$ with $\Sigma = \{a\}$, $A \in \Omega^{(2)}$, and P, the set made of the following rules:

$$\mathbf{r_0} \qquad S(x_1 x_2) \leftarrow A(x_1, x_2)$$
$$\mathbf{r_1} \qquad A(\epsilon, \epsilon)$$
$$\mathbf{r_2} \quad A(x_1 x_2 x_2 a, x_2 a) \leftarrow A(x_1, x_2)$$

It is easy to see that $\mathcal{L}(G, A) = \{(a^{n^2}, a^n) \mid n \in \mathbb{N}\}$ and thus $\mathcal{L}(G) = \{a^{n(n+1)} \mid n \in \mathbb{N}\}$. The string a^6 belongs to $\mathcal{L}(G)$ and a rule tree deriving it is $\mathbf{r_0}(\mathbf{r_2}(\mathbf{r_2}(\mathbf{r_1})))$.

A rule $\mathbf{r}$ as (1) is said *non-deleting* when, for every $1 \leq i \leq m$ and every $1 \leq j \leq p_i$, there exists $1 \leq k \leq p_0$ such that $|w_k|_{y_{i,j}} > 0$. A grammar is said *non-deleting* if all its rules are non-deleting.

Given a word w, and a symbol a such that $|w|_a \neq 0$, we define *the prefix of the first occurrence of a in w* as $lp(a, w) = w'$ when, for some w'', $w = w' a w''$ and $|w'|_a = 0$.

Definition 1. *Let $G = (\Sigma, \Omega, S, P)$ and let $\mathbf{r}$ be a rule of P as in (1). We define the partial order relation $<_{\mathbf{r}}$ on the symbols that occur in the right-hand side of $\mathbf{r}$, as $y_{i,j} <_{\mathbf{r}} y_{i,k}$ iff $|w_1 \ldots w_{p_0}|_{y_{i,j}} \neq 0$ and $|w_1 \ldots w_{p_0}|_{y_{i,k}} \neq 0$, and $|lp(y_{i,j}, w_1 \ldots w_{p_0})| < |lp(y_{i,k}, w_1 \ldots w_{p_0})|$ where $1 \leq i \leq m$ and $1 \leq j, k \leq p_i$.*

A rule $\mathbf{r}$ is said ordered if for all $1 \leq i \leq m$ and all $1 \leq j, k \leq p_i$, we have $y_{i,j} <_{\mathbf{r}} y_{i,k}$ implies $j < k$. A PMCFG is said ordered if all its rules are ordered; it is in normal form if ordered and non-deleting.

The grammar in Example 1 is in normal form. In the rest of the article, we assume that PMCFGs are in normal form (a standard procedure transforms a PMCFG into a weakly equivalent one in normal form that may be exponentially larger).

2.3 Parsing MCFGs with Datalog

A Datalog program is a logic program, where only atoms are used (while Prolog allows the use of compound terms). Such a program is made of rules of the form:

$$A_0(X_0) :- A_1(X_1), \ldots, A_p(X_p),$$

where, $A_0, A_1, \ldots, A_p$ are predicates; for $0 \leq i \leq p$, X_i is a list of variables and atoms $x_{i1}, \ldots, x_{in_i}$ (n_i being the arity of A_i); moreover, for $1 \leq j \leq n_0$, if x_{0j} is a variable, it must appear in the right-hand side of the rule (this is known as the *safety condition*). If $p = 0$, the rule is called extensional (and is part of the extensional database Edb); otherwise it is called intentional (and is part of the intentional database Idb). An Edb is a finite set of extensional rules and an Idb is a finite set of intentional rules.

Kanazawa [6] proposes a method for building CYK-like recognizers of MCFGs as Datalog programs. This method is based on the analogy between intentional Datalog rules and grammatical production rules. In order to apply this correspondence, one first transforms strings as ranges, in a similar fashion to RCGs [2]:

$$
\begin{array}{ccccc}
a_1 & a_2 & \ldots & & a_n \\
i_0 & i_1 & i_2 & i_{n-1} & i_n
\end{array}
$$

Any occurrence of a substring $a_k \ldots a_m$ in $a_1 \ldots a_n$ can now be uniquely identified by its corresponding range (i_{k-1}, i_m). As an example, consider an MCFG G defined by the production rules: $S(a, b, c)$ and $S(x_1 a, x_2 b, x_3 c) \leftarrow S(x_1, x_2, x_3)$. Then G is associated with the following intentional database $\mathtt{Idb}(G)$:

$$\mathtt{S}(i_0, i_2, j_0, j_2, k_0, k_2) :- \mathtt{S}(i_0, i_1, j_0, j_1, k_0, k_1), \mathtt{a}(i_1, i_2), \mathtt{b}(j_1, j_2), \mathtt{c}(k_1, k_2)$$
$$\mathtt{S}(i_0, i_1, j_0, j_1, k_0, k_1) :- \mathtt{a}(i_0, i_1), \mathtt{b}(j_0, j_1), \mathtt{c}(k_0, k_1)$$

The word for which we wish to test whether it is generated by the grammar serves as a basis to construct the extensional database. For instance, the word $w = abc$ would lead to the extensional database $\mathtt{Edb}(w)$ made of $\mathtt{a}(0, 1), \mathtt{b}(1, 2)$ and $\mathtt{c}(2, 3)$. The program made of $\mathtt{Idb}(G)$ and $\mathtt{Edb}(w)$ can derive the query $?- \mathtt{S}(0, 3)$ iff w is in $\mathcal{L}(G)$. Moreover, the seminaive bottom-up evaluation of the program implements a CYK-like algorithm for MCFGs.

In [7], a simple variation of the magic-set rewriting transformation [19] is proposed, and it is shown to elegantly lead to a prefix-correct algorithm for MCFGs that is arguably a generalization of Earley's algorithm [5] for CFGs to MCFGs (see section 5.2 for details).

3 Extended Datalog and Parsers

A parser differs from a recognizer in that it returns the parse forest, *i.e.* a finite representation of the set of derivation trees (in our case, rule trees) that derive the input word. So as to extend Kanazawa's method to parsing, we propose an extension of Datalog that uses terms in a restricted manner.

3.1 Compound Terms in Datalog

In our extension of Datalog, there are two kinds of objects (called atoms and terms) and predicates' arguments may be of the two kinds. As a convention we always write predicates as $A(X; T)$ where X denotes the usual Datalog atoms and T denotes the terms arguments of A which are built on a multi-sorted alphabet $\mathcal{T}$. We also fix a multi-sorted set of term variables $\mathcal{X}$. A rule $\mathbf{r}$ is now of the form:

$$A_0(X; T) :- A_1(X_1; T_1), \dots, A_n(X_n; T_n) \quad \text{where} \tag{2}$$

- $A_0(X) :- A_1(X_1), \dots, A_n(X_n)$ is a Datalog rule,
- each T_i is a sequence of elements of sorted variables of $\mathcal{X}$ each of which has a unique occurrence in $T_1, \dots, T_n$,
- T_0 is a sequence of terms in $\mathcal{T}(\mathcal{X})$ whose variables occur in some T_i for $1 \leq i \leq n$.

The distinction between extensional database and intentional database is as in Datalog. Given an extended Datalog program, the set of facts it derives is the smallest set such that, if the program contains a rule such as (2) (where $X_i = x_{i1}, \dots, x_{ip_i}$ and $T_i = y_{i1}, \dots, y_{im_i}$, for every $1 \leq i \leq n$; and $X = x_1 \dots x_p$ and $T = t_1, \dots, t_m$), and if

$$A_1(a_{11}, \dots, a_{1p_1}; t_{11}, \dots, t_{1m_1}), \dots, A_n(a_{n1}, \dots, a_{np_n}; t_{n1}, \dots, t_{nm_n})$$

are derivable facts, then $A(x_1 \cdot \sigma, \dots, x_m \cdot \sigma; t_1.\sigma', \cdot, t_m \cdot \sigma')$ is a derivable fact, for σ (*resp.* σ') the substitution mapping x_{ij} (*resp.* y_{ij}) to a_{ij} (*resp.* to $t_{i,j}$).

Given an extended Datalog program, a *query* is written

$$?- A(e_1, \dots, e_n; y_1, \dots, y_m),$$

where the e_i's are either Datalog variables or atoms of the *Edb*, the y_j's are elements of $\mathcal{X}$ and A is a predicate. The solutions of such a query are all the pairs of substitutions (σ, σ') so that $A(e_1 \cdot \sigma, \dots, e_n \cdot \sigma; x_1 \cdot \sigma', \dots, x_m \cdot \sigma')$ is a derivable fact. Notice that there may be infinitely many substitutions σ' that may be part of a solution to a query.

Continuing the analogy with PMCFGs, we use *rule trees* of extended Datalog programs to witness derivable facts. These trees can be seen as terms of a multi-sorted alphabet $\mathcal{P} = (A_P, S_P, \tau_P)$ where S_P is the set of intentional and extensional predicates, A_P the set of extensional and intentional rules, and a rule like (2) is of sort $A_1 \dots A_m A$.

3.2 PTIME Query Resolution for Extended Datalog Programs

We give a sketch of the proof that, despite the fact that queries to an extended Datalog program may have infinitely many solutions, it is computed in polynomial time. To do so, we need to represent in a finite manner all the possible solutions. For this we associate to an extended Datalog program P, a Datalog program P' that is obtained by removing the term components from the predicates: rules like (2) become $A(X) :- A_1(X_1), \ldots, A_n(X_n)$; rules $A(X;T)$ in the Edb become $A(X)$; and queries are transformed into $?- A(X)$. Since in the right-hand part of the intentional rules of an extended Datalog program the variables of terms occur at most once, the rule trees of P and P' are isomorphic. Now the rule trees solving a query in Datalog may be represented as a finite state tree automaton: indeed, the naive and the seminaive bottom-up evaluation algorithms consist in computing the fixpoint of derivable facts inductively. So each time a rule is applied, it uses derivable facts in its premise and outputs a possibly new derivable fact. Thus by taking facts as states of a tree automaton, each time we use a rule $\mathbf{r}$ to derive a fact $A(C)$ from the facts $A_1(C_1), \ldots, A_n(C_n)$, we may add a transition rule $\mathbf{r} : (A_1(C_1), \ldots, A_n(C_n)) \rightarrow A(C)$ to the automaton. In the case of the seminaive algorithm if $A(C)$ is a new fact, it is added to the agenda. Once the fixpoint is reached, each rule tree that is accepted by a state $A(C)$ is a rule tree representing a derivation of the fact $A(C)$. Thus, the rule trees that are solution of the query are those which are accepted by the automaton with accepting states $A(C)$. Therefore when solving a query for P' and storing the tree automaton during the naive or seminaive evaluation allows us to obtain a finite representation of the rule trees solving the query on P in polynomial time.

Moreover, consider the rule tree $\mathbf{t} = \mathbf{r}(\mathbf{t_1}, \ldots, \mathbf{t_n})$ that witnesses the derivability of the fact $A(X \cdot \sigma; T \cdot \sigma')$, where $\mathbf{r} : A(X;T) :- A_1(X_1;T_1), \ldots, A_n(X_n;T_n)$. The list of compound terms $T \cdot \sigma'$ can be recovered from $\mathbf{t}$ with a simple homomorphism $\mathcal{H}$ from terms to tuples of terms; the construction of $\mathcal{H}$ is straightforward from the shape of the rules. For instance, consider an extended rule $A(x; s(y_1, y_3), t(y_2)) :- A_1(x; y_1), A_2(x; y_2, y_3)$, and the following rule tree $\mathbf{r}(\mathbf{r_1}, \mathbf{r_2})$, then $\mathcal{H}(\mathbf{r}(\mathbf{r_1}, \mathbf{r_2})) = (s(\mathcal{H}(\mathbf{r_1}), \mathcal{H}_2(\mathbf{r_2})), t(\mathcal{H}_1(\mathbf{r_2})))$, where $\mathcal{H}_i(\mathbf{r_2})$ denotes the ith component in the tuple of terms $\mathcal{H}(\mathbf{r_2})$. Moreover, as regularity is preserved by inverse homomorphism, extractions of parse trees that have certain regular properties can be done at the level of the rule trees of the program.

4   A Bottom-up PMCFG Parser

Similarly to [6], we transform a PMCFG into an Idb and the string to parse into an Edb. Nevertheless, our transformation needs to take care of two points. First, we build parsers, and we use the compound terms of extended Datalog to compute the parse trees; second, we deal with copies of strings. We present two different methods to construct an extended Datalog program from a PMCFG.

4.1   Surface Equality

The first is rather straightforward and similar to the one proposed in [11]. We define string equality as a 4-ary predicate $eq(i, j, k, l)$, whose associated rules are[1]:

1. $eq(i, j, k, l) :- i = j, k = l$ and,
2. $eq(i, k, l, n) :- i \neq k, a(i, j), a(l, m), eq(j, k, m, n)$, for each letter a in the alphabet of the grammar.

---

[1] We assume that there are built-in predicates $=$ and $\neq$ for testing equality on the domain of the extensional database.

The first rule is testing the equality of occurrences of the empty strings. The rules of the second form are testing the equality of occurrences of strings that start with the same letter a. In those rules, we add the premise $i \neq k$ as an optimization of the evaluation of equalities: the program will not try to use rules of the second kind when it should use the first rule.

The transformation of a PMCFG rule into a Datalog rule is then performed similarly to MCFGs but using the predicate eq to check string equality. As an example, the Idb corresponding to the PMCFG in Example 1 is as follows:

$$S(i,k;r_0(u)) :- A(i,j,j,k;u) \qquad\qquad eq(i,j,k,l) :- i = j, k = l$$
$$A(i,j,k,l;r_1) :- i = j, k = l \qquad\qquad eq(i,k,l,n) :- i \neq k, a(i,j), a(l,m), eq(j,k,m,n)$$
$$A(i,m,n,p;r_2(u)) :- A(i,j,j,k;u), eq(j,k,k,l), a(l,m), eq(j,k,n,o), a(o,p)$$

4.2 Structural Equality

Consider the PMCFG rule $r_2 : A(x_1 x_2 x_2 a, x_2 a) \leftarrow A(x_1, x_2)$. Another way of implementing this rule in Datalog consists in verifying that there is a derivation of the non-terminal A whose second component spans the ranges of each occurrence of x_2 in the left-hand side of the rule. This would in particular imply that those ranges represent the same strings. To do so, we introduce the 4-ary predicate [2] eq_A_2 such that eq_A_2(i,j,k,l) is derivable iff there is a derivation of $A(x, y)$ in G such that y spans the ranges from i to j, and from k to l. The intentional Datalog rules defining that predicate are obtained using each rule of the PMCFG deriving A. For example the rule r_2 itself induces the Datalog rule:
eq_A_2$(i,k,l,n) :-$ eq_A_2$(i,j,l,m), a(j,k), a(n,m)$.

The conditions on the rule come from the fact that the second component of tuples derived by A in G within r_2 are the concatenation of a string x_2 derived as the second component of A and the letter a. Now, in the intentional rules obtained from the grammar, the predicate eq_A_2 may replace the predicate eq whenever eq tests for the equality of segments covered by a string derived as the second component of A (and similarly for other predicates eq_A_k). The complete definition of the predicate eq_A_2 is given by the rules:

1. eq_A_2$(i,k,l,n) :-$ eq_A_2$(i,j,l,m), a(j,k), a(n,m)$ and
2. eq_A_2$(i,j,k,l) :- i = j, k = l$.

4.3 Discussion

These two methods compile a PMCFG G into an extended intentional database $Idb(G)$ containing rules for production rules of G, and rules for defining equality. Given a word $w = a_1 \ldots a_n$ built on the alphabet of G, we can produce an extensional database $Edb(w)$ in the same way as in [6].

We write $P_{G,w}$ the extended Datalog program made of $Idb(G)$ and $Edb(w)$. If S is the starting symbol of G, then t is a rule tree witnessing that w is in

---

[2] More generally, we introduce for each non-terminal A and each of its kth argument, a 4-ary predicate eq_A_k. Of course we only keep the ones that are necessary to test the equalities required by the grammar.

the language of G iff $\mathsf{S}(0, \mathsf{n}; \mathsf{t})$ is a derivable fact of $P_{G,w}$. Moreover, if $P_{G,w}$ is constructed with the structural equality and if we represent a finite state string automaton in the Edb (see [8], § 4.2), the fact $\mathsf{S}(\mathsf{q}_0, \mathsf{q}_1; \mathsf{t})$ is derivable by the program iff the rule tree t witnesses that the string w it yields is in $\mathcal{L}(G)$ and labels a path from the state q_0 to the state q_1 in the automaton.

As a consequence, the seminaive algorithm (adapted to extended Datalog programs) performs parsing when solving the query $?-\mathsf{S}(0, \mathsf{n}; \mathsf{y})$ as it outputs a finite tree automaton that recognizes exactly those rules trees that witness that w is in the language of G. Moreover, the parser it implements has a similar behavior to the one of CYK-parsers for CFGs.

5   Earley Parser and Magic-Set Rewriting

The same program transformation as the one presented in [7] transforms the two CYK parsers we have seen above into Earley parsers verifying the prefix-correct property. Moreover, proving those properties can be done along the same lines as in [7]. Interestingly, the parsers obtained from programs based on structural equality are very close to those proposed by Angelov [1], in that structural equality mimics the CFG rules used by Angelov to keep track of copying. We explain here how Kanazawa's transformation can be adapted to cope with extended Datalog programs.

5.1   Redundancy Introduction and Structural Equality

The transformation in [7] is actually the composition of two transformations. Given a non-terminal A of arity n of the grammar, for each $0 < k < n$ the first transformation introduces a partial predicate $\mathsf{A_k}$ of arity $2k$, so that the following properties are equivalent:

1. $\mathsf{A_k}(\mathsf{i}_{1,1}, \mathsf{i}_{1,2}, \ldots, \mathsf{i}_{k,1}, \mathsf{i}_{k,2})$ is a derivable fact
2. there is a tuple $(w_1, \ldots, w_k, w_{k+1}, \ldots, w_n)$ in $L(G, A)$ so that for $1 \leq j \leq k$, w_j spans the range between $\mathsf{i}_{j,1}$ and $\mathsf{i}_{j,2}$.

In the context of PMCFGs, this transformation can be applied directly as in [7], and as these partial predicates are not relevant in the original grammar, we do not need to pass any compound term as argument in them. The program we would obtain for the PMCFG of Example 1, using structural equality is:

$\mathsf{S}(\mathsf{i}, \mathsf{k}; \mathsf{r}_0(\mathsf{u})) :- \mathsf{A}_{1,\mathsf{bf}}(\mathsf{i}, \mathsf{j}),$
     $\mathsf{A}_{\mathsf{bbbf}}(\mathsf{i}, \mathsf{j}, \mathsf{j}, \mathsf{k}; \mathsf{u})$

$\mathsf{A}(\mathsf{i}, \mathsf{j}, \mathsf{k}, 1; \mathsf{r}_1) :- \mathsf{aux}_{1,1,\mathsf{bf}}(\mathsf{i}, \mathsf{j}), \mathsf{k} = 1$
$\mathsf{A}_1(\mathsf{i}, \mathsf{j}) :- \mathsf{aux}_{1,1,\mathsf{bf}}(\mathsf{i}, \mathsf{j})$
$\mathsf{aux}_{1,1}(\mathsf{i}, \mathsf{j}) :- \mathsf{i} = \mathsf{j}$

$\mathsf{A}(\mathsf{i}, \mathsf{m}, \mathsf{n}, \mathsf{p}; \mathsf{r}_2(\mathsf{u})) :- \mathsf{aux}(\mathsf{i}, \mathsf{j}, \mathsf{k}, \mathsf{m}; \mathsf{u}),$
     $\mathsf{eq\_A\_2}(\mathsf{j}, \mathsf{k}, \mathsf{n}, \mathsf{o}), \mathsf{a}(\mathsf{o}, \mathsf{p})$
$\mathsf{A}_1(\mathsf{i}, \mathsf{m}) :- \mathsf{aux}_{2,1}(\mathsf{i}, \mathsf{j}, \mathsf{k}, \mathsf{m})$
$\mathsf{aux}_{2,1}(\mathsf{i}, \mathsf{j}, \mathsf{k}, \mathsf{m}; \mathsf{u}) :- \mathsf{A}_1(\mathsf{i}, \mathsf{j}), \mathsf{A}(\mathsf{i}, \mathsf{j}, \mathsf{j}, \mathsf{k}; \mathsf{u}),$
     $\mathsf{eq\_A\_2}(\mathsf{j}, \mathsf{k}, \mathsf{k}, 1), \mathsf{a}(1, \mathsf{m})$

$\mathsf{eq\_A\_2}(\mathsf{i}, \mathsf{j}, \mathsf{k}, 1) :- \mathsf{A}(\mathsf{i}, \mathsf{j}, \mathsf{k}, 1; \mathsf{t}), \mathsf{i} = \mathsf{j}, \mathsf{k} = 1$
$\mathsf{eq\_A\_2}(\mathsf{i}, \mathsf{k}, 1, \mathsf{n}) :- \mathsf{A}(\mathsf{i}, \mathsf{j}, \mathsf{k}, 1; \mathsf{t}), \mathsf{eq\_A\_2}(\mathsf{i}, \mathsf{j}, 1, \mathsf{m}),$
     $\mathsf{a}(\mathsf{j}, \mathsf{k}), \mathsf{a}(\mathsf{m}, \mathsf{n})$

As in [7], we create auxiliary predicates in order to remove some redundancy in the program which may appear when introducing partial predicates. One may remark that if necessary, the auxiliary predicates may have to pass terms so as to make sure that rule trees are constructed.

In presence of the structural equality, other partial predicates turn out to be useful so as to prune the equality test search tree. Indeed, structural equality intends to check the equality of the derivations of two strings. In the presence of partial predicates, the first string in the equality test must have already been processed. We may thus use partial predicates to derive specialized predicates which state whether it has been established that a segment has been processed as the kth component of a non-terminal A. For the non-terminal A of our example, this gives us two predicates pA_1 and pA_2 which are respectively defined with the rules $pA_1(i, j) :- A_1(i, j)$ and $pA_2(k, l) :- A(i, j, k, l; t)$.

Then we transform each structural equality rule related to A by adding a condition concerning $pA_k(i, j)$ in each rule deriving $eq\_A\_k(i, j, k, l)$. The effect is to stop the search of $eq\_A\_k(i, j, k, l)$ whenever we have not been able to derive that the segment from i to j is the kth component of some tuple derived by the non-terminal A. Now the Datalog rules defining $eq\_A\_2(i, j, k, l)$ become:

$$eq\_A\_2(i, k, l, n) :- pA_2(i, j), eq\_A\_2(i, j, l, m), a(j, k), a(m, n)$$
$$eq\_A\_2(i, j, k, l) :- pA_2(i, j), i = j, k = l$$

5.2 Adornment and Magic Set Rewriting

The second transformation used in [7] is magic set rewriting. This transformation is performed in two phases. The first one consists in analyzing the flow of the top-down evaluation of the program for a particular query. This is the *adornment phase*: predicates of arity n are labeled with a string in $(b \mid f)^n$ which indicates whether during resolution an argument is known –*i.e. bound*– in which case the corresponding position is tagged with b, or to be found –*i.e. free*– in which case the corresponding position is tagged with f. As during resolution, certain predicates may be called in different context, the adornment phase may duplicate predicates which need several adornments together with the rules that define them; certain premises of rules may also be reordered so as to reduce the number of possible adornments. Figure 1 shows the adorned version of the program in

$S_{bf}(i, k; r_0(u)) :- A_{1,bf}(i, j), A_{bbbf}(i, j, j, k; u)$

$A_{bbbf}(i, m, n, p; r_2(u)) :- aux_{2,1,bfff}(i, j, k, m; u),$
$\qquad\qquad eq\_A\_2_{bbbf}(j, k, n, o), a(o, p)$

$A_{1,bf}(i, m) :- aux_{2,1,bfff}(i, j, k, m)$

$aux_{2,1,bfff}(i, j, k, m; u) :- A_{1,bf}(i, j),$
$\qquad A_{bbbf}(i, j, j, k; u), eq\_A\_2_{bbbf}(j, k, k, l), a(1, m)$

$A_{bbbf}(i, j, k, l; r_1) :- aux_{1,1,bf}(i, j), k = 1$
$A_{1,bf}(i, j) :- aux_{1,1,bf}(i, j)$
$aux_{1,1,bf}(i, j) :- i = j$

$pA_{2,bf}(k, l) :- A_{bbbf}(i, j, k, l; t)$
$eq\_A\_2_{bbbf}(i, j, k, l) :- pA_{2,bf}(i, j), i = j,$
$\qquad\qquad k = 1$
$eq\_A\_2_{bbbf}(i, k, l, n) :- pA_{2,bf}(i, j),$
$\qquad\qquad eq\_A\_2(i, j, l, m), a(j, k), a(m, n)$

Fig. 1. Adorned parser with partial predicates

the previous page, for the query ?$- \mathsf{S}(0, \mathsf{x}; \mathsf{y})$, where x and y are variables. In this phase, the variables that correspond to compound terms are not taken into account.

The second phase is the magic set rewriting. For each adorned predicate, a magic predicate is introduced that only contains the bound coordinates of the predicate. Then a rule $\mathsf{A}(\mathsf{X}; \mathsf{T}) :- \mathsf{A}_1(\mathsf{X}_1; \mathsf{T}_1), \dots, \mathsf{A}_n(\mathsf{X}_n; \mathsf{T}_n)$ for a given adornment of A is guarded with the corresponding magic predicate $\mathsf{m\_A}(\mathsf{X}')$, and is transformed into a rule of the shape: $\mathsf{A}(\mathsf{X}; \mathsf{T}) :- \mathsf{m\_A}(\mathsf{X}'), \mathsf{A}_1(\mathsf{X}_1; \mathsf{T}_1), \dots, \mathsf{A}_n(\mathsf{X}_n; \mathsf{T}_n)$. Magic predicates make it impossible to use rules which are useless to derive new facts; they simulate and improve the *predict* rule of Earley's algorithm [5]. Then, the resulting rules are binarized, by introduction of supplementary predicates. So the rule we have seen above is replaced with a set of rules [3]:

- $\mathsf{r}_1 : \mathsf{sup}_1(\mathsf{X} \cup \mathsf{X}'; \mathsf{T}_1) :- \mathsf{m\_A}(\mathsf{X}'), \mathsf{A}_1(\mathsf{X}_1; \mathsf{T}_1)$
- $\mathsf{r}_i : \mathsf{sup}_i(\mathsf{Y} \cup \mathsf{X}'_i; \mathsf{U} \cup \mathsf{T}'_i) :- \mathsf{sup}_{i-1}(\mathsf{Y}; \mathsf{U}), \mathsf{A}_i(\mathsf{X}_i; \mathsf{T}_i)$, for $1 < i < n$ where X'_i and T'_i contain only those variables that either have an occurrence in some $\mathsf{A}_j(\mathsf{X}_j; \mathsf{T}_j)$ for $i < j \leq n$ or in $\mathsf{A}(\mathsf{X}; \mathsf{T})$,
- $\mathsf{r}_n : \mathsf{A}(\mathsf{X}; \mathsf{T}) :- \mathsf{sup}_{n-1}(\mathsf{Y}; \mathsf{U}), \mathsf{A}_n(\mathsf{X}_n; \mathsf{T}_n)$

Finally, when binarization produces a rule of the form $\mathsf{A}(\mathsf{X}; \mathsf{T}) :- \mathsf{B}(\mathsf{Y}; \mathsf{U}), \mathsf{C}(\mathsf{Z}; \mathsf{S})$ where C is an adorned version of an intentional predicate of the original program, we create a rule $\mathsf{m\_C}(\mathsf{Z}') :- \mathsf{B}(\mathsf{Y}; \mathsf{U})$, where $\mathsf{m\_C}$ is the magic predicate corresponding to the adornment of $\mathsf{C}(\mathsf{Z}; \mathsf{S})$. Figure 2 shows the magic set rewritten version of our example.

Remark that the compound terms the resulting program outputs are exactly the compound terms the original program outputs. Moreover and similarly to [7], the prefix-correctness property is witnessed by the shape of the adornment in Figure 1: only the last argument of each predicate is free.

6   Left Corner and Minimal Magic-Set Rewriting

Left-corner parsers (see [4,14]) consist in short-cutting series of applications of the *predict* rules of the Earley algorithm and try to construct a tree directly from its left-most leaf. When we look at the Earley algorithm through its presentation with magic set rewriting, the magic predicates are responsible of implementing the *predict* rules of the Earley algorithm. The short-cutting that the left-corner parsers perform may be seen as recursively unfolding and deleting the rules whose both sides are magic predicates, *i.e.* rules of the form $\mathsf{m\_A}(\mathsf{X}) :- \mathsf{m\_B}(\mathsf{Y})$. After those rules have been recursively unfolded, they can be removed without changing the semantics of the program. Then, the chains of *predictions* that these rules implemented are now short-cut. Nonetheless, a bit of care is necessary here, as, one of the role of magic predicate is also to prevent trying to derive several times the same goal.

---

[3] Given two lists of elements E and E', $E \cup E'$, denotes a list made of the union of the set of elements in E and E'.

$sup_{0,1}(i,j):-m\_S_{bf}(i), A_{1,bf}(i,j)$

$S_{bf}(i,k;r_0(u)):-sup_{0,1}(i,j), A_{bbbf}(i,j,j,k;u)$

$m\_A_{1,bf}(i):-m\_S_{bf}(i)$

$m\_A_{bbbf}(i,j,j):-sup_{0,1}(i,j)$

$sup_{1,1}(i,j,k):-m\_A_{bbbf}(i,j,k), aux_{1,1,bf}(i,j)$

$A_{bbbf}(i,j,k,1,r_1):-sup_{1,1}(i,j,k), = (k,1)$

$m\_aux_{1,1,bf}(i):-m\_A_{bbbf}(i,j,k)$

$A_{1,bf}(i,j):-m\_A_{1,bf}(i), aux_{1,1,bf}(i,j)$

$m\_aux_{1,1,bf}(i):-m\_A_{1,bf}(i)$

$aux_{1,1,bf}(i,j):-m\_aux_{1,1,bf}(i), = (i,j)$

$sup_{4,1}(i,m,n,j,k;u):-m\_A_{bbbf}(i,m,n),$

$\qquad\qquad\qquad\qquad aux_{2,1,bfff}(i,j,k,m;u)$

$sup_{4,2}(i,m,n,o;u):-sup_{4,1}(i,m,n,j,k;u),$

$eq\_A\_2_{bbbf}(j,k,n,o)$

$m\_aux_{2,1,bfff}(i):-m\_A_{bbbf}(i,m,n)$

$A_{bbbf}(i,m,n,p;r_2(u)):-sup_{4,2}(i,m,n,o;u),$

$a(o,p)$

$m\_eq\_A\_2_{bbbf}(j,k,n):-sup_{4,1}(i,m,n,j,k;u)$

$sup_{6,1}(i,j):-m\_aux_{2,1,bfff}(i), A_{1,bf}(i,j)$

$sup_{6,2}(i,j,k;u):-sup_{6,1}(i,j), A_{bbbf}(i,j,j,k;u)$

$sup_{6,3}(i,j,k,1;u):-sup_{6,2}(i,j,k;u),$

$\qquad\qquad\qquad\qquad eq\_A\_2_{bbbf}(j,k,k,1)$

$aux_{2,1,bfff}(i,j,k,m;u):-sup_{6,3}(i,j,k,1;u), a(1,m)$

$m\_A_{bbbf}(i,j,j):-sup_{6,1}(i,j)$

$m\_eq\_A\_2_{bbbf}(j,k,k):-sup_{6,2}(i,j,k)$

$pA_{2,bf}(k,1):-m\_pA_{2,bf}(k), A_{bbbf}(i,j,k,1;t)$

$sup_{8,1}(i,j,k):-m\_eq\_A\_2_{bbbf}(i,j,k), pA_{2,bf}(i,j)$

$sup_{8,2}(i,j,k):-sup_{8,1}(i,j,k), = (i,j)$

$eq\_A\_2_{bbbf}(i,j,k,1):-sup_{8,2}(i,j,k), = (k,1)$

$m\_pA_{2,bf}(i):-m\_eq\_A\_2_{bbbf}(i,j,k,1)$

$sup_{9,1}(i,j,k,1):-m\_eq\_A\_2_{bbbf}(i,k,1), pA_{2,bf}(i,j)$

$sup_{9,2}(i,j,k,1,m):-sup_{9,1}(i,j,k,1),$

$\qquad\qquad\qquad\qquad eq\_A\_2_{bbbf}(i,j,1,m)$

$sup_{9,3}(i,j,k,1,m):-sup_{9,2}(i,j,k,1,m), a(j,k)$

$eq\_A\_2_{bbbf}(i,k,1,n):-sup_{9,3}(i,j,k,1,m), a(m,n)$

$m\_eq\_A\_2_{bbbf}(i,j,1):-sup_{9,1}(i,j,k,1)$

$A_{1,bf}(i,m):-m\_A_{1,bf}(i), aux_{2,1,bfff}(i,j,k,m)$

$m\_A_{1,bf}(i):-m\_aux_{2,1,bfff}(i)$

$m\_aux_{2,1,bfff}(i):-m\_A_{1,bf}(i)$

Fig. 2. Magic set rewritten program

For example, let us unfold the rule $m\_aux_{1,1,bf}(i):-m\_A_{bbbf}(i,j,k)$ of the program of Figure 2, into the rule, $aux_{1,1,bf}(i,j):-m\_aux_{1,1,bf}(i), = (i,j)$ we would obtain the rule: $aux_{1,1,bf}(i,j):-m\_A_{bbbf}(i,k,1), = (i,j)$ that would be invoked during the seminaive evaluation for every possible derivable fact of the form $m\_A_{bbbf}(i,k,1)$. But, when the rule $m\_aux_{1,1,bf}(i):-m\_A_{bbbf}(i,j,k)$ is not unfolded, each newly derived fact $m\_A_{bbbf}(i,k,1)$ triggers an instantiation of the rule $aux_{1,1,bf}(i,j):-m\_aux_{1,1,bf}(i), = (i,j)$ only when it creates a new fact $m\_aux_{1,1,bf}(i)$ with the rule $m\_aux_{1,1,bf}(i):-m\_A_{bbbf}(i,j,k)$, that is only when it is the first fact derived with that particular i. Thus, it is preferable to unfold and remove only the rules $m\_A(X):-m\_B(Y)$ when the variables occurring in Y are included in those occurring in X, so as to avoid to trigger useless instantiations of complex rules. In the program of Figure 2, we would only recursively unfold and delete the rules:

$$m\_A_{1,bf}(i):-m\_S_{bf}(i) \qquad m\_aux_{1,1,bf}(i):-m\_A_{1,bf}(i)$$
$$m\_A_{1,bf}(i):-m\_aux_{2,1,bfff}(i) \quad m\_aux_{1,1,bf}(i):-m\_A_{1,bf}(i)$$

The unfolding would create the following new rules that implement the left-corner optimization:

$$A_{1,\text{bf}}(i,m) :- m\_S_{\text{bf}}(i), aux_{2,1,\text{bfff}}(i,j,k,m) \quad A_{1,\text{bf}}(i,m) :- m\_aux_{2,1,\text{bfff}}(i), aux_{2,1,\text{bfff}}(i,j,k,m)$$
$$aux_{1,1,\text{bf}}(i,j) :- m\_A_{1,\text{bf}}(i), = (i,j) \quad\quad sup_{6,1}(i,j) :- m\_A_{1,\text{bf}}(i), A_{1,\text{bf}}(i,j)$$
$$aux_{1,1,\text{bf}}(i,j) :- m\_S_{\text{bf}}(i), = (i,j) \quad\quad sup_{6,1}(i,j) :- m\_S_{\text{bf}}(i), A_{1,\text{bf}}(i,j)$$

7   Conclusion

In this article, we show how the constructions proposed in [6,7] for implementing recognizers for MCFGs can easily be extended to construct parsers for PMCFGs. With this method, we provide two kinds of prefix-correct parsers, one of which can also work on finite state automata and is similar to Angelov's [1] but arguably much simpler to present. Moreover, we show that a simple modification of the magic set rewriting transformation allows one to easily obtain left-corner parsers. By combining the two constructions, we obtain a prefix-correct parser with left-corner optimization for PMCFGs. As designing parsers is a very delicate task, one of the interest of the approach is its simplicity. Moreover, with this approach, the possibility of designing various transformations and combine them permits a high flexibility and modularity in parsers design. Finally, similarly to parsing schemata, this approach separates the Datalog solver that evaluates program from the actual definition of the algorithms. This separation between the evaluation machinery and the algorithms permits ones to make every improvement of the solver be a benefit for all the parsers implemented with this method.

References

1. Angelov, K.: Incremental parsing with parallel multiple context-free grammars. In: EACL, pp. 69–76 (2009)
2. Boullier, P.: Range concatenation grammars. In: Proceedings of the Sixth International Workshop on Parsing Technologies, pp. 53–64 (February 2000)
3. Colmerauer, A.: Metamorphosis grammars. In: Bolc, L. (ed.) Natural Language Communication with Computers. LNCS, vol. 63, pp. 133–188. Springer, Heidelberg (1978)
4. Demers, A.J.: Generalized left corner parsing. In: Proceedings of the 4th ACM SIGACT-SIGPLAN Symposium on Principles of Programming Languages, pp. 170–182. ACM, New York (1977), http://doi.acm.org/10.1145/512950.512966
5. Earley, J.: An efficient context-free parsing algorithm. Commun. ACM 13(2), 94–102 (1970)
6. Kanazawa, M.: Parsing and generation as Datalog queries. In: Proceedings of the 45th Annual Meeting of the Association for Computational Linguistics, pp. 176–183. Association for Computational Linguistics, Prague (2007)
7. Kanazawa, M.: A prefix-correct Earley recognizer for multiple context-free grammars. In: TAG+9, Proceedings of the Ninth International Workshop on Tree Adjoining Grammars and Related Frameworks, Tubingen, Germany (June 2008)
8. Kanazawa, M.: Parsing and generation as Datalog query evaluation (2012) (under review), http://research.nii.ac.jp/~kanazawa/publications/pagadqe.pdf

9. Kobele, G.M.: Generating Copies: An investigation into structural identity in language and grammar. Ph.D. thesis, UCLA (2006)
10. Ljunglöf, P.: Expressivity and complexity of the Grammatical Framework. Citeseer (2004)
11. Ljunglöf, P.: A polynomial time extension of parallel multiple context-free grammar. In: Blache, P., Stabler, E.P., Busquets, J.V., Moot, R. (eds.) LACL 2005. LNCS (LNAI), vol. 3492, pp. 177–188. Springer, Heidelberg (2005)
12. Ljunglöf, P.: Practical parsing of parallel multiple context-free grammars. In: TAG+11, 11th International Workshop on Tree Adjoining Grammar and Related Formalisms, Paris, France (2012)
13. Michaelis, J., Kracht, M.: Semilinearity as a syntactic invariant. In: Retoré, C. (ed.) LACL 1996. LNCS (LNAI), vol. 1328, pp. 329–345. Springer, Heidelberg (1997)
14. Nederhof, M.J.: Generalized left-corner parsing. In: Sixth Conference of the European Chapter of the Association for Computational Linguistics, Proceedings of the Conference, pp. 305–314 (1993)
15. Pereira, F.C., Shieber, S.M.: Prolog and Natural-Language Analysis. CSLI Lecture Notes Series, vol. 10. Center for the Study of Language and Information (1987), http://mtome.com/Publications/PNLA/pnla.html
16. Seki, H., Matsamura, T., Mamoru, F., Kasami, T.: On multiple context-free grammars. Theoretical Computer Science 88(2), 191–229 (1991)
17. Shieber, S.: Evidence against the context-freeness of natural language. Linguistics and Philosophy 8, 333–343 (1985), http://dx.doi.org/10.1007/BF00630917
18. Sikkel, K.: Parsing schemata - a framework for specification and analysis of parsing algorithms. Springer (1997)
19. Ullman, J.D.: Bottom-up beats top-down for datalog. In: Proceedings of the Eighth ACM SIGACT-SIGMOD-SIGART Symposium on Principles of Database Systems, pp. 140–149. ACM (1989)

Representing Anaphora with Dependent Types

Daisuke Bekki[1,2,3,*]

[1] Ochanomizu University, Graduate School of Humanities and Sciences,
2-1-1 Ohtsuka, Bunkyo-ku, Tokyo 112-8610, Japan
[2] National Institute of Informatics,
2-1-2 Hitotsubashi, Chiyoda-ku, Tokyo, 101-8430, Japan
[3] CREST, Japan Science and Technology Agency,
4-1-8 Honcho, Kawaguchi, Saitama, 332-0012, Japan

Abstract. Discourse semantics based on dependent type theory, such as Ranta's Type Theoretical Grammar, is expected to serve as a proof-theoretic alternative to standard, model-theoretic discourse semantics such as DRT and DPL. Its compositionality, however, with respect to anaphora and presupposition, has been left as an open problem, toward which several different approaches have been proposed. In this paper, I will point out that four problems still remain to be solved in the previous approaches, and present a compositional discourse theory that remedies this enterprise, by the combination of the following settings: 1) the context-passing mechanism, 2) @-operators for representing anaphora/presupposition triggers, 3) (bottom-up) semantic composition with raw terms, and 4) (top-down) anaphora resolution as type checking.

1 Introduction

One of the difficulties that has motivated and driven the school of dynamic, model-theoretic semantics over the past 30 years (DRT in Kamp [13], DPL in Groenendijk and Stokhof [10], and their successors) lies in the tension between dynamics and compositionality. In other words, we have sought for a semantic theory in which sentences with inter- and intra-sentential anaphoric/presuppositional links are given well-formed representations that keep their structures parallel to their syntactic derivations.

Since Sundholm [24] discovered that this is feasible with dependent type theories, such as constructive/Martin-Löf Type Theory in Martin-Löf [17] (henceforth MLTT), much of the subsequent research investigated the horizon of *Sundholmian* semantics and established a school of constructive, proof-theoretic semantics. Among others, Ranta [21]'s Type Theoretical Grammar (TTG) is notable for its broad empirical coverage. TTG also provoked many insightful discussions, including the proof-theoretic explanation of anaphora (in)accessibility,

---

* My sincere thanks to Koji Mineshima, Pascual Martínez Goméz, Ribeka Tanaka, Shunsuke Yatabe, Eric McCready, Kohei Kishida, and Stefan Kaufmann for many helpful discussions. I also thank the anonymous reviewers for their insightful comments. This research is partially supported by JST, CREST.

N. Asher and S. Soloviev (Eds.): LACL 2014, LNCS 8535, pp. 14–29, 2014.

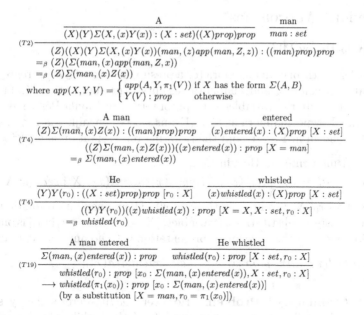

Fig. 1. A semantic composition of (1a) in Dávila-Pérez [4]

the data of which had been accumulated during the 1970s (as found in Karttunen [14]).

However, TTG is a *sugaring-oriented* theory (i.e., a theory for sentence generation). In terms of a semantic theory, this is one-sided: a proof-theoretic semantics theory ought to tell, for a given sentence, what should be known to utter it and what can be deduced from its utterance (cf. Prawitz [20]). TTG offers only the former. The latter, that is, a *parsing-oriented* theory, has been in demand, toward the establishment of which two different approaches have developed.

Dávila-Pérez [4] is one of few attempts to provide a parsing-oriented semantic theory[1] in MLTT. Dávila-Pérez's theory consists of semantic composition rules, defined in the style of Montague Grammar (namely, one rule for each syntactic configuration).

Krahmer and Piwek [15] and Piwek and Krahmer [19] (henceforth, K&P) presented an algorithm for anaphora resolution, presupposition binding, and accommodation. For the syntactic component, K&P adopts a set of translation rules from DRS to Sundholmian representations, which are proposed in Ahn and Kolb [1].

---

[1] Ranta [21] also presented a parsing-oriented theory based on MLTT in chapters 8 and 9, but I focus only on Dávila-Pérez's theory for the sake of space.

2   Previous Approaches

2.1   Dávila-Pérez [4]

In Dávila-Pérez's theory, an anaphora (or a presupposition trigger) is represented as a variable in context, and anaphora resolution/presupposition binding is a process to substitute the variables with proof terms. In Dávila-Pérez's theory, a sentence with E-type anaphora as (1a) (Evans [5], Groenedijk and Stokhof [10]) is derived as shown in **Fig. 1**, and the resulting representation is (1b).[2]

(1)   a. A man entered. He whistled.

       b. $whistled(r_0) : prop \ [x_0 : \Sigma(man, (x)entered(x)), X : set, r_0 : X]$

where variables x_0, X, r_0 remain in the context. Then, anaphora resolution takes place by a consistent substitution of variables; $[X = man, r_0 = \pi_1(x_0)]$ is one such substitution, yielding the following representation with no unresolved anaphora.

(2) $whistled(\pi_1(x_0)) : prop \ [x_0 : \Sigma(man, (x)entered(x))]$

"Lack of Asymmetry" Problem. However, Dávila-Pérez's theory suffers from two problems. The first problem arises from the inability to theoretically distinguish between unresolved anaphora (or presupposition triggers) and their antecedents. Both are uniformly represented as variables in contexts in MLTT, although the former are called *reference markers* and distinguished from the latter at the implementation level.

Therefore, Dávila-Pérez's theory does not prevent us from substituting a variable in a given context that is *not* supposed to be a reference marker, as the following simple discourse exemplifies.

(3)   A man was playing jazz. Then someone made a noise, and he made a furious exit.

The anaphora "he" in the second sentence is to be resolved under the following context:

$$[x_0 : \Sigma(man, (x)play(x, j)),$$
$$x_1 : \Sigma(man, (x)make(x, noise)),$$
$$X : set,$$
$$r_0 : X].$$

The intended anaphoric link is established with a substitution $[X = man, r_0 = \pi_1(x_0)]$. However, we may instead substitute x_1 with $(\pi_1(x_0), k(\pi_1(x_0))(\pi_2(x_0)))$, assuming that we share a world knowledge k that for any man, playing jazz makes a noise (which is quite sensible):

$$k : \Pi(man, (x)(play(x, j) \supset make(x, noise))).$$

---

[2] For details, see chapters 2 and 3 in Dávila-Pérez [4], where $T2$ is a Determiner-Noun rule (p. 43), $T4$ is a Subject-Predicate Rule (p. 45), and $T19$ is a Discourse Linking Rule (p. 62).

This is a legitimate operation in Dávila-Pérez's theory but empirically inaccurate: it interprets an existential quantifier as anaphoric.

In short, the setting of Dávila-Pérez [4] lacks asymmetry between context variables and reference markers, and therefore lacks asymmetry between anaphora and non-anaphora; this accidentally affords non-anaphoric expressions an anaphoric interpretation.

Ill-Formedness Problem. The second problem is that some semantic representations in Dávila-Pérez [4] are not well-formed in the sense of MLTT. For example, let us consider the following lexical item for the definite article "the" (Dávila-Pérez [4], p. 58).

$$(Y)Y(r_n) : ((X : set)prop)prop \ [r_n : X]$$

This representation is ill-formed because its well-formedness requires a proof as shown in (4), in which the application of the (ΠI) rule in the last line is prohibited because the variable r_0 that remains in the context still depends on the variable X, which blocks the abstraction of X.[3]

$$(4) \quad *(\Pi I) \frac{(\Pi I) \frac{(\Pi E) \frac{Y : (X)prop \ [X : set, \ Y : (X)prop] \quad r_0 : X \ [X : set, \ r_0 : X]}{Y(r_0) : prop \ [X : set, \ Y : (X)prop, \ r_0 : X]}}{(Y)Y(r_0) : ((X)prop)prop \ [X : set, \ r_0 : X]}}{(X)(Y)Y(r_0) : (X : set)((X)prop)prop \ [r_0 : X]}$$

An even more serious problem occurs when "the" is composed with a common noun. Suppose that "the" is to be composed with a common noun "dog", represented as $dog : set$. The beta reduction of the result substitutes the variable X in $(X)(Y)Y(r_n) : (X : set)((X)prop)prop$ and yields $(Y)Y(r_n) : ((dog)prop)prop$, as expected. However, X also occurs as *free* in the context $[r_n : X]$, which should not be substituted with dog, assuming the standard definition of beta reduction. But this means we lose the presuppositional content altogether.

This is not a technical problem exclusive to the definite article. It occurs whenever a presupposed semantic content contains a variable that is to be saturated by its argument. This includes cases like factive presuppositions and possessive presuppositions.

2.2   Krahmer and Piwek [15], Piwek and Krahmer [19]

K&P defined an extended language of MLTT with *annotated variables* as an extra construction that is intended to represent unresolved anaphora and presupposition triggers. For example, K&P's representation for (1a) is as follows.

---

[3] This is a general assumption in lambda calculi (cf. Martin-Löf [17], p. 27 has the following note on the Π-introduction rule for introducing a term of the form $(\lambda x \in A)M$: "we assume that the usual variable restriction is met, i.e. that x does not appear free in any assumption except (those of the form) $x \in A$.").

```
resolve(Φ, C, Φ)                          :- atomic(Φ).
resolve(ΠV : Φ.Ψ, C, ΠV : Φ' : Ψ') :- resolve(Φ, C, Φ'),
                                             C' := C ⊗ (Γ − C),
                                             resolve(Ψ, C' ⊗ V : Φ', Ψ').
resolve(Φ_χ, C, Φ')                       :- binder(χ, C, S),
                                             resolve(Φ[S], C, Φ').
resolve(Φ_χ, C, Φ')                       :- adequate(χ[S'], C),
                                             add(χ[S'], Γ),
                                             resolve(Φ[S'], C ⊗ χ[S'], Φ').
```

(and three more clauses for intermediate and local accommodation).[4]

Fig. 2. The Anaphora Resolution Algorithm of Krahmer and Piwek [15]

(5) $(\Sigma x_0 : (\Sigma u : (\Sigma x : \mathbf{entity})\mathbf{man}(x))\mathbf{enter}(\pi_1(u)))$

   $\mathbf{whistle}(X_{[X:\mathbf{entity}, m:\mathbf{man}(X)]})$

In this representation, $X_{[X:\mathbf{entity}, m:\mathbf{man}(X)]}$ is an annotated variable corresponding to the anaphora "He" in the second sentence, where $[X : \mathbf{entity}, m : \mathbf{man}(X)]$ is called an annotation (syntactically, an annotation is a context). In K&P's theory, anaphora resolution is understood as a substitution of annotated variables, which, in this case, fulfils the condition that each of the following judgments is simultaneously proven under the substitution.

(6)   a. $x_0 : (\Sigma u : (\Sigma x : \mathbf{entity})\mathbf{man}(x))\mathbf{enter}(\pi_1(u)) \vdash X : \mathbf{entity}$

   b. $x_0 : (\Sigma u : (\Sigma x : \mathbf{entity})\mathbf{man}(x))\mathbf{enter}(\pi_1(u)) \vdash m : \mathbf{man}(X)$

A substitution $X = \pi_1\pi_1(x_0)$, $m = \pi_2\pi_1(x_0)$ satisfies the condition, and the anaphora is thus resolved. Let us call the context responsible for a given anaphora resolution a *local context*. K&P's algorithm for deriving a resolution for a given representation under a given local context is partly shown in **Fig. 2**. Readers wanting details are referred to Appendix A in Krahmer and Piwek [15].

In K&P, anaphora resolution reduces to a search for a proof of a judgment from a given local context to the types in the annotations. Thus, K&P denominated this view behind the algorithm *anaphora resolution as proof construction*. This paradigm inherits the *presupposition as anaphora* paradigm by van der Sandt [22] and Geurts [9] in the sense that both regard anaphora resolution and presupposition binding as the same operation. However, K&P states a stronger claim with regard to the nature of anaphora and presupposition: namely, any anaphoric link is a proof. Moreover, K&P's theory is empirically superior to van der Sandt [22] and Geurts [9]'s DRT-based approach in cases such as bridging (Clark [3]) where an inference is required to establish an anaphoric link.[5]

(7)   If John$_i$ buys a car, he$_i$ checks the motor first.

---

[4] ⊗ denotes the *append* operation between two contexts, and Γ is a given context in which the presuppositions of Φ are to be resolved. The readers may be puzzled by the status of Γ as a global variable despite its Prolog-style notation. For details, refer to Krahmer and Piwek [15], the appendix A.

[5] Mineshima [18] pursued this analysis in the setting of Ranta [21].

Partiality Problem of Resolution Algorithm. Yet K&P's theory has left at least two problems unsolved. The first problem is that K&P's algorithm is not defined for all constructions of MLTT, but only for those listed in **Fig. 2**: atomic formulas, constructions of the form $\Pi V : \Phi$, and annotated variables. This means that the algorithm resolves anaphora that appears in certain forms only.

Note that this is not problematic for K&P's theory itself, which adopts Ahn and Kolb [1]'s translation from DRS so that it only yields permissible forms. However, this requirement is too strict if we try to extend the empirical coverage of K&P's theory or use K&P's theory in a compositional setting, where it is naturally expected that an annotated variable may occur within a functional application, projection, lambda abstraction, or other construction. For example, the following is a semantic representation of "John" and "loves his father", respectively.

(8)   a. $(\lambda p)p(j)$

      b. $(\lambda x)\textbf{love}(x, X_{[X:\textbf{entity}, f:\textbf{fatherOf}(x,j)]})$

The representation (8b) contains a variable with annotation $[X : \textbf{entity}, f : \textbf{fatherOf}(x,j)]$ within the lambda abstraction construction, on which K&P's anaphora resolution algorithm does not work. This may cause trouble when a construction such as generalized quantifiers uses a lambda-abstracted representation as its subformula, as in (9).

(9) $Most((\lambda x)\textbf{boy}(x))((\lambda x)\textbf{love}(x, X_{[X:\textbf{entity}, f:\textbf{fatherOf}(x,j)]}))$

Therefore, it is a natural urge to extend the algorithm to arbitrary forms as well so as to secure the empirical coverage of the theory.[6]

Copying Problem of Annotated Variable. The second problem occurs when a variable with annotation gets copied. This happens when operations such as the conjunction reduction take place due to the generalized conjunction (in the sense of Gazdar [7]). This occurs in the following sentence.

(10)   Each of John and Bill loves his father.

The reading for (10) is either (each of John and Bill loves his own father) or (both John and Bill love somebody's father (including John's and Bill's)). However, a *mixed* reading in which John only loves his own father and Bill only loves Sam's father, for example, does not seem available.

K&P's algorithm gives rise to the mixed reading as well as other legitimate readings, and so it overgenerates anaphoric links. Assume that the semantic

---

[6] However, there seems to exist an inherent difficulty in defining resolution rules for all constructions: in a semantic representation of the form $(\lambda P)P(...X_A...)$, where X_A is an annotated variable, the local context for a resolution of X_A depends on the content of P. Thus, the resolution algorithm has to delay the evaluation to the latter stage, where P is instantiated.

representation of (10) is as follows, where the annotated variable Y is copied and appears twice.

(11) $\textbf{love}(j, Y_{[X:\text{entity},Y:\text{entity},f:\textbf{fatherOf}(Y,X)]})$

$\wedge \textbf{love}(b, Y_{[X:\text{entity},Y:\text{entity},f:\textbf{fatherOf}(Y,X)]})$

In K&P's theory, anaphora is resolved *locally*; namely, each occurrence of a variable with annotation gets substituted under each local context. Thus, the resolution allows the first X to be substituted with John and the second X with some person other than John and Bill. Therefore, the semantic language that K&P suggests for unresolved representations empirically overgenerates.

3 Dependent Type Semantics

For the solution of various problems discussed in the last section, I present a framework that I will call *Dependent Type Semantics* (henceforth DTS). DTS is based on dependent type theory with Π, Σ constuctors, equation and natural number types (like MLTT), extended with an @-operator (unlike MLTT), whose syntax for raw terms is specified as follows:

$$\Lambda := x \mid c \mid () \mid (@_i : \Lambda)$$
$$\mid (\Pi x{:}\Lambda)\Lambda \mid (\lambda x)\Lambda \mid \Lambda\Lambda \mid (\Sigma x{:}\Lambda)\Lambda \mid (\Lambda, \Lambda) \mid \pi_1(\Lambda) \mid \pi_2(\Lambda)$$
$$\mid \textbf{eq}_\Lambda(\Lambda, \Lambda) \mid \textsf{r}_\Lambda(\Lambda, \Lambda) \mid \textsf{s}(\Lambda) \mid \textsf{R}(\Lambda, \Lambda, \Lambda)$$

where x is a variable, c is a constant symbol, () is a unit, $(@_i : \Lambda)$ is an @-operator (i is a natural number), $\textsf{r}_A(M, N)$ is a proof term of the equation between M and N of type A, $\textsf{s}$ is the successor operator in $\mathbb{N}$-introduction rule, and $\textsf{R}$ is the mathematical induction operator in $\mathbb{N}$-elimination rule, respectively.[7]

3.1 Concepts

DTS is characterized by the following four features, though the first one is shared by most of the other Sundholmian semantics.

1. From the Curry-Howard correspondence, where a proposition *is* a type and a proof *is* a term, a *static* proposition in DTS is a type. Under a given context, it is true if and only if it is inhabited (i.e., there exists a proof term of that type).
2. A *dynamic* proposition in DTS is a function from a proof of a static proposition that corresponds to its preceding discourse (a *context* in DTS) to a static proposition. A context is transferred either externally by the *context-passing* mechanism built into *dynamic conjunction and disjunction* (which are akin to continuation semantics (de Groote [11])), or internally in the lexical representations.

---

[7] Although the whole system of DTS is described by means of Martin-Löf type theory, our notation in this paper is inherited from Pure Type System (Barendregt [2]), which is more explicit about the status of contexts, substitutions, discharging, and other formal notions.

3. All the lexical representations are *raw terms* of dependent type theory, and composed as raw terms. This allows a context to be polymorphic.
4. When such raw terms are composed together to yield a representation for a syntactic category S (that is, a sentence), it must be of sort $\gamma \rightarrow$ type (for some new variable γ) in order to be uttered felicitously. This is called the *felicity condition* in DTS.

3.2   Static and Dynamic Propositions

In a dynamic proposition, a given context is discarded when the dynamic proposition does not contain any anaphora or presupposition triggers. For example, a semantic representation in DTS for "A man entered" is as $(12)^{8}$ where c is a variable for a proof of its left context, which is not used in this representation.

(12) $(\lambda c)(\Sigma u{:}(\Sigma x{:}\mathbf{e})\mathbf{M}(x))\mathbf{E}(\pi_1(u))$

3.3   The @-Operator and Anaphora/Presupposition Triggers

Anaphora and presupposition triggers are represented by @-operators that take the left context that is passed to a dynamic proposition that contains them. The representation for "He whistled" is (13), where the $@_0$-operator ($@_0 : \gamma_0 \rightarrow \mathbf{e}$) is fed its left context c (whose type is underspecified as γ_0) and returns an entity (of type $\mathbf{e}$) whom the pronoun refers to.

(13) $(\lambda c)\mathbf{W}((@_0 : \gamma_0 \rightarrow \mathbf{e})(c))$

@-operators have the following formation rule $(@F)$.

$$(@F)\frac{A : \mathsf{type} \qquad A \; true}{(@_i : A) : A}$$

---

[8] The constant symbol $\mathbf{e}$ is short for $\mathbf{entity}$, $\mathbf{M}$ is short for $\mathbf{Man}$, $\mathbf{E}$ is short for $\mathbf{Enter}$, and so forth. With respect to the representations of noun phrases, two different approaches have been adopted in previous works. For example, Sundholm [24] and Ranta [21] (and also Dávila-Pérez [4] in MLTT setting) encode the semantic representation of "A man laughs" as in (1), while Krahmer and Piwek [15] adopts the style in (2).

(1) $(\Sigma x{:}\mathbf{M})\mathbf{L}(x)$ (2) $(\Sigma u{:}(\Sigma x{:}\mathbf{e})\mathbf{M}(x))\mathbf{L}(\pi_1(u))$

DTS adopts the style in (2). One reason for this choice is to avoid the verbose use of the *app* operator of Dávila-Pérez [4] (see **Fig. 1**), which arises from polymorphism of noun phrases: the representation of "man" is *man* while that of "old man" is $\Sigma(man, (x)old(x))$.

This not only forces nominal modifiers to be polymorphic, but also requires a wrapper, such as an *app* operator, between noun phrases and verbs to absorb the polymorphism. Even worse, this polymorphism makes the definition of generalized quantifiers in Sundholm [25] notoriously polymorphic, as criticized in Fox and Lappin [6].

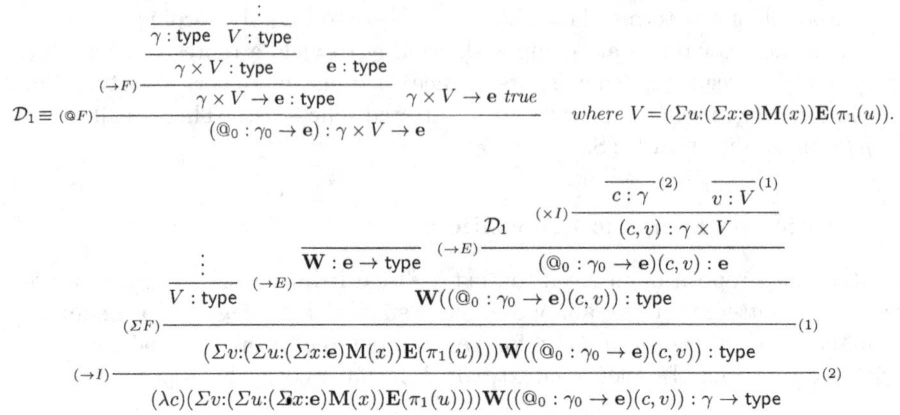

$$\mathcal{D}_1 \equiv (@F) \cfrac{(→F) \cfrac{\cfrac{\gamma : \text{type} \quad V : \text{type}}{\gamma \times V : \text{type}} \quad \mathbf{e} : \text{type}}{\gamma \times V → \mathbf{e} : \text{type}} \quad \gamma \times V → \mathbf{e} \ true}{(@_0 : \gamma_0 → \mathbf{e}) : \gamma \times V → \mathbf{e}} \quad where \ V = (\Sigma u{:}(\Sigma x{:}\mathbf{e})\mathbf{M}(x))\mathbf{E}(\pi_1(u)).$$

$$(→I) \cfrac{(\Sigma F) \cfrac{(→E) \cfrac{\vdots}{V : \text{type}} \quad (→E) \cfrac{\overline{\mathbf{W} : \mathbf{e} → \text{type}} \quad (×I) \cfrac{\mathcal{D}_1 \quad \cfrac{\overline{c : \gamma}^{(2)} \quad \overline{v : V}^{(1)}}{(c,v) : \gamma \times V}}{(@_0 : \gamma_0 → \mathbf{e})(c,v) : \mathbf{e}}}{\mathbf{W}((@_0 : \gamma_0 → \mathbf{e})(c,v)) : \text{type}}}{(\Sigma v{:}(\Sigma u{:}(\Sigma x{:}\mathbf{e})\mathbf{M}(x))\mathbf{E}(\pi_1(u))))\mathbf{W}((@_0 : \gamma_0 → \mathbf{e})(c,v)) : \text{type}}^{(1)}}{(\lambda c)(\Sigma v{:}(\Sigma u{:}(\Sigma x{:}\mathbf{e})\mathbf{M}(x))\mathbf{E}(\pi_1(u))))\mathbf{W}((@_0 : \gamma_0 → \mathbf{e})(c,v)) : \gamma → \text{type}}^{(2)}$$

Fig. 3. Type Checking for (1a)

The $(@F)$ rule requires that a certain type ($\gamma_0 → \mathbf{e}$, in the case of (13)) is inhabited, which is the presupposition triggered by the @-operator.[9] There is no introduction or elimination rule for @-operators. Free variables and substitution for @-operators are defined as follows.

$$fv((@_i : A)) \quad \overset{def}{\equiv} \quad fv(A)$$
$$(@_i : A)[M/x] \overset{def}{\equiv} (@_i : (A[M/x]))$$

A natural number i in $(@_i : A)$ is assigned for each occurrence of an anaphoric expression or presupposition trigger.

3.4   Context-Passing Mechanism

Then, two dynamic propositions are merged into one by either *dynamic conjunction* or *dynamic disjunction* (a dynamic version of equivalence in propositional logic: $A \vee B \equiv \neg A → B$).

Definition 1 (Dynamic conjunction and disjunction).

$$M; N \overset{def}{\equiv} (\lambda c)(\Sigma u{:}Mc)N(c,u)$$
$$M|N \overset{def}{\equiv} (\lambda c)(\Pi u{:}\neg Mc)N(c,u)$$

A left context c for $M; N$ (or $M|N$) is first passed to M (or $\neg M$), and then the pair (c, u) is passed to N; here, u is a proof of Mc (or $\neg Mc$). This means that the anaphora in N can refer to both antecedents in the left context and those introduced in M, but the anaphora in M can only refer to antecedents in the left context.

---

[9] This idea is in line with the use of the epsilon operator in Mineshima [18].

The types of the context c and the pair of contexts (c, u) are different, thus the two dynamic propositions M and N should be assigned different types. But this does not require a polymorphic setting at the object language level since M and N are raw terms and polymorphism is handled at the metalanguage level when type checking takes place.

The dynamic conjunction operator, if applied to the sequence of (12) and (13), yields a complex as follows.

$$((\lambda c)(\Sigma u{:}(\Sigma x{:}\mathbf{e})\mathbf{M}(x))\mathbf{E}(\pi_1(u))); \ ((\lambda c)\mathbf{W}((@_0 : \gamma_0 \to \mathbf{e})(c))))$$
$$= (\lambda c)(\Sigma v : (\Sigma u{:}(\Sigma x{:}\mathbf{e})\mathbf{M}(x))\mathbf{E}(\pi_1(u)))\mathbf{W}((@_0 : \gamma_0 \to \mathbf{e})(c, v))$$

3.5   The Felicity Condition and Anaphora Resolution

Since the last representation in the previous derivation is one for syntactic category S, it obeys the felicity condition of DTS. Checking the felicity condition for each sentential representation evokes its type checking algorithm (cf. the algorithm W in Hindley [12]) of dependent type theory, as shown in **Fig. 3**, which requires that the following judgment holds at the topmost node.

(14) $(\Sigma c{:}\gamma)(\Sigma u{:}(\Sigma x{:}\mathbf{e})\mathbf{M}(x))\mathbf{E}(\pi_1(u)))) \to \mathbf{e}$ *true*

This is true, since this type inhabits a proof term $(\lambda c)\pi_1\pi_1\pi_2(c)$. In words, there is an entity in a given context to which the pronoun "He" can refer. This exactly corresponds to the presupposition that the pronoun triggers.

Now, I declare the following statement for anaphora resolution and presupposition binding: anaphora resolution involves proof search, in line with K&P's theory.

Definition 2 (Anaphora Resolution / Presupposition Binding in DTS).
Suppose that $\Gamma \vdash (@_i : A) : A$ and $\Gamma \vdash a : A$. Then a resolution of $@_i$ by a under the context Γ is an equation $(@_i : A) = a : A$.

A proof such as $a : A$ always exists when the felicity condition is met, in which case there is a solution to anaphora resolution. In the above example, the following equation is a resolution:

$$(@_0 : \gamma_0 \to \mathbf{e}) = (\lambda c)\pi_1\pi_1\pi_2(c) : \gamma_0 \to \mathbf{e}$$

where $\gamma_0 = (\Sigma c{:}\gamma)(\Sigma u{:}(\Sigma x{:}\mathbf{e})\mathbf{M}(x))\mathbf{E}(\pi_1(u))))$.

Note that this equation is not a logical consequence deduced from the given representation; anaphora resolution (and presupposition binding) in DTS is understood as an *abduction* that infers the speaker's knowledge behind the utterance that contains anaphora or presupposition triggers, which makes it true (cf. Krause [16]).

4 Example Derivations: Donkey Sentences

As a compositional semantics, DTS is more *transparent* than Dávila-Pérez's theory where each composition rule is tightly bound to a particular syntactic configuration.

In order to provide a more detailed exposition of how the machinery of DTS works in general, this section will demonstrate a derivation of donkey sentence (Geach [8]) shown in (15), as one of the canonical benchmark tests that we expect any new discourse theory to cover.

(15)   Every farmer who owns [a donkey]$_1$ beats it$_1$.

The lexical items required to derive the sentence (15) are listed in Definition 3. Throughout this paper, DTS is presented as a semantic component of combinatory categorial grammar (Steedman [23]), but it naturally serves for other lexical grammars as well.[10]

Definition 3 (Lexical items in DTS).

PF	CCG categories	Semantic representations in DTS
if	$S/S/S$	$(\lambda p)(\lambda q)(\lambda c)(\Pi u{:}pc)(q(c,u))$
every$_{nom}$	$\boldsymbol{T}/(\boldsymbol{T}\backslash NP)/N$	$(\lambda n)(\lambda p)(\lambda c)(\Pi u{:}(\Sigma x{:}\mathbf{e})nxc)(p(\pi_1(u))(c,u))$
every$_{acc}$	$\boldsymbol{T}\backslash(\boldsymbol{T}/NP)/N$	$(\lambda n)(\lambda p)(\lambda x)(\lambda c)(\Pi v{:}(\Sigma y{:}\mathbf{e})nyc)(p(\pi_1(v))x(c,v))$
a$_{nom}$	$\boldsymbol{T}/(\boldsymbol{T}\backslash NP)/N$	$(\lambda n)(\lambda p)(\lambda c)(\Sigma u{:}(\Sigma x{:}\mathbf{e})nxc)p(\pi_1(u))(c,u)$
a$_{acc}$	$\boldsymbol{T}\backslash(\boldsymbol{T}/NP)/N$	$(\lambda n)(\lambda p)(\lambda x)(\lambda c)(\Sigma v{:}(\Sigma y{:}\mathbf{e})nyc)p(\pi_1(v))x(c,v)$
farmer	N	$(\lambda x)(\lambda c)\mathbf{F}(x)$
donkey	N	$(\lambda x)(\lambda c)\mathbf{D}(x)$
who	$N\backslash N/(S\backslash NP)$	$(\lambda p)(\lambda n)(\lambda x)(\lambda c)(nxc \wedge pxc)$
whom	$N\backslash N/(S/NP)$	$(\lambda p)(\lambda n)(\lambda x)(\lambda c)(nxc \wedge pxc)$
owns	$S\backslash NP/NP$	$(\lambda y)(\lambda x)(\lambda c)\mathbf{O}(x,y)$
beats	$S\backslash NP/NP$	$(\lambda y)(\lambda x)(\lambda c)\mathbf{B}(x,y)$
he$_{nom}^{i}$	$\boldsymbol{T}/(\boldsymbol{T}\backslash NP)$	$(\lambda p)(\lambda c)((\lambda x)px(c,x))((@_i : \gamma_i \to \mathbf{e})(c))$
it$_{acc}^{j}$	$\boldsymbol{T}\backslash(\boldsymbol{T}/NP)$	$(\lambda p)(\lambda x)(\lambda c)((\lambda y)pyx(c,y))((@_j : \gamma_j \to \mathbf{e})(c))$

The conditional "if" and the universal quantifier "every" are constructed from Π-operator, while the indefinite article "a" is from Σ-operator, following Sundholm [24].

The relativizer "who" takes a subjectless sentence and a common noun, and statically conjoins them. Pronouns are represented by means of @-operators, where each γ_i is a new variable.

The derivation of the relative donkey sentence (15) is as follows.

---

[10] Given that the semantic representations in DTS are raw terms, the result of semantic composition may not be typable. This problem can be avoided by adopting a categorial grammar for a syntactic component of DTS and by ensuring that each semantic representation in the lexicon is typable. The proof is routine (we only have to show that each rule of the adopted categorial grammar preserves typability). We also need Subject Reduction Theorem and Normalization Theorem of DTS with respect to the CCG categories in order to execute reductions during derivations.

$$\frac{\dfrac{\text{owns}}{\dfrac{S\backslash NP/NP}{:(\lambda y)(\lambda x)(\lambda c)\mathbf{O}(x,y)}} \quad \dfrac{\dfrac{\text{a}}{\dfrac{\boldsymbol{T}\backslash(\boldsymbol{T}/NP)/N}{:(\lambda n)(\lambda p)(\lambda x)(\lambda c)(\Sigma v{:}(\Sigma y{:}\mathbf{e})nyc)(p(\pi_1(v))x(c,v))}} \quad \dfrac{\text{donkey}}{\dfrac{N}{:(\lambda x)(\lambda c)\mathbf{D}(x)}}}{\dfrac{\boldsymbol{T}\backslash(\boldsymbol{T}/NP)}{:(\lambda p)(\lambda x)(\lambda c)(\Sigma v{:}(\Sigma y{:}\mathbf{e})\mathbf{D}(y))(p(\pi_1(v))x(c,v))}}}{\dfrac{S\backslash NP}{:(\lambda x)(\lambda c)(\Sigma v{:}(\Sigma y{:}\mathbf{e})\mathbf{D}(y))\mathbf{O}(x,\pi_1(v))}}$$

$$\frac{\dfrac{\text{farmer}}{\dfrac{N}{:(\lambda x)(\lambda c)\mathbf{F}(x)}} \quad \dfrac{\dfrac{\text{who}}{\dfrac{N\backslash N/(S\backslash NP)}{:(\lambda p)(\lambda n)(\lambda x)(\lambda c)(nxc \wedge pxc)}} \quad \dfrac{\text{owns a donkey}}{\dfrac{S\backslash NP}{:(\lambda x)(\lambda c)(\Sigma v{:}(\Sigma y{:}\mathbf{e})\mathbf{D}(y))\mathbf{O}(x,\pi_1(v))}}}{\dfrac{N\backslash N}{:(\lambda n)(\lambda x)(\lambda c)(nxc \wedge (\Sigma v{:}(\Sigma y{:}\mathbf{e})\mathbf{D}(y))\mathbf{O}(x,\pi_1(v)))}}}{\dfrac{N}{:(\lambda x)(\lambda c)(\mathbf{F}(x) \wedge (\Sigma v{:}(\Sigma y{:}\mathbf{e})\mathbf{D}(y))\mathbf{O}(x,\pi_1(v)))}}$$

$$\frac{\dfrac{\text{every}}{\dfrac{S/(S\backslash NP)/N}{:(\lambda n)(\lambda p)(\lambda c)(\Pi u{:}(\Sigma x{:}\mathbf{e})nxc)(p(\pi_1(u))(c,u))}} \quad \dfrac{\text{farmer who owns a donkey}}{\dfrac{N}{:(\lambda x)(\lambda c)(\mathbf{F}(x) \wedge (\Sigma v{:}(\Sigma y{:}\mathbf{e})\mathbf{D}(y))\mathbf{O}(x,\pi_1(v)))}}}{\dfrac{S/(S\backslash NP)}{:(\lambda p)(\lambda c)(\Pi u{:}(\Sigma x{:}\mathbf{e})(\mathbf{F}(x) \wedge (\Sigma v{:}(\Sigma y{:}\mathbf{e})\mathbf{D}(y))\mathbf{O}(x,\pi_1(v))))(p(\pi_1(u))(c,u))}}$$

$$\frac{\dfrac{\text{beats}}{\dfrac{S\backslash NP/NP}{:(\lambda y)(\lambda x)(\lambda c)\mathbf{B}(x,y)}} \quad \dfrac{\text{it}_1}{\dfrac{(S\backslash NP)\backslash(S\backslash NP/NP)}{:(\lambda p)(\lambda x)(\lambda c)p((@_1:\gamma_1 \to \mathbf{e})(c))xc}}}{\dfrac{S\backslash NP}{:(\lambda x)(\lambda c)\mathbf{B}(x,(@_1:\gamma_1 \to \mathbf{e})(c))}}$$

$$\frac{\dfrac{\text{every farmer who owns [a donkey]}_1}{\dfrac{S/(S\backslash NP)}{\begin{array}{c}(\lambda p)(\lambda c)(\Pi u:(\Sigma x{:}\mathbf{e})(\mathbf{F}(x) \wedge (\Sigma v{:}(\Sigma y{:}\mathbf{e})\mathbf{D}(y))\mathbf{O}(x,\pi_1(v)))) \\ (p(\pi_1(u))(c,u))\end{array}}} \quad \dfrac{\text{beats it}_1}{\dfrac{S\backslash NP}{:(\lambda x)(\lambda c)\mathbf{B}(x,(@_i:\gamma_1 \to \mathbf{e})(c))}}}{\dfrac{S}{:(\lambda c)(\Pi u{:}(\Sigma x{:}\mathbf{e})(\mathbf{F}(x) \wedge (\Sigma v{:}(\Sigma y{:}\mathbf{e})\mathbf{D}(y))\mathbf{O}(x,\pi_1(v))))\mathbf{B}(\pi_1(u),(@_1:\gamma_1 \to \mathbf{e})(c,u))}}$$

Thus we obtain (16) as a semantic representation of (15), from the last line of the above derivation.

(16) $(\lambda c)(\Pi u{:}(\Sigma x{:}\mathbf{e})(\mathbf{F}(x) \wedge (\Sigma v{:}(\Sigma y{:}\mathbf{e})\mathbf{D}(y))\mathbf{O}(x,\pi_1(v))))\mathbf{B}(\pi_1(u),(@_1:\gamma_1 \to \mathbf{e})(c,u))$

Then the felicity condition requires (16) to be of type $\gamma_0 \to \mathsf{type}$ (where γ_0 is a new variable), which is to be checked by the type checking algorithm.

We assume that the constant symbols are annotated as $\mathbf{F}:\mathbf{e} \to \mathsf{type}$, $\mathbf{D}:\mathbf{e} \to \mathsf{type}$, $\mathbf{O}:\mathbf{e} \times \mathbf{e} \to \mathsf{type}$, and $\mathbf{B}:\mathbf{e} \times \mathbf{e} \to \mathsf{type}$. Under this setting, the type setting algorithm requires, via the (@F) rule, that the following type is *true*, namely, it has a proof term[11]:

---

[11] We need a proof search to check this step, which gives rise to the undecidability of type checking in DTS. This is one potential problem of the current version of DTS, though the inhabitance of (17) is exactly what one has to check to decide the antecedent of the donkey anaphora in (15) which has to be calculated at some point or other.

(17) $\gamma_0 \times (\Sigma x{:}\mathbf{e})(\mathbf{F}(x) \wedge (\Sigma v{:}(\Sigma y{:}\mathbf{e})\mathbf{D}(y))\mathbf{O}(x, \pi_1(v))) \to \mathbf{e}$

As the following proof diagram shows, $(\lambda c)\pi_1\pi_1\pi_2\pi_2\pi_2(c)$ is a proof term that satisfies the felicity condition, which corresponds to the reading where "it" refers to the donkey.

$$
\cfrac{\cfrac{\cfrac{\cfrac{\cfrac{\cfrac{\overline{c : \gamma_0 \times (\Sigma x{:}\mathbf{e})(\mathbf{F}(x) \wedge (\Sigma v{:}(\Sigma y{:}\mathbf{e})\mathbf{D}(y))\mathbf{O}(x, \pi_1(v)))}^{(1)}}{\pi_2(c) : (\Sigma x{:}\mathbf{e})(\mathbf{F}(x) \wedge (\Sigma v{:}(\Sigma y{:}\mathbf{e})\mathbf{D}(y))\mathbf{O}(x, \pi_1(v)))} {\scriptstyle (\times E)}}{\pi_2\pi_2(c) : \mathbf{F}(\pi_1\pi_2(c)) \wedge (\Sigma v{:}(\Sigma y{:}\mathbf{e})\mathbf{D}(y))\mathbf{O}(\pi_1\pi_2(c), \pi_1(v))} {\scriptstyle (\Sigma E)}}{\pi_2\pi_2\pi_2(c) : (\Sigma v{:}(\Sigma y{:}\mathbf{e})\mathbf{D}(y))\mathbf{O}(\pi_1\pi_2(c), \pi_1(v))} {\scriptstyle (\Sigma E)}}{\pi_1\pi_2\pi_2\pi_2(c) : (\Sigma y{:}\mathbf{e})\mathbf{D}(y)} {\scriptstyle (\Sigma E)}}{\pi_1\pi_1\pi_2\pi_2\pi_2(c) : \mathbf{e}} {\scriptstyle (\Sigma E)}}{(\lambda c)\pi_1\pi_1\pi_2\pi_2\pi_2(c) : \gamma_0 \times (\Sigma x{:}\mathbf{e})(\mathbf{F}(x) \wedge (\Sigma v{:}(\Sigma y{:}\mathbf{e})\mathbf{D}(y))\mathbf{O}(x, \pi_1(v))) \to \mathbf{e}} {\scriptstyle (\to I)}^{(1)}
$$

Thus, the equation $(@_1 : \gamma_1 \to \mathbf{e}) = (\lambda c)\pi_1\pi_1\pi_2\pi_2\pi_2(c) : \gamma_1 \to \mathbf{e}$ is a resolution of $@_1$ under the given context in the sense of Definition 2. Assuming this equation in succeeding inferences allows us to substitute $(@_1 : \gamma_1 \to \mathbf{e})$ in the semantic representation of (15) with $(\lambda c)\pi_1\pi_1\pi_2\pi_2\pi_2(c)$, yielding the *resolved* semantic representation (18).

(18) $(\lambda c)(\Pi u{:}(\Sigma x{:}\mathbf{e})(\mathbf{F}(x) \wedge (\Sigma v{:}(\Sigma y{:}\mathbf{e})\mathbf{D}(y))\mathbf{O}(x, \pi_1(v))))\mathbf{B}(\pi_1(u), \pi_1\pi_1\pi_2\pi_2(u))$

5   Solutions to the Puzzles

5.1   "Lack of Asymmetry" Problem Solved

The first problem of Dávila-Pérez [4] does not occur in DTS in an obvious sense, since DTS distinguishes anaphora and non-anaphora by representing the former, but not the latter, by means of @-operators. For example, the representation for (3) is as (19), where an @-operator is used for only the pronoun "he"; thus, there is no danger that other terms are interpreted as anaphoric.

(19) $(\lambda c)(\Sigma x{:}\mathbf{e})(\mathbf{M}(x) \wedge \mathbf{P}(x, j)); (\lambda c)(\Sigma x{:}\mathbf{e})(\mathbf{M}(x) \wedge \mathbf{MK}(x, n)); (\lambda c)\mathbf{MFE}(@_0 : (\gamma_0 \to \mathbf{e})(c))$

5.2   Ill-Formedness Problem Solved

The second problem of Dávila-Pérez [4] is also avoided in DTS. The semantic representation for "the" in DTS is as (20), where the lambda abstraction with respect to the variable n is legitimate, since the occurrence of n in the @-operator is just that of a free variable and no other variables depend on n.

(20) $(\lambda n)(\lambda p)(\lambda c)p(\pi_1((@_i : (\Pi c{:}\gamma_i)(\Sigma x{:}\mathbf{e})nxc)(c)))c$

The semantic representation for a sentence in (21a) in DTS is (21b), as derived in **Fig. 4**.

$$\frac{\displaystyle \frac{\quad\text{the}\quad}{S/(S\backslash NP)/N : (\lambda n)(\lambda p)(\lambda c)p(\pi_1((@_0 : \gamma_0 \to (\Sigma x{:}e)nxc)(c)))c} \quad \frac{\text{dog}}{N : (\lambda x)(\lambda c)\mathbf{D}(x)}}{S/(S\backslash NP) : (\lambda p)(\lambda c)p(\pi_1((@_0 : \gamma_0 \to (\Sigma x{:}e)\mathbf{D}(x))(c)))c} {>} \quad \frac{\text{barks}}{S\backslash NP : (\lambda x)(\lambda c)\mathbf{B}(x)}}{S : (\lambda c)\mathbf{B}(\pi_1((@_0 : \gamma_0 \to (\Sigma x{:}e)\mathbf{D}(x))(c)))} {>}$$

Fig. 4. A Derivation of (21a)

$$\frac{\overline{c : \gamma_0}^{(1)}}{\vdots}$$

$$\text{(}@F\text{)}\frac{\gamma_0 \to (\Sigma x{:}e)\mathbf{D}(x) : \text{type} \quad \gamma_0 \to (\Sigma x{:}e)\mathbf{D}(x) \; \text{true}}{(@_1 : \gamma_1 \to (\Sigma x{:}e)\mathbf{D}(x)) : \gamma_0 \to (\Sigma x{:}e)\mathbf{D}(x)} \quad \overline{c : \gamma_0}^{(1)}$$

$$\text{(}\to E\text{)}\frac{}{(@_1 : \gamma_1 \to (\Sigma x{:}e)\mathbf{D}(x))(c) : (\Sigma x{:}e)\mathbf{D}(x)}$$

$$\overline{\mathbf{B} : e \to \text{type}} \quad (\Sigma E)\frac{}{\pi_1((@_1 : \gamma_1 \to (\Sigma x{:}e)\mathbf{D}(x))(c)) : e}$$

$$(\to E)\frac{}{\mathbf{B}(\pi_1((@_1 : \gamma_1 \to (\Sigma x{:}e)\mathbf{D}(x))(c))) : \text{type}}$$

$$(\to I)\frac{}{(\lambda c)\mathbf{B}(\pi_1((@_1 : \gamma_1 \to (\Sigma x{:}e)\mathbf{D}(x))(c))) : \gamma_0 \to \text{type}} {(1)}$$

Fig. 5. Type Checking for (21a)

(21)   a. The dog barks.

   b. $(\lambda c)\mathbf{B}(\pi_1((@_1 : \gamma_1 \to (\Sigma x{:}e)\mathbf{D}(x))(c)))$

Then, its felicity condition is checked as shown in **Fig. 5**, assuming the type of the given context as $c : \gamma_0$. Thus, all we need for the felicity condition to be satisfied is that the type $\gamma_0 \to (\Sigma x{:}e)\mathbf{D}(x)$ is inhabited (i.e., that there is a proof from a given left context of the existence of a dog), which is just as expected.

5.3   Partiality Problem Solved

The first problem of K&P is solved by the context-passing mechanism. DTS does not need to define a rule for each configuration in dependent type theory about how local contexts are passed since local contexts are explicitly passed around as arguments for dynamic propositions. Consider a semantic representation (22) for (8b) in DTS.

(22) $(\lambda x)(\lambda c)\mathbf{L}(x, \pi_1((@_1 : \gamma_1 \to (\Sigma y{:}e)\mathbf{fatherOf}(y, (@_0 : \gamma_0 \to e)(c, x)))(c, x)))$

In (22), the representation explicitly takes a context c as an argument and passes it (with x) to the @-operator, which presupposes that the existence of x's father is proven from c.

Thus we do not have to care about what kind of construction of dependent type theory we are dealing with because the relations between a local context and @-operators are always explicitly specified.

5.4 Copying Problem Solved

The second problem of K&P is circumvented by indexing @-operators. For example, assume that the representation of (10) in DTS is as (23).

(23) $(\lambda c)(\mathbf{L}(j, \pi_1((@_1 : \gamma_1 \rightarrow (\Sigma x{:}\mathbf{e})\mathbf{fatherOf}(x, (@_0 : \gamma_0 \rightarrow \mathbf{e})(c, j)))(c, j)))$
  $\wedge \mathbf{L}(b, \pi_1((@_1 : \gamma_1 \rightarrow (\Sigma x{:}\mathbf{e})\mathbf{fatherOf}(x, (@_0 : \gamma_0 \rightarrow \mathbf{e})(c, b)))(c, b)))$

In (23), an $@_0$ operator presupposed an existence of somebody that the pronoun "his" denotes, and the $@_1$ operator presupposes that of his father. Since the two occurrences of the $@_0$ operators in (23) share the same index, their resolution must substitute both occurrences of the $@_0$ operator at the same time. A possible substitution is that with π_2, which picks up John and Bill as antecedents of "his".

The same argument applies to the $@_1$ operators. As a result, they are to be substituted by the same proof term, which in turn picks up the same person as the father in question from a given context c. This way, the mixture of antecedent selection that troubled K&P's theory does not arise in DTS.

6 Conclusion

We presented the framework of DTS, a new compositional semantic theory based on dependent type theory (in line with Sundholm [24] and Ranta [21]) extended with @-operators. While inheriting the parsing-orientedness from Dávila-Pérez [4] and the "anaphora resolution as proof construction" paradigm from K&P, DTS differs from the previous constructive type theoretic approaches in four points: 1) DTS has a context-passing mechanism, 2) DTS uses an @-operator for anaphora and presupposition triggers, 3) semantic representations in DTS are raw terms, and 4) the felicity condition invokes a type checking of the semantic representation, which works as anaphora resolution and presupposition binding. With this setting, DTS gives a unified solution to the problems that the previous approaches left unsolved.

References

1. Ahn, R., Kolb, H.P.: Discourse representation meets constructive mathematics. In: Kalman, L., Polos, L. (eds.) Papers from the Second Symposium on Logic and Language (1990)
2. Barendregt, H.P.: Lambda calculi with types. In: Abramsky, S., Gabbay, D.M., Maibaum, T. (eds.) Handbook of Logic in Computer Science, vol. 2, pp. 117–309. Oxford Science Publications (1992)
3. Clark, H.H.: Bridging. In: Roger, S., L., N.W.B. (eds.) TINLAP 1975: Proceedings of the 1975 Workshop on Theoretical Issues in Natural Language Processing, pp. 169–174. Association for Computational Linguistics, Stroudsburg (1975)
4. Dávila-Pérez, R.: Semantics and Parsing in Intuitionistic Categorial Grammar. Ph.d. thesis, University of Essex (1995)

5. Evans, G.: Pronouns. Linguistic Inquiry 11, 337–362 (1980)
6. Fox, C., Lappin, S.: Type-theoretic approach to anaphora and ellipsis. In: Recent Advances in Natural Language Processing (RANLP 2003), Borovets, Bulgaria (2003)
7. Gazdar, G.: A cross-categorial semantics for conjunction. Linguistics and Philosophy 3, 407–409 (1980)
8. Geach, P.: Reference and Generality: An Examination of Some Medieval and Modern Theories. Cornell University Press, Ithaca (1962)
9. Geurts, B.: Presuppositions and pronouns. Elsevier, Oxford (1999)
10. Groenendijk, J., Stokhof, M.: Dynamic predicate logic. Linguistics and Philosophy 14, 39–100 (1991)
11. de Groote, P.: Towards a montagovian account of dynamics. In: Gibson, M., Howell, J. (eds.) 16th Semantics and Linguistic Theory Conference (SALT16), pp. 148–155. CLC Publications, University of Tokyo (2006)
12. Hindley, J.R.: The principal type-scheme of an object in combinatory logic. Transactions of the American Mathematical Society 146, 29–60 (1969)
13. Kamp, H.: A theory of truth and semantic representation. In: Groenendijk, J., Janssen, T.M., Stokhof, M. (eds.) Formal Methods in the Study of Language, Amsterdam (1981)
14. Karttunen, L.: Discourse referents. In: McCawley, J.D. (ed.) Syntax and Semantics 7: Notes from the Linguistic Underground, vol. 7, pp. 363–385. Academic Press, New York (1976)
15. Krahmer, E., Piwek, P.: Presupposition projection as proof construction. In: Bunt, H., Muskens, R. (eds.) Computing Meanings: Current Issues in Computational Semantics. Kluwer Academic Publishers, Dordrecht (1999)
16. Krause, P.: Presupposition and abduction in type theory. In: Klein, E., Manandhar, S., Nutt, W., Siekman, J. (eds.) Edinburgh Conference on Computational Logic and Natural Language Processing. HCRC, Edinburgh (1995)
17. Martin-Löf, P.: Intuitionistic Type Theory, vol. 17. Bibliopolis, Naples, Italy (1984), sambin, Giovanni (ed.)
18. Mineshima, K.: A presuppositional analysis of definite descriptions in proof theory. In: Satoh, K., Inokuchi, A., Nagao, K., Kawamura, T. (eds.) JSAI 2007. LNCS (LNAI), vol. 4914, pp. 214–227. Springer, Heidelberg (2008)
19. Piwek, P., Krahmer, E.: Presuppositions in context: Constructing bridges. In: Bonzon, P., Cavalcanti, M., Nossum, R. (eds.) Formal Aspects of Context. Applied Logic Series. Kluwer Academic Publishers, Dordrecht (2000)
20. Prawitz, D.: Intuitionistic logic: A philosophical challenge. In: von Wright, G. (ed.) Logics and Philosophy. Martinus Nijhoff, The Hague (1980)
21. Ranta, A.: Type-Theoretical Grammar. Oxford University Press (1994)
22. van der Sandt, R.: Presupposition projection as anaphora resolution. Journal of Semantics 9, 333–377 (1992)
23. Steedman, M.J.: The Syntactic Process (Language, Speech, and Communication). The MIT Press, Cambridge (2000)
24. Sundholm, G.: Proof theory and meaning. In: Gabbay, D., Guenthner, F. (eds.) Handbook of Philosophical Logic, vol. III, pp. 471–506. Kluwer, Reidel (1986)
25. Sundholm, G.: Constructive generalized quantifiers. Synthese 79, 1–12 (1989)

An Interpretation of Full Lambek Calculus in Its Variant without Empty Antecedents of Sequents

Wojciech Buszkowski

Faculty of Mathematics and Computer Science,
Adam Mickiewicz University, Poznań
buszko@amu.edu.pl

Abstract. We define a faithful interpretation of Full Lambek Calculus without the constant 1 [6] in its subsystem not allowing empty antecedents of sequents. We also define a multi-valued interpretation working for the multiplicative fragments. The interpretations are applied to obtain some general results on the complexity of substructural logics and the generative capacity of type grammars.

1 Introduction and Preliminaries

Full Lambek Calculus is a basic substructural logic. These logics are often defined as its extensions with additional axioms and rules [6,8]. In the present paper Full Lambek Calculus is denoted by FL_1, its 1-free fragment by FL^*, and the subsystem of FL^* not allowing empty antecedents of sequents by FL. This notation differs from a standard one in the literature on substructural logics, where FL stands for our FL_1. Substructural logicians, however, usually ignore logics like FL in our sense, and we need a notation discriminating these different systems.

FL_1 can be presented as a sequent system in language $(\cdot, \backslash, /, 1, \wedge, \vee)$. We reserve meta-variables p, q, r, s (possibly with subscripts, primes etc.) for variables, α, β, γ for formulae, and Γ, Δ, Φ for finite sequences of formulae. The empty sequence is denoted by ϵ. Sequents are of the form $\Gamma \Rightarrow \alpha$. FL_1 is based on the following axioms and rules:

$$(\text{Id})\ \alpha \Rightarrow \alpha,$$

$$(\text{L}\cdot)\ \frac{\Gamma, \alpha, \beta, \Gamma' \Rightarrow \gamma}{\Gamma, \alpha \cdot \beta, \Gamma' \Rightarrow \gamma}, \quad (\text{R}\cdot)\ \frac{\Gamma \Rightarrow \alpha; \ \Delta \Rightarrow \beta}{\Gamma, \Delta \Rightarrow \alpha \cdot \beta},$$

$$(\text{L}\backslash)\ \frac{\Gamma, \beta, \Gamma' \Rightarrow \gamma; \ \Delta \Rightarrow \alpha}{\Gamma, \Delta, \alpha\backslash\beta, \Gamma' \Rightarrow \gamma}, \quad (\text{L}/)\ \frac{\Gamma, \beta, \Gamma' \Rightarrow \gamma; \ \Delta \Rightarrow \alpha}{\Gamma, \beta/\alpha, \Delta, \Gamma' \Rightarrow \gamma},$$

$$(\text{R}\backslash)\ \frac{\alpha, \Gamma \Rightarrow \beta}{\Gamma \Rightarrow \alpha\backslash\beta}, \quad (\text{R}/)\ \frac{\Gamma, \alpha \Rightarrow \beta}{\Gamma \Rightarrow \beta/\alpha},$$

$$(\text{L1})\ \frac{\Gamma, \Gamma' \Rightarrow \alpha}{\Gamma, 1, \Gamma' \Rightarrow \alpha} \quad (\text{R1})\ \Rightarrow 1,$$

N. Asher and S. Soloviev (Eds.): LACL 2014, LNCS 8535, pp. 30–43, 2014.
© Springer-Verlag Berlin Heidelberg 2014

$$(\text{L}\wedge) \ \frac{\Gamma, \alpha_i, \Gamma' \Rightarrow \beta}{\Gamma, \alpha_1 \wedge \alpha_2, \Gamma' \Rightarrow \beta}, \ (\text{R}\wedge) \ \frac{\Gamma \Rightarrow \alpha; \ \Gamma \Rightarrow \beta}{\Gamma \Rightarrow \alpha \wedge \beta},$$

$$(\text{L}\vee) \ \frac{\Gamma, \alpha, \Gamma' \Rightarrow \gamma; \ \Gamma, \beta, \Gamma' \Rightarrow \gamma}{\Gamma, \alpha \vee \beta, \Gamma' \Rightarrow \gamma}, \ (\text{R}\vee) \ \frac{\Gamma \Rightarrow \alpha_i}{\Gamma \Rightarrow \alpha_1 \vee \alpha_2},$$

$$(\text{CUT}) \ \frac{\Gamma, \alpha, \Gamma' \Rightarrow \beta; \ \Delta \Rightarrow \alpha}{\Gamma, \Delta, \Gamma' \Rightarrow \beta},$$

where $i \in \{1, 2\}$ in $(\text{L}\wedge)$ and $(\text{R}\vee)$.

Optionally one can add a new constant 0 (no axioms or rules for 0) and the constants $\perp, \top$ with the axioms:

$$(\text{a}\perp) \ \Gamma, \perp, \Gamma' \Rightarrow \alpha \ (\text{a}\top) \ \Gamma \Rightarrow \top.$$

One defines (substructural) negations: $\sim \alpha = \alpha \backslash 0, \ -\alpha = 0/\alpha$.

A formula α is said to be provable, if $\Rightarrow \alpha$ is provable. Every sequent is deductively equivalent to a single formula: $\Gamma \Rightarrow \alpha$ and $\Rightarrow \Gamma \backslash \alpha$ are derivable from each other. Here $\Gamma \backslash \alpha$ is recursively defined as follows: $\epsilon \backslash \alpha = \alpha, (\Gamma\beta) \backslash \alpha = \beta \backslash (\Gamma \backslash \alpha)$. $\Gamma\beta$ denotes the concatenation of Γ and (β). In antecedents of sequents we write Γ, Δ for $\Gamma\Delta$.

FL^* is FL_1 restricted to sequents without 1; so (L1) and (R1) are dropped. FL is FL^* restricted to sequents $\Gamma \Rightarrow \alpha$ with $\Gamma \neq \epsilon$; this means, one requires $\Gamma \neq \epsilon$ in $(\text{R}\backslash), (\text{R}/), (\text{a}\top)$. According to the terminology of linear logics, $\cdot, \backslash, /, 1, 0$ are *multiplicative* connectives and constants, whereas $\wedge, \vee, \perp, \top$ are *additive* connectives and constants. In formulae we assume a higher priority of multiplicatives over additives. The multiplicative fragment of FL is called Lambek Calculus and denoted by L. L^* is the multiplicative fragment of FL^* and L_1 of FL_1. So L_1 is axiomatized by (Id), $(\text{L}\cdot), (\text{R}\cdot), (\text{L}\backslash), (\text{R}\backslash), (\text{L}/), (\text{R}/)$, (L1), (R1) and (CUT), L^* drops (L1) and (R1), and L additionally requires $\Gamma \neq \epsilon$ in $(\text{R}\backslash), (\text{R}/)$.

For any logic $\mathcal{L}, \vdash_{\mathcal{L}} \Gamma \Rightarrow \alpha$ means: $\Gamma \Rightarrow \alpha$ is provable in $\mathcal{L}$. $\vdash_{\mathcal{L}} \alpha \Leftrightarrow \beta$ means: $\vdash_{\mathcal{L}} \alpha \Rightarrow \beta$ and $\vdash_{\mathcal{L}} \beta \Rightarrow \alpha$; for all logics considered here, this relation is a congruence in the algebra of formulae. In logics, all axioms and rules, hence all provable sequents, are closed under substitutions. In opposition to axioms, *assumptions* are some particular sequents added to the logic: logics enriched with assumptions are called *theories* (they appear in Section 3).

Lambek [14] proves the cut-elimination theorem for L: every sequent provable in L is also provable in L without (CUT). The same theorem holds for all systems mentioned above; the first proof for a version of FL_1 is due to Ono and Komori [21]. This yields the decidability of these systems, since the proof search tree of any sequent is finite. This also yields *the subformula property*: every provable sequent has a proof such that all formulae appearing in this proof are subformulae of the formulae occurring in this sequent. As a consequence, FL_1 is a conservative extension of FL^* and L_1 of L^*; also FL^* (resp. FL) is a conservative extension of L^* (resp. L). L^* is not a conservative extension of L; e.g. $p/(q/q) \Rightarrow p$ is provable in L^* but not in L, and similarly FL^* is not a conservative extension of FL.

FL_1 and FL^* are complete with respect to residuated lattices, L_1 and L^* with respect to residuated monoids, and L (resp. FL) with respect to (resp. lattice-ordered) residuated semigroups; see [6,1]. Algebras do not play any essential role in the present paper, so we skip the precise definitions. We only recall that in algebraic models the antecedent sequence $(\alpha_1, \ldots, \alpha_n)$ is interpreted as the product $\alpha_1 \cdots \alpha_n$ (the empty antecedent as the unit element) and $\Rightarrow$ as $\leq$. Substructural logics are often defined as axiomatic and rule extensions of FL_1 (possibly with $0, \perp, \top$), and their classes of algebraic models are quasi-varieties of residuated lattices; see [6,8]. In this paper we regard a wider class of logics, containing such logics as FL, L, which are standard type logics in type grammars.

One also considers systems with structural rules of exchange (e), integrality (i) and contraction (c) of the following form:

$$\text{(e)} \ \frac{\Gamma, \alpha, \beta, \Gamma' \Rightarrow \gamma}{\Gamma, \beta, \alpha, \Gamma' \Rightarrow \gamma}, \ \text{(i)} \ \frac{\Gamma, \Gamma' \Rightarrow \beta}{\Gamma, \alpha, \Gamma' \Rightarrow \beta},$$

$$\text{(c)} \ \frac{\Gamma, \Delta, \Delta, \Gamma' \Rightarrow \alpha}{\Gamma, \Delta, \Gamma' \Rightarrow \alpha}.$$

A stronger form of contraction is the set of two rules:

$$\text{(c1)} \ \frac{\Gamma_1, \alpha, \Gamma_2, \alpha, \Gamma_3 \Rightarrow \gamma}{\Gamma_1, \Gamma_2, \alpha, \Gamma_3 \Rightarrow \gamma}, \ \text{(c2)} \ \frac{\Gamma_1, \alpha, \Gamma_2, \alpha, \Gamma_3 \Rightarrow \gamma}{\Gamma_1, \alpha, \Gamma_2, \Gamma_3 \Rightarrow \gamma}.$$

(c) is equivalent to $\{c1, c2\}$ in the presence of (e) or (i). Our further results involving (c) remain true for $\{c1, c2\}$.

If $S \subseteq \{e, i, c\}$, then FL_S denotes FL enriched with all rules from S, and similarly for FL_1 (we write: $FL_{1,S}$) and other systems. For example, L_{ei} stands for L enriched with (e) and (i). For systems with (e), $\alpha \cdot \beta \Leftrightarrow \beta \cdot \alpha$ and $\alpha \backslash \beta \Leftrightarrow \beta / \alpha$ are provable, and one writes $\alpha \to \beta$ for both $\alpha \backslash \beta$ and β / α.

[6] also admits sequents of the form $\Gamma \Rightarrow$ with the axiom (0) $0 \Rightarrow$ and the rule of right weakening (o): from $\Gamma \Rightarrow$ infer $\Gamma \Rightarrow \alpha$. Here we do not admit such sequents; (o) with (0) can be replaced by the definition $0 = \perp$.

In the literature on substructural logics, systems like FL_1 are more popular than systems like FL. In FL no single formula is a theorem, hence it lacks sense to formalize FL as a Hilbert-style system and makes it difficult to compare this logic with other nonclassical logics. It is well known that many important nonclassical logics, e.g. Łukasiewicz multi-valued logics, Hajek fuzzy logics, relevant logics, linear logics and others, can be presented as axiomatic extensions of FL_1 with 0; see [6].

A type grammar based on the logic $\mathcal{L}$ (an $\mathcal{L}$–grammar) is defined as a triple $G = (\Sigma_G, I_G, \delta_G)$ such that Σ_G is a nonempty finite alphabet (lexicon), I_G is a map assigning a finite set of formulae (types) to any element of Σ_G, and δ_G is a formula; I_G is called the lexical type assignment and δ_G the designated type of G. One says that G assigns type α to the string $a_1 \ldots a_n$, where each $a_i \in \Sigma_G$, if for any $i = 1, \ldots, n$, there exists $\alpha_i \in I_G(a_i)$ such that $\alpha_1, \ldots, \alpha_n \Rightarrow \alpha$ is provable in $\mathcal{L}$; we write: $a_1 \ldots a_n : \alpha$ in G. $L(G, \alpha)$ denotes the set of all strings u such that $u : \alpha$ in G. $L(G, \delta_G)$ is called the language of G (or: generated by G) and denoted $L(G)$. The designated type is often a variable, and one denotes it by s_G. For natural language, $L(G, s_G)$ is intended to consist of all correct sentences of the language. In the definition of $a_1 \ldots a_n : \alpha$ one usually stipulates $n > 0$, and consequently $L(G, \alpha)$ does not contain ϵ. If $\mathcal{L}$ allows empty antecedents of sequents, this definition can be extended for $n = 0$, and consequently, $\epsilon \in L(G, \alpha)$ is admitted.

Type grammars mostly employ systems without empty antecedents of sequents. Although mathematical linguistics accepts languages containing ϵ, in type grammars one usually assigns types to nonempty strings only. This is motivated by: (1) semantics (e.g. the empty string has no meaning), (2) economy (the type assignment is simpler). Let us comment more on this matter.

$\alpha/\alpha \Leftrightarrow (\alpha/\alpha)/(\alpha/\alpha)$ is provable in L^*. As a consequence, the adverb 'very', if typed $(N/N)/(N/N)$ (N is the type of common nouns), would be indistinguishable from adjectives, typed N/N, which is a linguistic nonsense; see [20]. One can overcome these problems by making the type assignment more complex, e.g. assigning a special atomic type to adjectives, but this is less satisfactory from the semantical point of view. Lambek's pregroup grammars, based on a logic with 1, employ a great number of atomic types: 33 for a fragment of English (see [17]).

Here is an example of a formal language. The language $L = \{a^n b^n : n \geq 1\}$ is generated by the L-grammar which assigns $a : s/p, (s/p)/s$ and $b : p$ (the grammar assigns s to precisely all strings from L). The language $L' = \{a^n b^n : n \geq 0\}$ requires a more involved type assignment on the basis of L^*; see a general solution in [12]. A seemingly easy solution, namely substitution of s/s for s in the above (s/s is the designated type), does not work, because $s/s, s/s \Rightarrow s/s$ is provable in L^*, hence the grammar assigns s/s also to strings from $L' \cdot L'$. (This typing, however, is good for Nonassociative Lambek Calculus.)

To unify the research in type grammars and substructural logics one needs a closer examination of the connections between systems like FL and systems like FL*. This is the aim of the present paper.

In Section 2 we translate every formula α in the language $(\cdot, \backslash, /, \wedge, \vee)$, optionally containing $0, \bot, \top$, into two formulae $N(\alpha), P(\alpha)$ (the negative and the positive translation of α) of this language. We prove (N-P): for any sequent $\alpha_1, \ldots, \alpha_n \Rightarrow \alpha$ ($n > 0$), this sequent is provable in FL* if and only if $N(\alpha_1), \ldots, N(\alpha_n) \Rightarrow P(\alpha)$ is provable in FL. The same holds for systems enriched with structural rules. In the proof of (N-P) it is essential that the logics allow cut elimination.

The translations N, P essentially employ additives and cannot be defined for the multiplicative fragments. For the latter, N, P are replaced by multi-valued maps which send a formula to a finite set of formulae. An analogue of (N-P) is proved. For the $(\backslash, /)$–fragment of L^*, N, P were already defined in [2].

As a consequence, we infer that every ϵ–free language generated by a type grammar based on a logic $\mathcal{L}^*$, allowing empty antecedents and satisfying (N-P) with respect to a subsystem $\mathcal{L}$, not allowing empty antecedents, is also generated by some type grammar based on $\mathcal{L}$.

In Section 3 we apply (N-P) to obtain some new results on the complexity of substructural logics. Recall that a logic is said to be *consistent*, if not every sequent is provable. An extension of FL* is consistent if and only if p is not provable (p is an arbitrary variable); an extension of FL is consistent if and only if $p \Rightarrow q$ is not provable (p, q are arbitrary, distinct variables). *The disjunction property* (DP) states: if $\alpha \vee \beta$ is provable, then α or β is provable. Notice that (DP) evidently holds for all logics FL_S^*, $FL_{1,S}$, since in the cut-free proof of $\Rightarrow \alpha \vee \beta$ the last rule must be (R$\vee$). This, however, need not be true for logics not allowing cut elimination.

Horčik and Terui [8] prove: every consistent substructural logic (an extension of FL_1, possibly in a different language) satisfying (DP) is PSPACE-hard. (Some positive examples are FL_1 and intuitionistic logic IL; a negative example is classical logic CL, which does not satisfy (DP) and is coNP-complete.) These authors apply a reduction of the validity of quantified boolean formulae to the provability of sequents in the given logic.

It is easy to see that their proof yields a stronger result: every logic between FL_1 and some arbitrary consistent substructural logic satisfying (DP) is PSPACE-hard (a logic is identified with its set of provable sequents; so 'between' refers to set inclusion). In particular, all logics between FL_1 and IL are PSPACE-hard. Recall that $IL=FL_{1,\perp,eic}$ (in fact, '=' means the identity of Lindenbaum-Tarski algebras). This result cannot directly be extended to logics without empty antecedents of sequents. (DP) lacks sense for such logics (one might say that (DP) trivially holds, since $\alpha \vee \beta$ is never provable, but the proof from [8] does not go for this case). Furthermore, this proof essentially relies on sequents with empty antecedents and the presence of 1 in models, e.g. it uses the provability of $\alpha/(\beta\backslash\beta) \Rightarrow \alpha$ (not true for FL-like logics) and single formulae p (i.e. sequents $\Rightarrow p$) as assumptions.

By a modification of the proof from [8], with the aid of (N-P) we prove: every logic between FL and some arbitrary consistent substructural logic satisfying (DP) is PSPACE-hard. (By a refinement of the proof in [8] one can prove the same result without (N-P).) This implies the PSPACE-hardness of FL, all systems FL_S (subsystems of IL), DFL, i.e. FL with the distributive laws for $\wedge, \vee$ (a subsystem of IL), all logics between FL and MALL (Mutiplicative-Additive Linear Logic; i.e. $FL_{1,0,e}$ with the axiom $(\alpha \to 0) \to 0 \Rightarrow \alpha$), and others. Some of them satisfy (DP), e.g. all systems FL_S, IL and MALL, some do not, or (DP) is not meaningful for them. An advantage of our statement of the theorem is that one need not worry about (DP) for each particular logic.

If the given PSPACE-hard logic is PSPACE, then it is PSPACE-complete. This holds for all systems FL_S, $FL_{1,S}$, where S either does not contain (c), or contains both (c) and (i), and for linear logics MALL, NMALL (i.e. Noncommutative MALL), CyMALL (i.e. Cyclic MALL). It is not known whether DFL is PSPACE.

The PSPACE-completeness of several substructural logics was proved earlier. Early results on linear logics are discussed in [18,10]. Kanazawa [10] proves the PSPACE-completeness of FL^*, using an encoding of quantifiers different from that in [8]. Kanazawa's proof works for FL as well, but it is not clear whether it works for other systems FL_S and DFL ([10] skips all proofs of lemmata). As noted in [8], it does not work for logics containing $(\alpha \cdot \beta) \wedge (\alpha \cdot \gamma) \Rightarrow \alpha \cdot (\beta \wedge \gamma)$.

Hence it certainly does not work for IL (satisfying this law, since · collapses with ∧; the PSPACE-completeness of IL was proved by Statman [24]), nor infinitely many other logics, being covered by the results of [8] and the present paper (covering more).

At the end, we briefly discuss the role of logics with ∧, ∨ in type grammars. Their applications in this role are not very frequent, but there are good reasons to regard them. Some recent contributions were presented on Formal Grammars 2012, 2013.

Types with ∧ were already applied in [15] in order to replace a multi-valued type assignment $a : \alpha_1, \ldots, \alpha_n$ by the one-valued assignment $a : \alpha_1 \wedge \cdots \wedge \alpha_n$ (Lambek writes $[\alpha, \beta]$ for $\alpha \wedge \beta$). Lambek [16] decomposes some atomic types in subtypes, e.g. π (subject) is decomposed in π_1, π_2, π_3 (subject in k−th person). Lambek's non-lexical assumptions $\pi_k \Rightarrow \pi$, $k = 1, 2, 3$, can be replaced by the definition $\pi = \pi_1 \vee \pi_2 \vee \pi_3$. Kanazawa [9] considers a feature-decomposition, e.g. the type np (noun phrase) is decomposed in np ∧ sing (singular noun phrase) and np ∧ pl (plural noun phrase).

These examples suggest that ∧, ∨ are interpreted as the set-theoretic intersection and union of languages; the corresponding language models are distributive lattices (even boolean lattices). FL is not complete with respect to these models, since it does not prove the distributive laws for ∧, ∨. The complete logic for residuated semigroups based on distributive lattices is DFL.

Let us note an interesting linguistic interpretation of FL. Clark [5] proposes a particular kind of concept lattices, called *syntactic concept lattices* (SCLs). Let Σ be a finite alphabet. A context is a pair (u, v), where $u, v \in \Sigma^*$. We fix a language $L \subseteq \Sigma^*$. Every set of contexts S determines the S−category (concept) $\{w \in \Sigma^* : \text{for all } (u, v) \in S, uwv \in L\}$; in particular, L is the category determined by $\{(\epsilon, \epsilon)\}$. (This approach to grammatical categories is close to *contextual grammars* of S. Marcus.) One shows that all S−categories form a closure system, and the corresponding closure operation C is a nucleus on $\mathcal{P}(\Sigma^*)$. The family of C−closed sets is a complete residuated lattice, called the SCL determined by the language L. Clark applies this notion in some learning procedures for context-free grammars. Wurm [25] shows that FL* is strongly complete with respect to SCLs, and a similar result can be proved for FL and appropriately modified SCLs.

2 Interpretations

In what follows ⊢ and ⊢* denote the provability relations in FL and FL*, respectively. For any formula α of FL (hence also FL*) we define two formulae $N(\alpha)$ and $P(\alpha)$ of FL (the negative and the positive translation of α), by the following recursion on α.

(I1) $N(p) = P(p) = p$, for variables p,
(I2) $N(\alpha \circ \beta) = N(\alpha) \circ N(\beta)$, for $\circ \in \{\cdot, \wedge, \vee\}$,
(I3) $N(\alpha \backslash \beta) = P(\alpha) \backslash N(\beta)$ and $N(\beta/\alpha) = N(\beta)/P(\alpha)$, if $\nvdash^* \alpha$,
(I4) $N(\alpha \backslash \beta) = P(\alpha) \backslash N(\beta) \wedge N(\beta)$ and $N(\beta/\alpha) = N(\beta)/P(\alpha) \wedge N(\beta)$, if $\vdash^* \alpha$,

(I5) $P(\alpha \circ \beta) = P(\alpha) \circ P(\beta)$, for $\circ \in \{\wedge, \vee\}$,

(I6) $P(\alpha \backslash \beta) = N(\alpha) \backslash P(\beta)$ and $P(\beta / \alpha) = P(\beta) / N(\alpha)$,

(I7) $P(\alpha \cdot \beta) = P(\alpha) \cdot P(\beta)$, if $\nvdash^* \alpha$ and $\nvdash^* \beta$,

(I8) $P(\alpha \cdot \beta) = P(\alpha) \cdot P(\beta) \vee P(\beta)$, if $\vdash^* \alpha$ and $\nvdash^* \beta$,

(I9) $P(\alpha \cdot \beta) = P(\alpha) \cdot P(\beta) \vee P(\alpha)$, if $\nvdash^* \alpha$ and $\vdash^* \beta$,

(I10) $P(\alpha \cdot \beta) = (P(\alpha) \cdot P(\beta) \vee P(\alpha)) \vee P(\beta)$, if $\vdash^* \alpha$ and $\vdash^* \beta$.

The constants $0, \bot, \top$ are treated as p in (I1).

Lemma 1. *For any formula γ: (i) $\vdash N(\gamma) \Rightarrow \gamma$, (ii) $\vdash \gamma \Rightarrow P(\gamma)$, (iii) $\vdash^* \gamma \Rightarrow N(\gamma)$, (iv) $\vdash^* P(\gamma) \Rightarrow \gamma$.*

Proof. We prove (i), (ii) by simultaneous induction on γ. For atoms we use (I1), (Id).

Let $\gamma = \alpha \cdot \beta$. Since $\vdash N(\alpha) \Rightarrow \alpha$ and $\vdash N(\beta) \Rightarrow \beta$ and $N(\gamma) = N(\alpha) \cdot N(\beta)$, we obtain (i), by (R·), (L·). In a similar way we get $\vdash \gamma \Rightarrow P(\alpha) \cdot P(\beta)$, which yields (ii) with the aid of (R∨).

Let $\gamma = \alpha \backslash \beta$. Then, $P(\gamma) = N(\alpha) \backslash P(\beta)$, and (ii) holds by the induction hypothesis, (L\) and (R\). In a similar way we obtain $\vdash P(\alpha) \backslash N(\beta) \Rightarrow \gamma$. If $\vdash^* \alpha$, then $N(\gamma) = P(\alpha) \backslash N(\beta) \wedge N(\beta)$, and (i) holds, by (L∧); otherwise (i) holds immediately. For $\gamma = \beta / \alpha$ the argument is similar.

Let $\gamma = \alpha \wedge \beta$. Then, $N(\gamma) = N(\alpha) \wedge N(\beta)$ and $P(\gamma) = P(\alpha) \wedge P(\beta)$. Consequently, (i) and (ii) hold, by the induction hypothesis, (L∧), (R∧). For $\gamma = \alpha \vee \beta$ the argument is similar.

We prove (iii) and (iv) by simultaneous induction on γ. The argument goes as above. We only write two interesting cases. We prove (iii) for $\gamma = \alpha \backslash \beta$. By the induction hypothesis, (L\), (R\), we get $\vdash^* \gamma \Rightarrow P(\alpha) \backslash N(\beta)$, so (iii) holds provided that $\nvdash^* \alpha$. If $\vdash^* \alpha$, then $\vdash^* \gamma \Rightarrow N(\beta)$, by (L\), and consequently, $\vdash^* \gamma \Rightarrow P(\alpha) \backslash N(\beta) \wedge N(\beta)$, by (R∧), which yields (iii). We prove (iv) for $\gamma = \alpha \cdot \beta$. Again $\vdash^* P(\alpha) \cdot P(\beta) \Rightarrow \gamma$ holds, by the induction hypothesis, (R·), (L·). If $\nvdash^* \alpha$ and $\nvdash^* \beta$, this yields (iv). If $\nvdash^* \alpha$ and $\vdash^* \beta$, then $\vdash^* P(\alpha) \Rightarrow \gamma$, by the induction hypothesis and (R·), and consequently, $\vdash^* P(\alpha) \cdot P(\beta) \vee P(\alpha) \Rightarrow \gamma$, by (L∨), which yields (iv). The two remaining subcases are handled similarly. □

Corollary 1. *For any formula γ, $\vdash^* N(\gamma) \Leftrightarrow \gamma$ and $\vdash^* P(\gamma) \Leftrightarrow \gamma$.*

For $\Gamma = (\alpha_1, \ldots, \alpha_n)$, we define $N(\Gamma) = (N(\alpha_1), \ldots, N(\alpha_n))$.

Theorem 1. *For any sequent $\Phi \Rightarrow \gamma$ with $\Phi \neq \epsilon$, there holds: $\vdash^* \Phi \Rightarrow \gamma$ if and only if $\vdash N(\Phi) \Rightarrow P(\gamma)$.*

Proof. The implication ($\Leftarrow$) follows from Lemma 1 ((iii), (iv)), by (CUT). The implication ($\Rightarrow$) is proved by induction on cut-free proofs in FL*. For axioms $\alpha \Rightarrow \alpha$, we get $\vdash N(\alpha) \Rightarrow P(\alpha)$, by Lemma 1 ((i), (ii)) and (CUT).

We consider rule (L\). Let $\Delta \neq \epsilon$. By the induction hypothesis, $\vdash N(\Gamma \beta \Gamma') \Rightarrow P(\gamma)$ and $\vdash N(\Delta) \Rightarrow P(\alpha)$, hence $\vdash N(\Gamma \Delta), P(\alpha) \backslash N(\beta), N(\Gamma') \Rightarrow P(\gamma)$, by (L\). $P(\alpha) \backslash N(\beta)$ can be replaced with $N(\alpha \backslash \beta)$, by applying (L∧) (if needed).

Let $\Delta = \epsilon$. As above, we have $\vdash N(\Gamma\beta\Gamma') \Rightarrow P(\gamma)$, hence $\vdash N(\Gamma(\alpha\backslash\beta)\Gamma') \Rightarrow P(\gamma)$, by (L$\wedge$). For (L/) the argument is similar.

We consider rule (R$\cdot$). Then $\Gamma\Delta \neq \epsilon$, so we consider three subcases. (1) $\Gamma \neq \epsilon$, $\Delta \neq \epsilon$. By the induction hypothesis, we get $\vdash N(\Gamma) \Rightarrow P(\alpha)$ and $\vdash N(\Delta) \Rightarrow P(\beta)$. Hence $\vdash N(\Gamma\Delta) \Rightarrow P(\alpha)\cdot P(\beta)$, by (R$\cdot$), which yields $\vdash N(\Gamma\Delta) \Rightarrow P(\alpha\cdot\beta)$, by (R$\vee$) (if needed). (2) $\Gamma \neq \epsilon$, $\Delta = \epsilon$. As above, $\vdash N(\Gamma) \Rightarrow P(\alpha)$, which yields $\vdash N(\Gamma) \Rightarrow P(\alpha \cdot \beta)$, by (R$\vee$). (3) $\Gamma = \epsilon$, $\Delta \neq \epsilon$. As above, $\vdash N(\Delta) \Rightarrow P(\beta)$, which yields $\vdash N(\Delta) \Rightarrow P(\alpha \cdot \beta)$, by (R$\vee$).

The arguments for other rules and axioms (a$\perp$), (a$\top$) are easy. $\square$

Lemma 2. *For any formula* γ, $\vdash N(N(\gamma)) \Leftrightarrow N(\gamma)$ *and* $\vdash P(P(\gamma)) \Leftrightarrow P(\gamma)$.

Proof. The proof proceeds by simultaneous induction on γ. We only consider the case: $\gamma = \alpha\backslash\beta$. Let $\vdash^* \alpha$. Then, $\vdash^* P(\alpha)$, by Corollary 1. We compute:

$$N(N(\gamma)) = N(P(\alpha)\backslash N(\beta) \wedge N(\beta)) = N(P(\alpha)\backslash N(\beta)) \wedge N(N(\beta)) =$$

$$P(P(\alpha))\backslash N(N(\beta)) \wedge N(N(\beta)) \wedge N(N(\beta)) \Leftrightarrow P(\alpha)\backslash N(\beta) \wedge N(\beta) = N(\gamma).$$

Let $\not\vdash^* \alpha$. As above, $\not\vdash^* P(\alpha)$, and we compute:

$$N(N(\gamma)) = N(P(\alpha)\backslash N(\beta)) = P(P(\alpha))\backslash N(N(\beta)) \Leftrightarrow P(\alpha)\backslash N(\beta) = N(\gamma).$$

The proof of $P(P(\gamma)) \Leftrightarrow P(\gamma)$ is similar to the latter. $\square$

Sequents of the form $N(\Gamma) \Rightarrow P(\alpha)$, where $\Gamma \neq \epsilon$, are said to be *stable*. By Corollary 1, every sequent $\Gamma \Rightarrow \alpha$ with $\Gamma \neq \epsilon$ is deductively equivalent in FL* to a stable sequent.

Corollary 2. *A stable sequent is provable in* FL* *if and only if it is provable in* FL.

Proof. The implication ($\Leftarrow$) is obvious, since FL is a subsystem of FL*. For ($\Rightarrow$), consider a stable sequent $N(\Gamma) \Rightarrow P(\alpha)$, provable in FL*. By Theorem 1, $N(N(\Gamma)) \Rightarrow P(P(\alpha))$ is provable in FL. By Lemma 2 and (CUT), $N(\Gamma) \Rightarrow P(\alpha)$ is provable in FL. $\square$

The provability of single formulae in FL* can be reduced to the provability in FL. In other words, a decision method for FL yields a decision method for FL*. One uses the facts: (1) $\vdash^* \alpha \cdot \beta$ iff $\vdash^* \alpha$ and $\vdash^* \beta$, (2) the same for $\alpha \wedge \beta$, (3) $\vdash^* \alpha \vee \beta$ iff $\vdash^* \alpha$ or $\vdash^* \beta$, (4) $\vdash^* \alpha\backslash\beta$ iff $\vdash N(\alpha) \Rightarrow P(\beta)$, (5) the same for β/α, (7) $\not\vdash^* p$, $\not\vdash^* 0$, $\not\vdash^* \perp$, $\vdash^* \top$.

Structural rules cause no difficulty for the above arguments. Only (i) needs the additional lemma: if $\vdash^* \gamma$, then $\vdash \Gamma \Rightarrow \gamma$, for any $\Gamma \neq \epsilon$, which can be proved by induction of γ (here $\vdash^*$ denotes the probability in FL$^*_S$ and $\vdash$ the provability in FL$_S$, where S contains (i)).

Consequently, Theorem 1 and other results remain true for all systems FL$^*_S$. DFL can be presented as a sequent system with cut elimination [11], and our interpretation works for DFL and its version without empty antecedents.

Clearly it works for some language-restricted fragments, e.g. $(\backslash, \wedge)$, $(\backslash, /, \wedge, \vee)$, $(\cdot, \vee)$ and others, but not for the multiplicative fragments (see below). Associativity plays no essential role, hence the interpretation can be applied for nonassociative versions of Full Lambek Calculus, i.e. FNL (also denoted by GL) and its extensions; see [4,3,7] for more information on these logics.

The precise generative capacity of type grammars based on FL and its companions is not known; Kanazawa [9] shows that FL-grammars generate all finite intersections of ϵ-free context-free languages. On the contrary, the languages of FNL-grammars (also with assumptions) are context-free; see [4].

We state a general result. Let $\mathcal{L}^*$ be a logic allowing empty antecedents of sequents and satisfying Theorem 1, where $\vdash^*$ denotes the provability in $\mathcal{L}^*$ and $\vdash$ denotes the provability in a logic $\mathcal{L}$.

Corollary 3. *Every ϵ-free language generated by an $\mathcal{L}^*$-grammar is also generated by an $\mathcal{L}$-grammar.*

Proof. Let G be an $\mathcal{L}^*$-grammar such that $\epsilon \notin L(G)$. We define an $\mathcal{L}$-grammar G': $\Sigma_{G'} = \Sigma_G$, $\delta_{G'} = P(\delta_G)$ and for any $a \in \Sigma_G$, $I_{G'}(a) = \{N(\alpha) : \alpha \in I_G(a)\}$. By Theorem 1, $L(G) = L(G')$. □

For L* and its variants, N, P are defined as multi-valued maps; for any formula α, we define finite sets of formulae $N(\alpha), P(\alpha)$, both containing α. If X, Y are sets of formulae and $\circ$ is a binary connective, then one defines $X \circ Y = \{\alpha \circ \beta : \alpha \in X, \beta \in Y\}$. The new definition of N, P can be formulated by clauses looking like (I1)-(I10) except that $N(p) = P(p) = \{p\}$, the clauses for $\wedge, \vee$ are omitted, and (I4), (I8)-(I10) take the following form:

(I4') $N(\alpha\backslash\beta) = P(\alpha)\backslash N(\beta) \cup N(\beta)$ and $N(\beta/\alpha) = N(\beta)/P(\alpha) \cup N(\beta)$, if $\vdash^* \alpha$,
(I8') $P(\alpha \cdot \beta) = P(\alpha) \cdot P(\beta) \cup P(\beta)$, if $\vdash^* \alpha, \nvdash^* \beta$,
(I9') $P(\alpha \cdot \beta) = P(\alpha) \cdot P(\beta) \cup P(\alpha)$, if $\nvdash^* \alpha, \vdash^* \beta$,
(I10') $P(\alpha \cdot \beta) = P(\alpha) \cdot P(\beta) \cup P(\alpha) \cup P(\beta)$, if $\vdash^* \alpha, \vdash^* \beta$.

Theorem 2. *For any sequent $\gamma_1, \ldots, \gamma_n \Rightarrow \gamma$ ($n \geq 1$) in language $(\cdot, \backslash, /)$, this sequent is provable in L* if and only if for any $1 \leq i \leq n$ there exists $\beta_i \in N(\gamma_i)$ and there exists $\beta \in P(\gamma)$ such that $\beta_1, \ldots, \beta_n \Rightarrow \beta$ is provable in L.*

The proof is similar to that of Theorem 1. The implication ($\Leftarrow$) follows from an analogue of Lemma 1 (iii): if $\beta \in N(\gamma)$ then $\vdash^* \gamma \Rightarrow \beta$, (iv): if $\beta \in P(\gamma)$ then $\vdash^* \beta \Rightarrow \gamma$. Theorem 2 remains true for systems with structural rules.

An analogue of Corollary 3 holds, if δ_G is atomic; one defines $I_{G'} = \bigcup\{N(\alpha) : \alpha \in I_G(a)\}$. If δ_G is not atomic, then, in general, $L(G)$ is the union of finitely many languages generated by $\mathcal{L}$-grammars. We note an application. From the Pentus theorem [22] that L-grammars generate context-free languages it follows immediately that also L*-grammars generate context-free languages (the dissertation of M. Pentus contains a direct proof of the latter).

Kuznetsov [13] defines a reduction of L_1 to L*. In $\Gamma \Rightarrow \gamma$ one replaces every occurrence of 1 by q/q and every occurrence of a variable p by $((q/q) \cdot p) \cdot (q/q)$, where q is a fixed new variable. The resulting sequence is provable in L* if and only if $\Gamma \Rightarrow \gamma$ is provable in L_1. It is easy to see that this reduction also works for systems with $\wedge, \vee$ and structural rules. The superposition of Kuznetsov's reduction with ours yields a reduction of $FL_{1,S}$ to FL_S.

3   PSPACE-Hardness

Horčik and Terui [8] reduce the validity problem for quantified boolean formulae (QBFs) to the provability problem for some substructural logics. Following their notation (with minor changes), a QBF is a formula of the form $Q_n x_n \ldots Q_1 x_1 \varphi_0$ such that $Q_i \in \{\forall, \exists\}$, for $i = 1, \ldots, n$, and φ_0 is a propositional formula in DNF, i.e. a finite disjunction of finite conjunctions of literals; $x_1, \ldots, x_n$ stand here for propositional (boolean) variables occurring in φ_0 (the reverse order in the prefix is a purely technical trick, making proofs by induction more elegant). It is well-known that the validity problem for closed QBFs is PSPACE-complete.

We briefly recall the proof from [8]. Fix a closed QBF φ, presented as above. $\varphi_0 = \psi_1 \vee \cdots \vee \psi_m$, where each ψ_j is a finite conjunction of literals. We fix different variables $p_1, \ldots, p_n, \bar{p}_1, \ldots, \bar{p}_n, q_1, \ldots, q_n$ (not all q_i are really needed). ψ_j is encoded as $\beta_j = l_1 \cdot l_2 \cdots l_n$, where $l_i = p_i$ if x_i occurs in ψ_j (as a literal), $l_i = \bar{p}_i$ if $\neg x_i$ occurs in ψ_j, and $l_i = p_i \vee \bar{p}_i$ otherwise. φ_0 is encoded as $\alpha_0 = \beta_1 \vee \cdots \vee \beta_m$. This encoding is the same as in [10], the encoding of quantifiers is different. For any $1 \le k \le n$, the formula $\varphi_k = Q_k x_k \ldots Q_1 x_1 \varphi_0$ is encoded by α_k defined as follows. If $Q_k = \forall$, then $\alpha_k = (p_k \vee \bar{p}_k) \backslash \alpha_{k-1}$. If $Q_k = \exists$, then $\alpha_k = (p_k \backslash q_k \vee \bar{p}_k \backslash q_k)/(\alpha_{k-1} \backslash q_k)$. (A simpler encoding could be $\alpha_k = p_k \backslash \alpha_{k-1} \vee \bar{p}_k \backslash \alpha_{k-1}$, but the size of α_k would be exponential in k.)

A partial valuation e_k assigns truth values 0, 1 to the variables $x_{k+1}, \ldots, x_n$. It is encoded by the sequence of variables $\varepsilon_k = (e_{k+1}^k, \ldots, e_n^k)$ such that $e_i^k = p_i$ if $e_k(x_i) = 1$, $e_i^k = \bar{p}_i$ if $e_k(x_i) = 0$. e_n is the empty valuation, and $\varepsilon_n = \epsilon$. We write $(r_1, \ldots, r_j) \vdash_{\mathcal{L}} \chi$, if χ is provable in $\mathcal{L}$ from the assumptions $r_1, \ldots, r_j$ (so the sequence is understood as a set of atomic assumptions).

We recall the main lemma in [8]. Let $\mathcal{L}$ be a consistent substructural logic satisfying (DP). By a substructural logic one means here an axiomatic extension of FL_1 (possibly in a richer language). [8] admits axiomatic and rule extensions, but it makes no difference, since for the complexity results, discussed here, a logic can be identified with its set of provable sequents. So every extension of FL_1 in the sense of [8] is an axiomatic extension of FL_1: one adds to FL_1 all sequents provable in this extension as new axioms.

(T1) For any $k \le n$, the following conditions are equivalent: (i) e_k satisfies φ_k, (ii) $\vdash_{\mathcal{L}} \varepsilon_k \Rightarrow \alpha_k$, (iii) $\varepsilon_k \vdash_{\mathcal{L}} \alpha_k$.

For $k = n$ this yields: φ is valid if and only if $\vdash_{\mathcal{L}} \alpha_n$, which entails the PSPACE-hardness of $\mathcal{L}$. (T1) is proved in [8] by induction on k, using algebraic tools, (DP) and the closure of $\mathcal{L}$ under the rules of FL_1.

It is easy to see that this proof yields the PSPACE-hardness of any substructural logic $\mathcal{L}$ such that $FL_1 \subseteq \mathcal{L} \subseteq \mathcal{L}'$, for some consistent substructural logic $\mathcal{L}'$ satisfying (DP). We show: φ is valid if and only if $\vdash_{\mathcal{L}} \alpha_n$. If φ is valid, then α_n

is provable in FL_1, hence in $\mathcal{L}$. If $\vdash_{\mathcal{L}} \alpha_n$, then α_n is provable in $\mathcal{L}'$, hence φ is valid.

We extend this result for axiomatic extensions of FL. In Theorem 3, $\mathcal{L}$ is understood as an axiomatic extension of FL (possibly in a richer language, also with sequents $\Rightarrow \alpha$), and $\mathcal{L}'$ is understood as an axiomatic extension of FL_1. (Here FL_1 can be replaced by FL^*, since every consistent axiomatic extension of FL^* remains consistent, after one has added 1 with (L1), (R1).) On the other hand, there exist consistent axiomatic extensions of FL, which become inconsistent, if empty antecedents are admitted. For instance, FL with the axiom $\alpha, \beta \Rightarrow \gamma$ is consistent. In models, the axiom means $a \cdot b = \bot$, for all a, b, hence $a\backslash b = b/a = \top$, for all a, b. The multiplicative part of this logic is degenerate, but the additive part is not, and $p \Rightarrow q$ is not provable. With empty antecedents, from $p, p\backslash p \Rightarrow q$ we infer $p \Rightarrow q$, by (CUT); the substitution of q/q for p and (R$\backslash$) yield $\Rightarrow (q/q)\backslash q$, hence $\Rightarrow q$, since $(q/q)\backslash q \Rightarrow q$ is provable in L^*. So the resulting logic is inconsistent.

In general, the size of $N(\alpha)$ and $P(\alpha)$ is exponential in the size of α. For instance, for $\alpha = (q\backslash q)^n\backslash p$ (here $(q\backslash q)^n$ denotes the sequence of n copies of $q\backslash q$), the size of α is linear in n, but $N(\alpha)$ contains 2^n occurrences of p. For some formulae α, however, $P(\alpha) = \alpha$, which is applied in the proof below.

Theorem 3. *If $FL \subseteq \mathcal{L} \subseteq \mathcal{L}'$, for some consistent substructural logic $\mathcal{L}'$ satisfying (DP), then $\mathcal{L}$ is PSPACE-hard.*

Proof. We fix a consistent substructural logic $\mathcal{L}'$, satisfying (DP). We slightly modify the encoding from [8]. Let φ be as above. Let p_0 be a new variable. ψ_j is encoded by $\beta_j^\varphi = \beta_j \cdot p_0$. φ_0 is encoded by $\alpha_0^\varphi = \beta_1^\varphi \vee \cdots \vee \beta_m^\varphi$. α_k^φ, for $k = 1, \ldots, n$, is defined as above. The explicit reference to φ will be needed below.

Notice that our encoding is the same as the former one for the formula χ which adds x_{n+1} (as a literal) to every elementary conjunction ψ_j in φ (p_0 encodes x_{n+1}). Evidently e_k satisfies φ_k if and only if the extended valuation which assigns 1 to x_{n+1} satisfies χ_k. Accordingly (T1) yields the following.

(T2) For any $k \leq n$, e_k satisfies φ_k if and only if $\vdash_{\mathcal{L}'} \varepsilon_k, p_0 \Rightarrow \alpha_k^\varphi$.

For $k = n$, we obtain:

$$\varphi \text{ is valid if and only if } \vdash_{\mathcal{L}'} p_0 \Rightarrow \alpha_n^\varphi. \tag{1}$$

In particular, (1) holds for $\mathcal{L}' = FL_1$. Since α_n^φ does not contain 1 and FL_1 is a conservative extension of FL^*, this equivalence also holds for $\mathcal{L}' = FL^*$. By Theorem 1, we obtain:

$$\varphi \text{ is valid if and only if } p_0 \Rightarrow P(\alpha_n^\varphi) \text{ is provable in FL.} \tag{2}$$

CLAIM 1. For any $k \leq n$, α_k^φ is not provable in FL^*.

By induction on k, we prove the stronger claim: for any formula φ with variables $x_1, \ldots, x_n$ (n depends on φ), if $k \leq n$, then α_k^φ is not provable in FL^*. For $n = 0$, we set $\alpha_0^\varphi = p_0$, taking $\varphi = 1$ (the empty conjunction).

Let $k = 0$. Assume that α_0^φ is provable in FL*. Then, it is provable in FL$_1$. We substitute 1 for all variables $p_i, \bar{p}_i$, $i = 1, \ldots, n$, which yields a provable formula γ such that $\gamma \Leftrightarrow p_0$ is provable in FL$_1$. Consequently p_0 is provable, which is impossible, since FL$_1$ is consistent.

Assume that α_k^φ, where $0 < k \leq n$, is provable in FL*. We consider two cases. (1) $Q_k = \forall$. Then $\alpha_k^\varphi = (p_k \vee \bar{p}_k)\backslash\alpha_{k-1}^\varphi$. We substitute 1 for p_k and $\bar{p}_k$, which yields a formula γ provable in FL$_1$ such that $\gamma \Leftrightarrow \alpha_{k-1}^\chi$ is also provable, where χ results from φ by dropping Q_k and all occurrences of x_k and $\neg x_k$. Consequently, α_{k-1}^χ is provable in FL*, against the induction hypothesis. (2) $Q_k = \exists$. Then $\alpha_k^\varphi = (p_k\backslash q_k \vee \bar{p}_k\backslash q_k)/(\alpha_{k-1}^\varphi\backslash q_k)$. We substitute 1 for p_k and $\bar{p}_k$, which yields a formula γ provable in FL$_1$ and such that $\gamma \Leftrightarrow q_k/(\alpha_{k-1}^\chi\backslash q_k)$ is provable, where χ is as above. Consequently $q_k/(\alpha_{k-1}^\chi\backslash q_k)$ is provable in FL*, hence α_{k-1}^χ is provable (substitute α_{k-1}^χ for q_k in the former and use the provable law $\alpha/(\alpha\backslash\alpha) \Rightarrow \alpha$). This contradicts the induction hypothesis.

CLAIM 2. For any $k \leq n$, $P(\alpha_k^\varphi) = \alpha_k^\varphi$, where P is computed for FL*.

We proceed by induction on k. For $k = 0$ the claim holds, by (I1), (I5), (I7) ((I8)-(I10) are not applicable, since no variable is provable in FL*). Let $k > 0$. For $Q_k = \forall$, we compute:

$$P(\alpha_k^\varphi) = N(p_k \vee \bar{p}_k)\backslash P(\alpha_{k-1}^\varphi) = (p_k \vee \bar{p}_k)\backslash\alpha_{k-1}^\varphi = \alpha_k^\varphi .$$

For $Q_k = \exists$, using Claim 1, we compute:

$$P(\alpha_k^\varphi) = P(p_k\backslash q_k \vee \bar{p}_k\backslash q_k)/N(\alpha_{k-1}^\varphi\backslash q_k) = (p_k\backslash q_k \vee \bar{p}_k\backslash q_k)/(P(\alpha_{k-1}^\varphi)\backslash q_k) = \alpha_k^\varphi .$$

By Claim 2 and (2), we obtain:

$$\varphi \text{ is valid if and only if } p_0 \Rightarrow \alpha_n^\varphi \text{ is provable in FL.} \tag{3}$$

Since this equivalence holds for both FL, by (3), and $\mathcal{L}'$, by (1), then it also holds for any logic $\mathcal{L}$ such that FL $\subseteq \mathcal{L} \subseteq \mathcal{L}'$; see the remarks under (T1). □

The application of Theorem 1 can be eliminated from the proof of Theorem 3 by a refinement of (T1) with our encoding of the QBF. The new proof, however, must repeat (with essential refinements) the whole proof of (T1) from [8], whereas only the formulation of (T1) is used in the proof, given above.

Theorem 3 can be used to show that many particular logics are PSPACE-hard. Some examples were presented in Section 1. Let us give one more. The associative full Lambek-Grishin calculus, i.e. FL (or FL$_1$ with 0) enriched with dual multiplicative connectives and the corresponding axioms and rules for them, is PSPACE-hard; this follows from Theorem 3, since the calculus is a subsystem of MALL. Its PSPACE-hardness is not a direct consequence of the result of [8], because: (1) we do not know whether this logic fulfils (DP), (2) we can consider this logic without 1, nor empty antecedents..

Moortgat [19] studies a similar (multiplicative) logic, not assuming the associativity of product. It is not known whether Theorem 3 remains true for nonassociative logics. The proof of (T1) in [8] uses associativity, while proving (i) $\Rightarrow$ (ii) for $Q_k = \exists$; associativity is also essential for the proof in [10].

If one simplifies the encoding of $\exists$, as it has been mentioned above, then one can prove the PSPACE-hardness of definitional extensions of FNL* and FNL. More precisely, one proves the PSPACE-hardness of the provability from assumptions, which are a finite set of definitions. The definitions form a sequence of assumptions $r_k \Leftrightarrow \alpha_k$ $(k \le n)$, where $r_1, \ldots, r_k$ are new variables and, for $k = 1, \ldots, n$, $\alpha_k = (p_k \vee \bar{p}_k) \backslash r_{k-1}$, if $Q_k = \forall$, $\alpha_k = p_k \backslash r_{k-1} \vee \bar{p}_k \backslash r_{k-1}$, if $Q_k = \exists$.

The multiplicative logics L, L*, MLL, Noncommutative MLL and others are NP-complete; see [18,23].

References

1. Buszkowski, W.: Completeness results for Lambek syntactic calculus. Zeitschrift f. mathematische Logik und Grundlagen der Mathematik 32(1), 13–28 (1986)
2. Buszkowski, W.: On generative capacity of the Lambek calculus. In: van Eijck, J. (ed.) Logics in AI. LNCS, vol. 478, pp. 139–152. Springer, Heidelberg (1991)
3. Buszkowski, W.: Interpolation and FEP for logics of residuated algebras. Logic Journal of the IGPL 19(3), 437–454 (2011)
4. Buszkowski, W., Farulewski, M.: Nonassociative Lambek Calculus with Additives and Context-Free Languages. In: Grumberg, O., Kaminski, M., Katz, S., Wintner, S. (eds.) Francez Festschrift. LNCS, vol. 5533, pp. 45–58. Springer, Heidelberg (2009)
5. Clark, A.: A learnable representation for syntax using residuated lattices. In: de Groote, P., Egg, M., Kallmeyer, L. (eds.) Formal Grammar. LNCS, vol. 5591, pp. 183–198. Springer, Heidelberg (2011)
6. Galatos, N., Jipsen, P., Kowalski, T., Ono, H.: Residuated Lattices: An Algebraic Glimpse at Substructural Logics. In: Studies in Logic and the Foundations of Mathematics. Elsevier (2007)
7. Galatos, N., Ono, H.: Cut elimination and strong separation for substructural logics: an algebraic approach. Annals of Pure and Applied Logic 161(9), 1097–1133 (2010)
8. Horčik, R., Terui, K.: Disjunction property and complexity of substructural logics. Theoretical Computer Science 412, 3992–4006 (2011)
9. Kanazawa, M.: The Lambek calculus enriched with additional connectives. Journal of Logic, Language and Information 1(2) (1992)
10. Kanazawa, M.: Lambek calculus: recognizing power and complexity. In: JFAK. Esays Dedicated to Johan van Benthem on the Occasion of his 50th Birthday. Amsterdam University Press (1999)
11. Kozak, M.: Distributive Full Lambek Calculus has the finite model property. Studia Logica 91(2), 201–216 (2009)
12. Kuznetsov, S.: Lambek grammars with one division and one primitive type. Logic Journal of the IGPL 20(1), 207–221 (2012)
13. Kuznetsov, S.: Lambek Grammars with the Unit. In: de Groote, P., Nederhof, M.-J. (eds.) Formal Grammar 2010/2011. LNCS, vol. 7395, pp. 262–266. Springer, Heidelberg (2012)
14. Lambek, J.: The mathematics of sentence structure. American Mathematical Monthly 65, 154–170 (1958)
15. Lambek, J.: On the calculus of syntactic types. In: Jakobson, R. (ed.) Structure of Language and Its Mathematical Aspects, pp. 166–178. American Mathematical Society, Providence (1961)

16. Lambek, J.: Type Grammar Revisited. In: Lecomte, A., Perrier, G., Lamarche, F. (eds.) LACL 1997. LNCS (LNAI), vol. 1582, pp. 1–27. Springer, Heidelberg (1999)
17. Lambek, J.: From Word to Sentence: a computational algebraic approach to grammar. Polimetrica (2008)
18. Lincoln, P.D.: Deciding provability of linear logic formulas. In: Girard, J.-Y., Lafont, Y., Regnier, L. (eds.) Advances in Linear Logic, pp. 109–122. Cambridge University Press (1995)
19. Moortgat, M.: Symmetric categorial grammar. Journal of Philosophical Logic 38(6), 681–710 (2009)
20. Moortgat, M., Oehrle, R.T.: Pregroups and type-logical grammar: Searching for convergence. In: Casadio, C., Scott, P.J., Seely, R.A. (eds.) Language and Grammar. Studies in Mathematical Linguistics and Natural Language, pp. 141–160. CSLI Publications (2005)
21. Ono, H., Komori, Y.: Logics without the contraction rule. Journal of Symbolic Logic 50, 169–201 (1985)
22. Pentus, M.: Lambek grammars are context-free. In: Proceedings of the 8th IEEE Symposium on Logic in Computer Science, pp. 429–433 (1993)
23. Pentus, M.: Lambek calculus is NP-complete. Theoretical Computer Science 357, 186–201 (2006)
24. Statman, R.: Intuitionistic propositional logic is polynomial-space complete. Theoretical Computer Science 9(1), 67–72 (1979)
25. Wurm, C.: Completeness of Full Lambek Calculus for Syntactic Concept Lattices. In: Morrill, G., Nederhof, M.-J. (eds.) Formal Grammar 2012 and 2013. LNCS, vol. 8036, pp. 126–141. Springer, Heidelberg (2013)

Adverbs in a Modern Type Theory

Stergios Chatzikyriakidis

Dept. of Computer Science, Royal Holloway,
Univ of London Egham, Surrey TW20 0EX, U.K, Open University of Cyprus
stergios.chatzikyriakidis@cs.rhul.ac.uk

Abstract. This paper is the first attempt to deal with aspects of the semantics of adverbs within a modern type theoretical setting. A number of issues pertaining to the semantics of different classes of adverbs like verididality and intensionality will be discussed and further shown to be captured straightforwardly within a modern type theoretical setting. In particular, I look at the issue of veridicality and show that the inferences associated with veridical adverbs can be dealt with via typing alone, i.e. without the aid of meaning postulates. In case of intensional adverbs like *intentionally* or *allegedly*, I show that these can be captured by making use of the type theoretical notion of context, i.e. without the use of possible worlds.

1 Introduction

The linguistic class of adverbs is a well-known example where members of a single category exhibit a vast non-homogeneity as regards their semantic interpretation. A number of different semantic classes can be distinguished for adverbs according to the semantics they give rise to. However, it seems that an abstraction to a tripartite classification can be made possible in the sense of [21]. According to this classification, there are three basic classes of adverbials with further subclassifications for each class: a) predicational, b) participant oriented and c) functional adverbials. [1] Note that this classification is for adverbials in general, and not adverbs only. In this paper, we concentrate on a subset of predicational adverbs that constitute the main bulk of adverbs. Predicational adverbs comprise a class of adverbs that are further subcategorized into: a) sentence adverbs and b) verb-related adverbs. In the former category, we further find: a) subject oriented adverbs like *arrogantly*, b) speaker-oriented adverbs like *honestly*, *intentionally* and *surprisingly*, and c) domain adverbs like *botanically* and *mathematically*. Verb related adverbs on the other hand include: a) mental attitude adverbs like *reluctantly*, b) manner adverbs like *skilfully* and *slowly*, and c) degree adverbs like *deeply*.[2]

---

[1] There are also syntactic criteria that are used in the literature to distinguish between the types of adverbs. We do not discuss syntax in this paper, and as such, no such criteria are discussed. See [11,6,8,9] among many others for discussions of syntactic relevance.

[2] See [21] for more details on the classification.

N. Asher and S. Soloviev (Eds.): LACL 2014, LNCS 8535, pp. 44–56, 2014.

There are various proposals pertaining to the semantics of adverbs. However, most of the approaches boil down to two major ways of looking at adverbs. The first of these is the operator approach proposed within the Montagovian tradition, while the latter concerns approaches within the (neo)-Davidsonian event-related tradition. Both lines of approach have their merits as well as their disadvantages. According to the operator approach (see [24,28,12] among others), adverbs are seen as functors which return the same type as that of their argument, further distinguishing between adverbs that take a truth value (or a proposition) to return a truth value (or proposition) and adverbs that take a set (or concept) to return a set (or concept):[3]

(1) Extensional:$(e \to t) \to (e \to t)$
    Intensional:$(s \to (e \to t)) \to (s \to (e \to t))$
(2) Extensional:$(t \to t)$
    Intensional:$(s \to t) \to (s \to t)$

The typings above correspond to the distinction between sentence type adverbs (e.g. evaluative adverbs like *fortunately*) and VP-adverbs (e.g. manner adverbs), while the intensionalized versions of the typings make the rather welcoming prediction that in VP-adverbs, opaque contexts should arise for the object but not for the subject, a prediction which is borne out from the facts (see [12,28] and [21] for a summary).[4]

On the other hand, approaches within the tradition initiated by Davidson [7], argue for an analysis where adverbs can be seen as providing restrictions w.r.t the event denoted by the sentence/proposition in each case. In effect, adverbs in these approaches are assumed to modify the event in some way. According to Davidson, each sentence involves an implicit event argument. This event argument is then assumed to be modified by adverbs and adverbials forming a simple conjunction in a first-order logic language. For example, a sentence like *John walks slowly* will receive the following semantics in a Davidsonian setting:[5]

(3) $\exists e: WALKING(e) \land AGENT(e, John) \land SLOW(e)$

In this paper, I present a first account of some aspects og the semantics of adverbs based on modern type theories, i.e. type theories within the tradition of Martin-Löf. In particular, an expressive and computationally attractive language, that of UTT with coercive subtyping [16,15,18] will be used in order

---

[3] Within the simple type theory used in Montague Grammar, e is the type of individuals, t is the type of truth-values and s the type of world-time pairs.

[4] An example in case would involve a VP-adverb like *intentionally* in a sentence like *Oedipus intentionally married Jocaste*. Under the intensionalized VP-adverb typing, it does not follow that *Oedipus intentionally married his mother*. See the analysis and discussion in §(3.2).

[5] e stands for event here, not to be conflated with the type e of individuals used in MG.

to present an account of various aspects of adverbial modification that, as it will be argued, fares well with respect to a number of well-known semantic issues associated with adverbial modification.

2   MTT Semantics: A Brief Intro

A Modern Type Theory (MTT) is a variant of a class of type theories in the tradition initiated by the work of Martin-Löf [22,23], which have dependent and inductive types, among others. We choose to call them Modern Type Theories in order to distinguish them from Church's simple type theory [5] that is commonly employed within the Montagovian tradition in formal semantics.

Among the variants of MTTs, we are going to employ the Unified Theory of dependent Types (UTT) [13] with the addition of the coercive subtyping mechanism (see, for example, [14,19] and below). UTT is an impredicative type theory in which a type *Prop* of all logical propositions exists.[6] This stands as part of the study of linguistic semantics using MTTs rather than simply typed ones. These issues have already been discussed in [16,17,1,2,4] among others. In what follows I provide a brief discussion on some of the features of MTTs relevant to the paper.

2.1   Type Many-Sortedness and CNs as Types

In Montague Grammar (MG, [25]), the underlying logic (Church's simple type theory [5]) can be seen as 'single-sorted' in the sense that there is only one type e of all entities. The other types such as t of truth values and the function types generated from e and t do not stand for types of entities. Thus, there are no fine-grained distinctions between the elements of type e and as such all individuals are interpreted using the same type. For example, *John* and *Mary* have the same type in simple type theories, the type e of individuals. An MTT, on the other hand, can be regarded as a 'many-sorted' logical system in that it contains many types and as such one can make fine-grained distinctions between individuals and further use those different types to interpret subclasses of individuals. For example, one can have *John* : [*man*] and *Mary* : [*woman*], where [*man*] and [*woman*] are different types.

An important trait of MTT-based semantics is the interpretation of common nouns (CNs) as *types* [27] rather than sets or predicates (i.e., objects of type $e \rightarrow t$) as it is the case within the Montagovian tradition. The CNs *man, human, table* and *book* are interpreted as types [*man*], [*human*], [*table*] and [*book*], respectively. Then, individuals are interpreted as being of one of the types used to interpret CNs. The interpretation of CNs as Types is also a prerequisite in

---

[6] This is similar to simple type theory where a type t of truth values exists.

order for the subtyping mechanism to work. This is because, assuming CNs to be predicates, subtyping would go wrong given contravariance of function types.[7]

2.2 Dependent Typing and Universes

One of the basic features of MTTs is the use of Dependent Types. A dependent type is a family of types depending on some values. Here two basic constructors for dependent types are explained, Σ and Π, both highly relevant for the study of linguistic semantics.

The constructor/operator Σ is a generalization of the Cartesian product of two sets that allows the second set to depend on values of the first. For instance, if $[\![human]\!]$ is a type and $male : [\![human]\!] \rightarrow Prop$, then the Σ-type $\Sigma h : [\![human]\!] . male(h)$ is intuitively the type of humans who are male.

More formally, if A is a type and B is an A-indexed family of types, then $\Sigma(A, B)$, or sometimes written as $\Sigma x{:}A.B(x)$, is a type, consisting of pairs (a, b) such that a is of type A and b is of type $B(a)$. When $B(x)$ is a constant type (i.e., always the same type no matter what x is), the Σ-type degenerates into product type $A \times B$ of non-dependent pairs. Σ-types (and product types) are associated projection operations π_1 and π_2 so that $\pi_1(a, b) = a$ and $\pi_2(a, b) = b$, for every (a, b) of type $\Sigma(A, B)$ or $A \times B$.

The linguistic relevance of Σ-types can be directly appreciated once we understand that in its dependent case, Σ-types can be used to interpret linguistic phenomena of central importance, like for example adjectival modification [27]. For example, *handsome man* is interpreted as a Σ-type (4), the type of handsome men (or more precisely, of those men together with proofs that they are handsome):[8]

(4) $\Sigma m : [\![man]\!] . [\![handsome]\!](m)$

---

[7] See [3] for more information. See also [17] for further philosophical argumentation on the choosing to represent CNs as types. Furthermore, one anonymous reviewer asks about any potential drawbacks of assuming CNs to be types. He mentions cases of noun compounding, asking how such cases would be treated. As far as I am concerned, these cases have not been dealt with yet under such an approach. Thus, I would be reluctant to answer such a question. The idea of defining type constructors that correspond to noun constructors seems viable, but the exact details of these constructors, given the compositionality issues abound in noun compounding, are unknown to me. On a more general note, it seems to me that noun compounding is a problematic issue for any formal semantic theory and not only for the approach pursued here. It is thus undeniable that a formal semantic theory should be able to address these cases. However, for the moment such an account does not exist within the framework discussed in this paper. I leave this issue as a subject of future research.

[8] It should be kept in mind that every proposition $P{:}Prop$ is a type and that an object of a proposition is called a proof.

where $[\![handsome]\!](m)$ is a family of propositions/types that depends on the man m.[9]

The other basic constructor for dependent types is Π. Π-types can be seen as a generalization of the normal function space where the second type is a family of types that might be dependent on the values of the first. A Π-type $\Pi(A, B)$ degenerates to the function type $A \to B$ in the non-dependent case. In more detail, when A is a type and P is a predicate over A, $\Pi x{:}A.P(x)$ is the dependent function type that, in the embedded logic, stands for the universally quantified proposition $\forall x{:}A.P(x)$.[10] For example, the following sentence (5) is interpreted as (6):

(5) Every man walks.

(6) $\Pi x : [\![man]\!] . [\![walk]\!](x)$

Type Universes. An advanced feature of MTTs, which will be shown to be very relevant in interpreting NL semantics, is that of universes. Informally, a universe is a collection of (the names of) types put into a type [23].[11] For example, one may want to collect all the names of the types that interpret common nouns into a universe CN : *Type*. The idea is that for each type A that interprets a common noun, there is a name $\overline{A}$ in CN. For example,

$$\overline{[\![man]\!]} : \text{CN} \quad \text{and} \quad T_{\text{CN}}(\overline{[\![man]\!]}) = [\![man]\!].$$

In practice, we do not distinguish a type in CN and its name by omitting the overlines and the operator T_{CN} by simply writing, for instance, $[\![man]\!]$: CN. Thus, the universe CNincludes the collection of the names that interpret common nouns. For example, in CN, we shall find the following types:

(7) $[\![man]\!], [\![woman]\!], [\![book]\!], ...$

(8) $\Sigma m : [\![man]\!] . [\![handsome]\!](m)$

(9) $G_R + G_F$

where the Σ-type in (8 is the proposed interpretation of 'handsome man' and the disjoint sum type in (9) is that of 'gun' (the sum of real guns and fake guns).[12]

---

[9] Adjectival modification is a notoriously difficult issue and as such not all cases of adjectives can be captured using a Σ type analysis. For a proper treatment of adjectival modification within this framework, see [2].

[10] The meticulous reader will notice that I make use of both Π and $\forall$ in this paper. Formally $\forall$ is just a notation for Π. When $\Pi x{:}A.P{:}Prop$ we write $\forall x{:}A.P$ instead.

[11] There is quite a long discussion on how these universes should be like. In particular, the debate is largely concentrated on whether a universe should be predicative or impredicative. A strongly impredicative universe U of all types (with $U : U$ and Π-types) is shown to be paradoxical [10] and as such logically inconsistent. The theory UTT used here has only one impredicative universe $Prop$ (representing the world of logical formulas) together with infinitely many predicative universes which as such avoids Girard's paradox (see [13] for more details).

[12] The use of disjoint sum types was proposed by [2] in order to deal with privative modification. The interested reader is directed there for details.

Interesting applications of the use of universes can be proposed. For example, we can propose types for quantifiers and VP adverbs that extend over the universe CN [20] as well as a type for coordination extending over the universe of all linguistic types LType [1]. We will see the relevance of universes further on in this paper, when VP-adverbs are going to be discussed.

2.3   Subtyping

Coercive subtyping [14,19] provides an adequate framework to be employed for MTT-based formal semantics [15,18].[13] It can be seen as an abbreviation mechanism: A is a (proper) subtype of B ($A < B$) if there is a unique implicit coercion c from type A to type B and, if so, an object a of type A can be used in any context $\mathfrak{C}_B[\_]$ that expects an object of type B: $\mathfrak{C}_B[a]$ is legal (well-typed) and equal to $\mathfrak{C}_B[c(a)]$.

As an example, assuming that both $[\![man]\!]$ and $[\![human]\!]$ are base types, one may introduce the following as a basic subtyping relation:

(10) $[\![man]\!] < [\![human]\!]$

In case that $[\![man]\!]$ is defined as a composite Σ-type (see §2.2 below for details), where $male : [\![human]\!] \to Prop$:

(11) $[\![man]\!] = \Sigma h : [\![human]\!] . male(h)$

we have that (10) is the case because the above Σ-type is a subtype of $[\![human]\!]$ via the first projection π_1:

(12) $(\Sigma h : [\![human]\!] . male(h)) <_{\pi_1} [\![human]\!]$

3   Adverbs in MTTs

A proper treatment of adverbs is lacking in the literature on MTTs. The classic work on MTT semantics, i.e. [27] only discusses time adverbials, and these not *per se*, but in order to deal with tense. No explicit discussion on either the typing or the semantics of adverbs is done. The first discussion, though in passing, of the correspondence of the typings of sentence and VP level adverbs in MTTs was proposed by Luo [16], followed by work on inference by [3,4]. In the latter two papers, adverbs are discussed in order to deal with quantifier inference cases involving adverbs like the one shown below:

(13) Some delegates finished the survey on time.
    Did any delegate finish the survey? [Yes]

---

[13] It is worth mentioning that subsumptive subtyping, i.e. the traditional notion of subtyping that adopts the subsumption rule (if $A \leq B$, then every object of type A is also of type B), is inadequate for MTTs in the sense that it would destroy some important metatheoretical properties of MTTs (see, for example, §4 of [19] for details).

According to these researchers, VP adverbs receive a polymorphic type extending over the universe CN (14), while sentence level adverbs are just functions from propositions to propositions (15):[14]

(14) $\Pi A : \text{CN}. (A \to Prop) \to (A \to Prop)$

(15) $Prop \to Prop$

In order to take care of the veridical inference associated with manner adverbs like *on time*, the authors propose to use an auxiliary object, which they call ADV, in effect a Σ type:

(16) $ADV : \Pi A : \text{CN}.\Pi v : A \to Prop. \Sigma p : A \to Prop.\forall x{:}A.p(x) \supset v(x)$

The above reads as follows: for any common noun A and any predicate v over A, $ADV(A, v)$ is a pair (p, m) such that for any $x : A$, such that $m(x)$, $p(x)$ implies $v(x)$. Then, adverbs like *on time* or in general adverbs that give rise to this sort of inference can be defined as the first projection of the previous Σ type:

(17) $on\ time = \lambda A : \text{CN}.\lambda v : A \to Prop.\ \pi_1(ADV(A, v))$

This line of approach, as the authors show, can effectively take care of the inferences associated with veridical adverbs.[15] In what follows, I present an account of different types of adverbs, concentrating on predicational adverbs and a number of their properties. The veridical/non-veridical distinction is first discussed, followed by a discussion on various other issues associated with the semantics of adverbs like opacity and rich typing. .

3.1 Veridical Adverbs

A very basic distinction as regards the inference that the semantics of different adverbs give rise to, concerns veridicality. In simple terms, veridical adverbs are adverbs that entail the sentence formed after omitting the adverb. Veridicality is not particular to sentence or VP adverbs and veridical adverbs can be found in both cases. Predicational adverbs involve adverbs of both kinds. Thus, one finds sentence level predicational adverbs like *fortunately* and *frankly*, as well as VP adverbs like *intentionally* and *slowly*.[16] The former function on the level of

---

[14] One can see the typing in (14) as a more fine-grained version of Montague's VP-adverb typing $(e \to t) \to (e \to t)$. A here stands for the syntactic subject.

[15] It has to be noted that the inference associated with manner adverbs like the one discussed, has been tried out in the Coq proof-assistant [3,4]. There it was shown that using a lexical entry for *on_time* like the one proposed in (17), one can formally verify/prove that (13) is a valid inference. See [3,4] for more details.

[16] Actually, predicational adverbs are further classified as sentence and verb related adverbs according to [21], with further classifications for each case. See [21] for more details. See also [8] for a slightly different classification.

the sentence while the latter at the level of the VP. The Σ type account used in [3] for manner adverbs can be adapted to veridical sentence adverbs. This account involves the use of an auxiliary object, followed by the definition of the adverb as the first projection of this auxiliary object. I consider this to be non-satisfactory for at least two reasons a) redundancy, i.e. every adverb will need two typings and b) the definition shown (17) involves an equality relation, i.e. it says roughly that these are the semantics of the specific adjective. However, this is just an aspect of the semantics of these adjectives (veridicality). For this reason, I propose to use a single entry for adverbs while still maintaining the Σ type mechanism in order to get the veridicality facts right. Thus, the typing for a sentence level adverb like *fortunately* will be the following:

(18) $Fortunately : \Sigma f : Prop \to Prop.\forall P{:}Prop.f(P) \supset P$

In the case of veridical VP-adverbs like for example *slowly, fast*, the same line of reasoning can be used. However, in this case as well, one has to modify the account proposed in [3,4] for the reasons discussed above. Thus, the new entry for a VP-adverb like *slowly* will be the one shown below:

(19) $Slowly : \Sigma f : \forall A{:}CN.(A \to Prop) \to (A \to Prop).\forall A{:}CN.\forall v{:}A \to Prop,$
$\quad \forall x{:}A.f(A, v, x) \supset v(x)$

Notice that given Σ types are a form of generalized conjunction one can also pursue a davidsonian kind of analysis in case s/he wants to introduce an explicit event argument in the semantics. To give an example, assume, in the spirit of Davidson, that every sentence involves an event argument, with $Event : Type$. In this case then an intransitive verb like $Walk$ will have the following type:

(20) $Walk : Human \to Event \to Prop$

With the presence of an explicit event argument, the typing in (19) will be modified as follows:[17]

(21) $Slowly : \Sigma f : \forall A{:}CN.(A \to Event \to Prop) \to (A \to Event \to Prop).$
$\quad \forall A{:}CN.\forall v{:}A \to Event \to Prop.\forall x{:}A.\forall e : Event.f(A, v, e, x) \supset v(e, x) \wedge$
$\quad SLOW(e)$

Of course, veridicality is one of the aspects of adverbs and a number of other issues should be discussed in order to give a complete account of the semantics of various types of adverbs, like e.g. evaluative or subject-oriented adverbs. It is impossible to discuss all these issues here, but however some proposals pertaining to some of these cases will be discussed later on in this paper.

3.2 Non-Veridical Adverbs

It is clear from the above discussion, that non-veridical adverbs should not involve the Σ type treatment as this is presented for veridical adverbs, since this

---

[17] With $SLOW : Event \to Prop$.

will incorrectly predict veridicality. Let us look at some examples in order to see how cases of non-veridical adverbs can be approached. If one is interested in veridicality only, and does not care about the specific semantics of each adverb in each case, a simple assumption as regards the two typings (sentence and VP-adverbs) suffices to prevent unwanted inferences:

(22) $\Pi A : \text{CN.} \ (A \rightarrow Prop) \rightarrow (A \rightarrow Prop)$

(23) $Prop \rightarrow Prop$

However, one has to say more at least for cases of adverbs like *intentionally* or epistemic adverbs like *possibly* or *allegedly*. The latter case, i.e. epistemic adverbs, creates opaque contexts for both the subject and the object, while the former, i.e *intentionally*, only for the object:

(24) Oedipus allegedly married Jocaste

(25) Oedipus intentionally married Jocaste

From (24), it does not follow that:

(26) Oedipus allegedly married Jocaste $\not\Rightarrow$ the son of Laius allegedly married Jocaste

(27) Oedipus married Jocaste $\not\Rightarrow$ Oedipus allegedly married his mother

On the other hand, from (25) we have:

(28) Oedipus intentionally married Jocaste $\Rightarrow$ The son of Laius intentionally married Jocaste

(29) Oedipus intentionally married Jocaste $\not\Rightarrow$ Oedipus intentionally married his mother

In order to make sense of these examples, we have to look at how the modal notions associated with adverbs like *intentionally* and *allegedly* should be represented. In the first case, one can assume that the meaning of *intentionally* can be represented as follows: there is an agent p, that intentionally did something x, in effect meaning that agent p believes that he did x. Now, following [27], we can represent p's belief context as a number of judgments $x{:}A$ with $A : Prop$, this agent has made. In case this agent p is *Oedipus*, this will be the following:

(30) $\Gamma_{oed} = x_1 : A_1, ..., x_n : A_n(x_1, ..., x_{n-1})$

From this, one can construct a generalized belief operator $B_p A$ standing for agent p believes A. The construction of this operator, is made out of binding all the variables in Γ_p:

(31) $B_p A = \Pi \Gamma_p.A = \Pi x_1{:}A_1...\Pi x_n{:}A_n(x_1, ..., x_{n-1}).A$

Given our knowledge of the story of Oedipus, he does not know neither that he is the son of Laius nor that his mother is Jocaste. In this sense, the required equality relations shown below are not part of Oedipus' belief context:

(32) $Eq(Person, Oed, SoL)$

$(33)Eq(Person, J, MoO)$

Thus, in this case one can assume something like the following for *intentionally*:

(34) *Intentionally* $= \lambda A : CN.\lambda P : A \rightarrow Prop. \forall x{:}A, B_x(P(x))$

The above definition says that given a predicate of type $A \rightarrow Prop$ and for all $x{:}A$ (x the subject here), the proposition $P(x)$ is true in x's belief context. Thus, in the case of *Oedipus intentionally married Jocaste*, we get a paraphrase that Oedipus believes/knows that he married Jocaste. Now, how do we derive the non-opacity of the subject, i.e. cases like *the son of Laius* is Oedipus $\Rightarrow$ The son of Laius married Jocaste? Notice that in (34), the x is not bound by the belief operator. In this sense, given an equality relation $Eq(Person, Oed, SoL)$ and given $x = Oed$, substitution of Oed with SoL is possible and thus the interpretation where the son of Laius intentionally married Jocaste arises. What one cannot get (correctly) is that Oedipus believes/knows that the son of Laius married Jocaste, according to fact. So, in this sense, the semantics of the adverb are captured as well as the behaviour with respect to opaque contexts. On the other hand, for adjectives like *allegedly*, one needs a different treatment given the opacity for both subject and object position. *Allegedly* can then be taken to mean that a given proposition, say P, is true in the belief context of an agent $p{:}Human$ and p is free in P. What one needs in this case is a sentence modifer type like the following:

(35) *Allegedly* $= \lambda P : Prop. \exists p{:}Human, B_p(P)$

In effect, we can deal with these kinds of adjectives without the need of postulating intensions or assuming possible world semantics. This type of approach has the welcoming result that cases of domain adverbs like the ones shown below can receive a similar treatment:

(36) Botanically, tomato is a fruit

(37) Mathematically, the proposition is not correct

These types of adjectives are not veridical, since the proposition expressed is only relevant for the relevant domain in each case (botanology and mathematics respectively). Thus, tomatoes are only fruits only in the context of botanology. These types of adjectives are sentence level adverbs that can be seen to hold in a specified context (i.e. domain).For example, let us assume a context Γ_B standing for the context representing the collection of facts pertaining to botanology. In this case, *botanically* will be defined as follows:

(38) *Botanically* $= \lambda P : Prop.\Gamma_B P$

A similar treatment can be given for (37).

Remark 1. Note that the approach proposed here, similarly to accounts like [26] and [28], predicts that in cases like (39) the only correct interpretation is with *painstakingly* taking wide scope over *intellibly*, a fact following from typing given that the former is a sentence adverb while the latter a VP-adverb:

(39) John painstakingly wrote illegibly.

Further differences in interpretation of manner adverbs like the ones shown below can be accounted assuming that in the second case the quantifier takes scope over the adverb while in the first the opposite happens:

(40) Sam carefully sliced all the bagels.
(41) Sam sliced all the bagels carefully.

One can then link, the minimally different interpretations to be dependent on syntactic positioning. One can actually propose a unit type in the sense of [16], encoding the two different interpretations for the same adverb. Then, one can assume that given syntactic positioning, the right type is chosen for each case. The exact mechanism of how this can be done is left for future research.

Remark 2. A note on typing is in place here. Note that the type of VP adverbs, extends over the universe CN. However, in some cases, e.g. with adverbs like *intentionally*, this will overgenerate since it will predict that non-human or even inanimate entities can be seen as bearing intentions! Fortunately, there is an easy solution in this case. It suffices to assume that besides the universe of common nouns CN that collects the names of all common noun denotations into a type, there are smaller common noun universes, which are further subuniverses of the already introduced CN universe. This has been already used by [2] in order to deal with a similar type of problem pertaining to adjectives like *skilful*. In this case, *skilful* was taken to extend not over the universe CN but over a subuniverse CN_H, i.e the universe containing the names of the types *Human* and its subtypes. The relevant introduction rules are shown below:

$$\frac{}{Human : \text{CN}_H} \qquad \frac{A < Human}{A : \text{CN}_H}$$

. The new entry with this minimal modification is shown below:

(42) *Intentionally* $= \lambda A : CN_H.\lambda P : A \rightarrow Prop. \ \forall x{:}A, B_x(P(x))$

Given the above typing, examples like the one shown below are ruled out:

(43) # The rock intentionally rolled down the hill.

More work on this issue should be done in order to see how the use of such subuniverses can be a useful tool of MTTs in the study of NL semantics.

3.3 Conclusions

This paper presented the first investigation into the semantics of adverbs from a MTT perspective. It was shown that using an expressive formal language like MTTs can have a number of welcoming results with respect to adverb typing. In particular, the issue of veridicality was discussed and a generalized Σ type mechanism was proposed for these types of adverbs. Furthermore, the semantics for a number of other cases of adverbs like epistemic, mental-attitude and domain adverbs were proposed by exploiting the type-theoretic notion of context, a notion free of the hyperintensional problems associated with possible world semantics, in order to provide adequate semantics for these cases.

References

1. Chatzikyriakidis, S., Luo, Z.: An account of natural language coordination in type theory with coercive subtyping. In: Duchier, D., Parmentier, Y. (eds.) Constraint Solving and Language Processing. LNCS, vol. 8114, pp. 31–51. Springer, Heidelberg (2013)
2. Chatzikyriakidis, S., Luo, Z.: Adjectives in a modern type-theoretical setting. In: Morrill, G., Nederhof, M.-J. (eds.) Formal Grammar 2012 and 2013. LNCS, vol. 8036, pp. 159–174. Springer, Heidelberg (2013)
3. Chatzikyriakidis, S., Luo, Z.: Natural language inference in coq (2013) (submitted)
4. Chatzikyriakidis, S., Luo, Z.: Natural language reasoning using proof-assistant technology: Rich typing and beyond. In: Proceedings of EACL 2014 (2014)
5. Church, A.: A formulation of the simple theory of types. J. Symbolic Logic 5(1) (1940)
6. Cinque, G.: Adverbs and Functional Heads: A Cross-Linguistic Perspective. Oxford University Press (1999)
7. Davidson, D.: Compositionality and coercion in semantics: The semantics of adjective meaning. In: Rescher, N. (ed.) The Logical Form of Action Sentences, pp. 81–95. University of Pittsburgh Press (1967)
8. Ernst, T.: The Syntax of Adjuncts. Cambridge press (2002)
9. Ernst, T.: On the role of semantics in a theory of adverb syntax. Lingua 117(6) (2007)
10. Girard, J.Y.: Une extension de l'interpretation fonctionelle de gödel à l'analyse et son application à l'élimination des coupures dans et la thèorie des types'. In: Proc. 2nd Scandinavian Logic Symposium. North-Holland (1971)
11. Jackendoff, R.: Semantic Interpretation in Generative Grammar. MIT Press (1972)
12. Kamp, H.: Formal semantics of natural language. In: Keenan, E. (ed.) Two Theories About Adjectives, pp. 123–155. Cambridge University Press (1975)
13. Luo, Z.: Computation and Reasoning: A Type Theory for Computer Science. Oxford Univ. Press (1994)
14. Luo, Z.: Coercive subtyping. Journal of Logic and Computation 9(1), 105–130 (1999)
15. Luo, Z.: Type-theoretical semantics with coercive subtyping. Semantics and Linguistic Theory 20 (SALT20), Vancouver 84(2), 28–56 (2010)
16. Luo, Z.: Contextual analysis of word meanings in type-theoretical semantics. In: Pogodalla, S., Prost, J.-P. (eds.) LACL 2011. LNCS, vol. 6736, pp. 159–174. Springer, Heidelberg (2011)

17. Luo, Z.: Common nouns as types. In: Béchet, D., Dikovsky, A. (eds.) LACL 2012. LNCS, vol. 7351, pp. 173–185. Springer, Heidelberg (2012)
18. Luo, Z.: Formal semantics in modern type theories with coercive subtyping. Linguistics and Philosophy 35(6), 491–513 (2012)
19. Luo, Z., Soloviev, S., Xue, T.: Coercive subtyping: theory and implementation. Information and Computation 223, 18–42 (2012)
20. Luo, Z.: Adjectives and adverbs in type-theoretical semantics. Notes (2011)
21. Maienborn, C., Schafer, M.: Adverbs and adverbials. In: Maienborn, C., von Heusinger, K., Portner, P. (eds.) Semantics. An International Handbook of Natural Language Meaning, pp. 1390–1420. De Gruyter, Mouton (2011)
22. Martin-Löf, P.: An intuitionistic theory of types: predicative part. In: Rose, H., Shepherdson, J.C. (eds.) Logic Colloquium 1973 (1975)
23. Martin-Löf, P.: Intuitionistic Type Theory. Bibliopolis (1984)
24. Montague, R.: English as a formal language. In: Visentini, B. (ed.) Linguaggi Nella Societe Nella. Edizioni di Comunitl, Milan (1970)
25. Montague, R.: Formal Philosophy. Yale University Press (1974)
26. Parsons, T.: Some problems concerning the logic of grammatical modifiers. In: Davidson, D., Harman, G. (eds.) Semantics of Natural Language, pp. 127–141. Reidel, Dordrecht (1972)
27. Ranta, A.: Type-Theoretical Grammar. Oxford University Press (1994)
28. Thomason, R., R.C.S.: A semantic theory of adverbs. Linguistic Inquiry 4(2), 195–220 (1973)

An Algebraic Approach to Multiple Context-Free Grammars

Alexander Clark[1] and Ryo Yoshinaka[2]

[1] Department of Philosophy, King's College London
alexander.clark@kcl.ac.uk
[2] Graduate School of Informatics, Kyoto University
ry@i.kyoto-u.ac.jp

Abstract. We define an algebraic structure, Paired Complete Idempotent Semirings (PCIS), which are appropriate for defining a denotational semantics for multiple context-free grammars of dimension 2 (2-MCFG). We demonstrate that homomorphisms of this structure will induce well-behaved morphisms of the grammar, and generalize the syntactic concept lattice from context-free grammars to the 2-MCFG case. We show that this lattice is the unique minimal structure that will interpret the grammar faithfully and that therefore 2-MCFGs without mergeable nonterminals will have nonterminals that correspond to elements of this structure.

1 Introduction

Denotational semantics[1] have been provided before for MCFGs and indeed for richer formalisms [6,7] but they have never specified precisely what the operations or algebraic structures that provide are. When defining denotational semantics for CFGs [5] this is well known: the appropriate structure is a complete idempotent semiring (CIS) [4]. Recently it has been shown [2] that homomorphisms of this structure induce nice grammar morphisms and that there is a unique smallest structure that interprets the CFG faithfully. As a result, CFGs without mergeable nonterminals will have nonterminals that correspond to elements of this structure. This structure, the Syntactic Concept Lattice, is also very important from the perspective of grammatical inference, as it gives rise to a number of algorithms for learning grammars using *distributional* techniques [1,12]. It consists of the collection of all sets of strings that are distributionally definable with respect to the language in question.

Given the central importance of mildly context-sensitive grammars in mathematical linguistics, it is clearly desirable to extend these techniques beyond the class of CFGS; here we take the next step to the class of 2-MCFGs. For a 2-MCFG, unsurprisingly, we need a richer structure than a CIS; which we define in this paper, and which we call a Paired Complete Idempotent Semiring (PCIS). We add a tupling operation and some nontrivial additional axioms. We then define the

---

[1] Here we refer to the semantics of the meta-grammar rather than the meanings of natural language sentences [8].

N. Asher and S. Soloviev (Eds.): LACL 2014, LNCS 8535, pp. 57–69, 2014.
© Springer-Verlag Berlin Heidelberg 2014

natural extension of the Syntactic Concept Lattice, which we call the Syntactic Concept Lattice of order 2, which consists of all distributionally definable sets of strings and sets of pairs of strings, where the notion of distribution is extended appropriately to account for the richer set of derivation contexts in a 2-MCFG. As a result we can show that every grammar without mergeable nonterminals for a language defined by a 2-MCFG will have nonterminals that correspond to the elements of this concept lattice.

A brief roadmap for the paper: we start (Section 2) by defining MCFGs and morphisms of these grammars in a fairly standard way. These grammars use a certain (infinite) family of linear regular functions. We then define in Section 3 the algebraic structures, Paired Complete Idempotent Semirings (PCIS) that we use to interpret these grammars, and show (Section 4) how can define the relevant linear regular functions in this structure. At this point we also define the standard Ginsburg and Rice-style fixed point semantics for 2-MCFGs. The generalization of the syntactic concept lattice is then defined in Section 5. At this point we can unify these two rather independent strands by showing that PCIS-homomorphisms induce well-behaved MCFG-morphisms, and that in particular the homomorphism into the syntactic concept lattice gives a grammar morphism that does not increase the language (Section 6). Moreover we show that it is the unique up to isomorphism simplest structure with this property.

2   Definitions

We assume a fixed nonempty finite set as an alphabet, Σ, and we write Σ^* for the set of finite strings over Σ, and λ for the empty string. We write $\mathcal{P}(X)$ for the power set of a set X. A language is a subset of Σ^*. Given two languages A, B we define $A \cdot B$ to be the standard concatenation of languages, and $A \times B$ to be the Cartesian product.

We recall the definition of a complete idempotent semiring (CIS), which is a tuple

$$\langle M, \circ, \vee, \epsilon, \bot \rangle$$

where M is a set, $\epsilon, \bot \in M$, $\circ$ is a binary operation such that $\langle M, \circ, \epsilon \rangle$ is a monoid, $\vee$ is an commutative idempotent operation with $\bot$ as identity, together with the infinitary variant of $\vee$ and so where $\langle M, \vee, \bot \rangle$ is a complete semilattice with zero. Moreover we require that $x \circ \bot = \bot = \bot \circ x$ for all $x \in M$ and that $\circ$ distributes left and right over $\vee$ so that for any $Y \subseteq M$, $x \circ \bigvee Y = \bigvee \{x \circ y \mid y \in Y\}$ and $\bigvee Y \circ x = \bigvee \{y \circ x \mid y \in Y\}$.

Given the $\vee$ operation we can naturally define a partial order $\leq$ by $x \leq y$ iff $y = x \vee y$.

The free CIS over a finite set Σ is defined to be

$$\langle \mathcal{P}(\Sigma^*), \cdot, \cup, \{\lambda\}, \emptyset \rangle$$

which we can easily verify to be a CIS. These provide the standard denotational semantics for CFGS [5,4].

For reasons of space, we assume that the reader is familiar with the MCFG formalism [10]. We denote an MCFG by $G = \langle \Sigma, V, S, P \rangle$, where Σ is the set of terminal symbols, V is the set of nonterminal symbols, S is the start symbol and P is the set of production rules. Each nonterminal in V is assigned a positive integer called *dimension* and we let V_d be the set of nonterminals of dimension d. We write $\dim(N) = d$ if $N \in V_d$. Each nonterminal of dimension k derives k-tuples of strings. The start symbol S has dimension 1, so it generates usual strings. There are different ways to describe rules of P.

For example, the rules of a grammar $G = \langle \Sigma, V, S, P \rangle$ can be described as

$$S(z_{1,1}z_{2,1}z_{1,2}z_{2,2}) :- N(z_{1,1}, z_{1,2}), M(z_{2,1}, z_{2,2}); \quad N(a, c); \quad M(b, d);$$
$$N(z_{1,1}a, z_{1,2}c) :- N(z_{1,1}, z_{1,2}); \quad M(z_{1,1}b, z_{1,2}d) :- M(z_{1,1}, z_{1,2}),$$

where each $z_{i,j}$ is a variable representing the jth element of the ith argument. In the above example, $N(a, c) \in P$ means that N generates a pair (a, c). The rule $S(z_{1,1}z_{2,1}z_{1,2}z_{2,2}) :- N(z_{1,1}, z_{1,2}), M(z_{2,1}, z_{2,2})$ means that if N generates a pair $(z_{1,1}, z_{1,2})$ and M generates $(z_{2,1}, z_{2,2})$ then S generates the string of the form $z_{1,1}z_{2,1}z_{1,2}z_{2,2}$ by concatenating these strings. This grammar generates the language $\{ a^m b^n c^m d^n \mid m, n \geq 1 \}$. In general, a rule has the following form:

$$N_0(\alpha_1, \ldots, \alpha_{d_0}) :- N_1(z_{1,1}, \ldots, z_{1,d_1}), \ldots, N_m(z_{m,1}, \ldots, z_{m,d_m})$$

where $\dim(N_i) = d_i$ for $i = 0, \ldots, m$ and $\alpha_k \in (\Sigma \cup \{ z_{i,j} \mid 1 \leq i \leq m, 1 \leq j \leq d_i \})^*$ for $k = 1, \ldots, d_0$ such that no variable $z_{i,j}$ occurs in $\alpha_1 \ldots \alpha_{d_0}$ twice or more.

Alternatively, the above rules can be written using *linear functions*:

$$S \to f(N, M), \quad N \to \langle a, c \rangle, \quad M \to \langle b, d \rangle, \quad N \to g(N), \quad M \to h(M),$$

where f, g, h are linear functions satisfying that for any $u_{i,j} \in \Sigma^*$

$$f(\langle u_{1,1}, u_{1,2} \rangle, \langle u_{2,1}, u_{2,2} \rangle) = u_{1,1}u_{2,1}u_{1,2}u_{2,2},$$
$$g(\langle u_{1,1}, u_{1,2} \rangle) = \langle u_{1,1}a, u_{1,2}c \rangle, \quad h(\langle u_{1,1}, u_{1,2} \rangle) = \langle u_{1,1}b, u_{1,2}d \rangle.$$

We often identify a linear function and its specification as a tuple of strings of terminals and variables. In the above examples, g is identified with $\langle z_{1,1}a, z_{1,2}c \rangle$.

We write the set of $\dim(N)$-tuples of strings generated by a nonterminal N of G by $\mathcal{L}(G, N) \subseteq (\Sigma^*)^{\dim(N)}$, which is recursively defined as follow: if a rule $N_0 \to f(N_1, \ldots, N_m)$ is in P and $\boldsymbol{u}_i \in \mathcal{L}(G, N_i)$ for $i = 1, \ldots, m$, then $f(\boldsymbol{u}_1, \ldots, \boldsymbol{u}_m) \in \mathcal{L}(G, N_0)$. The language of G is $\mathcal{L}(G) = \mathcal{L}(G, S)$.

A linear function uses each element of arguments at most once. We say that a linear function is *regular* or *non-deleting* if every argument appears as a part of the output. Moreover a linear regular function is *non-permuting* if $z_{i,j+1}$ never occurs left to $z_{i,j}$ in its specification.

In this paper, we assume that all linear functions are non-deleting and non-permuting and moreover those functions introduce terminal symbols only when the arity is 0, so their specifications are either variable-free or terminal-free.

It is known that those restrictions on linear functions do not affect the generative power of the MCFG formalism. In addition, we concern ourselves here with MCFGs whose nonterminals have dimension at most 2, i.e, $V = V_1 \cup V_2$. We define this class of grammars as 2-MCFG.

3   Paired Complete Idempotent Semirings

We use a multi-sorted algebra which has two types of elements: roughly sets of strings (sort 1) and sets of pairs of strings (sort 2).

Definition 1. *A Paired Complete Idempotent Semiring (PCIS) is a tuple*

$$\langle A_1, A_2, \circ, \otimes, \vee^1, \vee^2, \epsilon, \bot \rangle$$

where A_1, A_2 are two disjoint[2] sets, and $\epsilon, \bot \in A_1$. We call these the sets of elements of sort 1 and sort 2 respectively. We also have operations defined on elements of various sorts, $\vee^1, \vee^2$ which are commutative and idempotent, together with their infinitary variants, $\bigvee^1, \bigvee^2$, a binary concatenation operation $\circ$ on A_1, and a pairing operation that constructs elements of sort 2 from two elements of sort 1, $\otimes$. We will often drop the sortal superscripts on $\vee$ as they are clear from the context and overload the symbol $\vee$ or $\bigvee$.

These satisfy the following axioms:

- *$\langle A_1, \circ, \vee^1, \epsilon, \bot \rangle$ is a CIS;*
- *$\langle A_2, \vee^2, \bot \otimes \bot \rangle$ is a complete join semi-lattice with bottom element;*
- *$\vee^1$ and $\vee^2$ distribute over $\otimes$ that is to say we have the following identities:*
  - *$(x \vee^1 y) \otimes z = (x \otimes z) \vee^2 (y \otimes z)$ and $(\bigvee_i x_i) \otimes y = \bigvee_i (x_i \otimes y)$,*
  - *$x \otimes (y \vee^1 z) = (x \otimes y) \vee^2 (x \otimes z)$ and $x \otimes (\bigvee_i y_i) = \bigvee_i (x \otimes y_i)$.*

We define partial orders on the two sorts, $x \leq_1 y$ iff $y = x \vee^1 y$, $x \leq_2 y$ iff $y = x \vee^2 y$. Note that $\bot_1$ is a minimal element with respect to $\leq_1$ and $\bot_2 = \bot_1 \otimes \bot_1$ with respect to $\leq_2$.

Axiom E: *For all $x \in A_2$,*

$$x = \bigvee^2 \{u \otimes v \mid u, v \in A_1, u \otimes v \leq_2 x\}.$$

Axiom V: *For any set $J \subseteq A_1 \times A_1$, and any $p, q, a, b, c, d \in A_1$ if*

$$p \otimes q \leq_2 \bigvee \{u \otimes v \mid (u, v) \in J\}$$

then

$$p \circ q \leq_1 \bigvee \{u \circ v \mid (u, v) \in J\}$$

and

$$(a \circ p \circ b) \otimes (c \circ q \circ d) \leq_2 \bigvee \{(a \circ u \circ b) \otimes (c \circ v \circ d) \mid (u, v) \in J\}.$$

---

[2] We allow a slight violation of this criterion later as the empty set may be a member of both sets. This can be resolved with some technical modifications or notational variant.

Axioms E and V require some explanation. Axiom E excludes the case where there may be elements of sort 2 that are not formed from elements of sort 1. Axiom V can best be thought of as a generalization of the other distributivity axioms. From the CIS axioms we have that ∘ distributes over $\vee^1$. From Axiom V we can show that the general family of intercalation operations that we use in MCFG derivations distribute over $\vee_1$ and $\vee_2$ using the two clauses of the axiom respectively.

We use repeatedly the convention that d is a variable ranging over 1 and 2, which allows us to state conditions that both sorts satisfy. If A is a PCIS, then we write A_d for the set of elements of sort d, $\perp_A$ or $\perp_1$ for the bottom element of A_1 and ϵ_A for the ∘-identity.

The most basic type of PCIS which will help to understand the definition is the free structure over a finite set which will be very familiar.

Definition 2. *Given a finite set Σ we define the free structure $\mathfrak{F}(\Sigma)$ to be the structure:*

$$\langle \mathcal{P}(\Sigma^*), \mathcal{P}(\Sigma^* \times \Sigma^*), \cdot, \times, \cup, \cup, \{\lambda\}, \emptyset \rangle$$

The elements of sort 1 are just sets of strings, the elements of sort 2 are sets of pairs of strings, the pairing operation is the cartesian product and so on.

We define homomorphisms standardly.

Definition 3. *Given two PCISs A and B, a PCIS-homomorphism h is a pair of functions $h_1 : A_1 \to B_1$ and $h_2 : A_2 \to B_2$ such that:*

- *$h_1(\perp_A) = \perp_B$*
- *$h_1(\epsilon_A) = \epsilon_B$*
- *For all $u, v \in A_1$, $h_1(u \circ v) = h_1(u) \circ h_1(v)$*
- *For all $u, v \in A_1$, $h_2(u \otimes v) = h_1(u) \otimes h_1(v)$*
- *For all $X \subseteq A_d$, $h_d(\bigvee^d X) = \bigvee^d \{h_d(x) \mid x \in X\}$*

Definition 4. *Suppose we have a PCIS-homomorphism $h : A \to B$; we define $h^* : B \to A$ as a pair of functions $h_d^* : B_d \to A_d$ with $d = 1, 2$, where for all $y \in B_d$ we define*

$$h_d^*(y) = \bigvee^d \{x \in A_d \mid h_d(x) \leq y\} \,.$$

This function h^* is called the residual of the map h, which is a weak sort of inverse.

4   Algebraic Semantics for MCFGs

The PCIS only has the single concatenation operation ∘, but we can define linear regular functions in a natural way. We will illustrate this with a simple example. Consider the MCFG production

$$N(z_{1,1}z_{2,1}, z_{2,2}z_{1,2}) :- P(z_{1,1}, z_{1,2}), Q(z_{2,1}, z_{2,2})$$

which uses the linear regular function

$$f((z_{1,1}, z_{1,2}), (z_{2,1}, z_{2,2})) = (z_{1,1}z_{2,1}, z_{2,2}z_{1,2}).$$

We can extend these functions naturally from strings into a PCIS.

Definition 5. *For all $x, y \in A_2$ we define $x \ominus y$ to be*

$$x \ominus y = \bigvee \{(z_{1,1} \circ z_{2,1}) \otimes (z_{2,2} \circ z_{1,2}) \mid (z_{1,1} \otimes z_{1,2}) \leq x, (z_{2,1} \otimes z_{2,2}) \leq y\}$$

where the z variables range over elements of A_1. This defines a binary operation on A_2.

Here we implicitly rely on Axiom E; we apply the linear regular function to all of the sort 1 components of x and y, and then combine the results with $\bigvee$. Crucially, these operations, given the axioms of the PCIS, are "homomorphic".

Lemma 1. *If h is a PCIS-homomorphism then $h(x \ominus y) = h(x) \ominus h(y)$.*

Proof. (Sketch) It is immediate from the definitions that $h(x \ominus y) \leq h(x) \ominus h(y)$. Now $h(x) \ominus h(y) = \bigvee Z$ where $Z = \{(z_{1,1} \circ z_{2,1}) \otimes (z_{2,2} \circ z_{1,2}) \mid (z_{1,1} \otimes z_{1,2}) \leq h(x), (z_{2,1} \otimes z_{2,2}) \leq h(y)\}$. Using Axiom V we can show that every element of Z is bounded by $h(x \ominus y)$, which gives the result.   □

In a similar way we can define for any linear regular function f, a corresponding operation on a PCIS. These operations coincide in the trivial cases with primitive operations: for example, if f is the function $f(z_{1,1}, z_{2,1}) = z_{1,1}z_{2,1}$, then $f(x, y) = x \circ y$. Additionally we can prove that they are homomorphic.

Lemma 2. *If h is a PCIS-homomorphism and f is a k-ary linear regular function, with $k > 0$, then:*

$$h(f(\boldsymbol{x}_1, \ldots, \boldsymbol{x}_k)) = f(h(\boldsymbol{x}_1), \ldots, h(\boldsymbol{x}_k)).$$

For reasons of space we omit the full proofs; but the proofs require that the functions be non-deleting and non-permuting and require Axioms E and V in the definition of the PCIS. In the case where $k = 0$ and f is variable free this property is trivial.

We can now define the least fixed point semantics of a 2-MCFG in a non-standard way: rather than defining them directly in $\mathfrak{F}(\Sigma)$ which would be completely standard, we will define them in an arbitrary PCIS.

Definition 6. *Suppose we have an MCFG G with nonterminals V and a PCIS A. Let Ξ_A^V be the set of all functions from nonterminals to elements of A; where nonterminals of dimension d are mapped to elements of A_d. We define $\bigvee$ and $\leq$ componentwise on Ξ_A^V.*
In particular we define $\xi_\perp$ by $\xi_\perp(N) = \perp_{\dim(N)}$, for all $N \in V$.

Let h be a homomorphism from $\mathfrak{F}(\Sigma)$ to A. Each production $\pi \in P$ in the grammar then defines a function Φ_π^h from $\Xi_A^V \to \Xi_A^V$. If π is the k-ary production $(k > 0)$

$$N_0 \to f(N_1, \ldots, N_k)$$

then $\Phi_\pi^h(\xi) = \xi'$ is the element of Ξ_A^V which assigns $\perp_d$ to all nonterminals that are not N_0, and to the element N_0 assigns $f(\xi(N_1), \ldots, \xi(N_k))$.

$$\xi'(N) = \begin{cases} f(\xi(N_1), \ldots, \xi(N_k)) & \text{if } N = N_0, \\ \perp_{\dim(N)} & \text{otherwise.} \end{cases}$$

If $k = 0$ and π is of the form $N_0 \to w$, where $w \in (\Sigma^*)^{\dim(N_0)}$, then we use the homomorphism h to define ξ' to be

$$\xi'(N) = \begin{cases} h_{\dim(N)}(\{w\}) & \text{if } N = N_0, \\ \perp_{\dim(N)} & \text{otherwise.} \end{cases}$$

Definition 7. *For a grammar G, with set of productions P we define a function Φ_G^h from Ξ_A^V to Ξ_A^V.*

$$\Phi_G^h(\xi) = \bigvee \{ \Phi_\pi^h(\xi) \mid \pi \in P \}$$

We define recursively $\Phi_G^{h,n}(\xi) = \Phi_G^h(\Phi_G^{h,n-1}(\xi))$. By Kleene's fixed point theorem, the least fixed point, ξ_G^h, of this function exists and is equal to $\bigvee_n \Phi_G^{h,n}(\xi_\perp)$. This least fixed point coincides with the standard derivational semantics of MCFGS when the homomorphism h is the identity: for every nonterminal N, $\mathcal{L}(G, N) = \xi_G(N)$. On its own, this result is not very surprising: we have merely defined the derivation process in another way, as has been done before [6] and derived the same result. In order to say something interesting we need to use the homomorphism.

Lemma 3. *Suppose we have a homomorphism h from $\mathfrak{F}(\Sigma)$ to some PCIS A. Then write Φ_G^h for the interpretation function in A with h. Then for any $\xi \in \Xi_{\mathfrak{F}(\Sigma)}^V$*

$$h(\Phi_G^\iota(\xi)) = \Phi_G^h(h(\xi)),$$

where ι is the identity.

The proof is immediate given Lemma 2.

5   The Syntactic Concept Lattice

We now extend the syntactic concept lattice [2], from the structure appropriate to CFGS which is a CIS, to the structure appropriate for 2-MCFGS which is a PCIS.

We fix a language L over Σ. We have a distinguished symbol $\square \notin \Sigma$. A 2-word is an ordered pair of strings (u, v), an element of $\Sigma^* \times \Sigma^*$. A 1-context is a string in $\Sigma^* \square \Sigma^*$ and a 2-context is a string in $\Sigma^* \square \Sigma^* \square \Sigma^*$. See for example [11].

We can combine a d-context and a d-word using the wrap operation $\odot$. This is defined as $l\square r \odot u = lur$ and $l\square m\square r \odot (u, v) = lumvr$. We extend this to sets of d-words and d-contexts in the usual way.

Definition 8. *We define polar maps: we will use* $(\cdot)^{\triangleright}$ *for the maps from sets of d-words to sets of d-contexts and* $(\cdot)^{\triangleleft}$ *for the maps from sets of d-contexts to sets of d-words*
Given a set of 1-words x $(x \in \mathcal{P}(\Sigma^*))$ *define*

$$x^{\triangleright} = \{l\Box r \in \Sigma^*\Box\Sigma^* \mid l\Box r \odot x \subseteq L\}.$$

Given a set of 2-words x *define*

$$x^{\triangleright} = \{l\Box m\Box r \in \Sigma^*\Box\Sigma^*\Box\Sigma^* \mid l\Box m\Box r \odot x \subseteq L\}.$$

Given a set of 1-contexts t *we define*

$$t^{\triangleleft} = \{u \in \Sigma^* \mid t \odot u \subseteq L\}.$$

Given a set of 2-contexts t *we define*

$$t^{\triangleleft} = \{(u, v) \in \Sigma^* \times \Sigma^* \mid t \odot (u, v) \subseteq L\}.$$

This gives a pair of Galois connections, which as is well known give rise to a lattice [3]. We are interested in the closed sets of d-words, which are those sets x such that $x = x^{\triangleright\triangleleft}$. These sets naturally form a PCIS.

Definition 9. *The syntactic concept lattice of order 2 of the language* L, *written* $\mathfrak{B}(L)$ *is the following structure.*

- $A_1 = \mathfrak{B}^1(L) = \{x \in \mathcal{P}(\Sigma^*) \mid x = x^{\triangleright\triangleleft}\}$
- $A_2 = \mathfrak{B}^2(L) = \{x \in \mathcal{P}(\Sigma^* \times \Sigma^*) \mid x = x^{\triangleright\triangleleft}\}$
- $\epsilon = \{\lambda\}^{\triangleright\triangleleft}$ *and* $\bot = \emptyset^{\triangleright\triangleleft}$ *(in sort 1).*
- *For* $x, y \in A_1$, $x \circ y = (x \cdot y)^{\triangleright\triangleleft}$ *and* $x \otimes y = (x \times y)^{\triangleright\triangleleft}$
- *For* $X \subseteq A_d$, $\bigvee_d X = (\bigcup X)^{\triangleright\triangleleft}$

Lemma 4. $\mathfrak{B}(L)$ *is a* PCIS *and the map from* $\mathfrak{F}(\Sigma)$ *given by* $x \to x^{\triangleright\triangleleft}$ *is a* PCIS-*homomorphism.*

Proof. (Sketch) Suppose $x, y \in \mathcal{P}(\Sigma^*)$. Observe that $(x \cdot y)^{\triangleright\triangleleft} = (x^{\triangleright\triangleleft} \cdot y^{\triangleright\triangleleft})^{\triangleright\triangleleft}$, and $(x \times y)^{\triangleright\triangleleft} = (x^{\triangleright\triangleleft} \times y^{\triangleright\triangleleft})^{\triangleright\triangleleft}$.
    Moreover if $X \subseteq \mathcal{P}(\Sigma^*)$ then $(\bigcup X)^{\triangleright\triangleleft} = (\bigcup\{x^{\triangleright\triangleleft} \mid x \in X\})^{\triangleright\triangleleft}$.   □

Note that this will be finite, by an application of the Myhill-Nerode theorem, if and only if the language L is regular. It is easy to see that if $L = \Sigma^*$, then $\mathfrak{B}(L)$ is isomorphic to 1; and the only elements are Σ^* and $\Sigma^* \times \Sigma^*$.

Example 1. $L = a^*b^*$. This is regular and thus $\mathfrak{B}(L)$ is finite. Then $\mathfrak{B}^1(L) = \{\emptyset, \Sigma^*, \{\lambda\}, a^*, b^*, a^*b^*\}$ and $\mathfrak{B}^2(L) = \{\emptyset, \Sigma^* \times \Sigma^*, \{\langle\lambda, \lambda\rangle\}, a^* \times \{\lambda\}, \{\lambda\} \times b^*, a^* \times b^*, a^* \times a^*, b^* \times b^*, a^* \times a^*b^*, a^*b^* \times b^*\}$. Figure 1 contains a diagram showing these lattices.

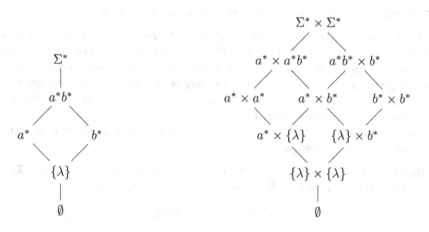

Fig. 1. The syntactic concept lattice of order 2 for the regular language $L = a^*b^*$; on the left is a Hasse diagram for $\mathfrak{B}^1(L)$, and on the right for $\mathfrak{B}^2(L)$

Example 2. Suppose $L = \{\,a^m b^n c^m d^n \mid m, n \geq 1\,\}$. Since this language is not regular $\mathfrak{B}(L)$ has an infinite number of elements. Sort 1 contains L, Σ^*, $\emptyset$, $\{\lambda\}$, as well as $\{a^n bc^n \mid n \geq 1\}$, $\{a^n bbc^n \mid n \geq 1\}$, and many others such as $\{a^m b^{i+j} c^m d^i \mid m \geq 1\}$.

Sort 2 is more complex and contains the infinite sets $\{(a^m, c^m) \mid m \geq 1\}$, $\{(a^{m+k}, c^m) \mid m \geq 1\}$, $\{(a^m, c^{m+k}) \mid m \geq 1\}$ for all $k \geq 1$, and so on, as well as $\{(b^{m+k}, d^m) \mid m \geq 1\}$ and so on. Note that $\mathfrak{B}(L)$ has only countably many elements though $\mathfrak{F}(\Sigma)$ is uncountable.

Example 3. Recently Salvati [9] showed that

$$\mathrm{MIX} = \{\,u \in \{a, b, c\}^* \mid |u|_a = |u|_b = |u|_c\,\},$$

where $|u|_a$ denotes the number of occurrences of a in u, is a 2-MCFL. Sort 1 ($\mathfrak{B}^1(\mathrm{MIX})$) consists of the sets $x_{i,j} = \{\,u \mid |u|_a - |u|_b = i$ and $|u|_a - |u|_c = j\,\}$ for all $(i, j) \in \mathbb{Z} \times \mathbb{Z}$. Sort 2 ($\mathfrak{B}^2(\mathrm{MIX})$) consists of the sets $y_{i,j} = \{\,(u, v) \mid |uv|_a - |uv|_b = i$ and $|uv|_a - |uv|_c = j\,\}$ for all $(i, j) \in \mathbb{Z} \times \mathbb{Z}$.

6 Homomorphisms and Grammar Morphisms

We will take a standard notion of grammar morphism as applied to MCFGs. Given a function ϕ from the set of nonterminals V_d to two disjoint sets X_d, we define the image of the grammar G, written $\phi(G)$. We extend ϕ to a function on productions, mapping

$$\phi(N_0 \to f(N_1, \dots, N_k)) = \phi(N_0) \to f(\phi(N_1), \dots, \phi(N_k))$$

and $\phi(N_0 \to w) = \phi(N_0) \to w$. Then $\phi(\langle \Sigma, V, S, P \rangle) = \langle \Sigma, \phi(V), \phi(S), \phi(P) \rangle$.

If ϕ is injective then the G is isomorphic to $\phi(G)$. If not, then two nonterminals must have been merged; it is easy to see that in any event $\mathcal{L}(G) \subseteq \mathcal{L}(\phi(G))$.

Definition 10. *If $\mathcal{L}(G) = \mathcal{L}(\phi(G))$ then ϕ is an* exact *morphism.*

If we have two distinct nonterminals M, N that are merged by an exact morphism ϕ, (i.e. $\phi(M) = \phi(N)$), then $\phi(G)$ is strictly smaller than G yet defines the same language. In this case we say that G has mergeable nonterminals. Requiring that a grammar does not have mergeable nonterminals is a very weak and natural condition on the grammars that we might want to use in practice or output from a learning algorithm.

Now we come to a crucial point: homomorphisms from $\mathfrak{F}(\Sigma)$ to some other PCIS induce an MCFG-morphism.

Definition 11. *Suppose A is a PCIS and h a PCIS-homomorphism from $\mathfrak{F}(\Sigma)$ to A. Then define ϕ_h to be a function from $V \to A$ defined by*

$$\phi_h(N) = h(\mathcal{L}(G, N)).$$

This morphism will merge two nonterminals iff their languages are mapped to the same element of A by h. Thus we can merge elements *algebraically*. As a special case of this morphism, we have the case where h is the identity. In this case, it merges two nonterminals of dimension d only if they generate exactly the same set of d-words. Clearly in this case the language generated by the grammar will be unchanged.

Given that the derivation operations of the grammar are homomorphic with respect to the algebra we can prove the following theorem.

Theorem 1. *Suppose we have a 2-MCFG, G, and a PCIS A and a homomorphism h from $\mathfrak{F}(\Sigma) \to A$. Then for all nonterminals N in G:*

$$h(\mathcal{L}(\phi_h(G), \phi_h(N))) = h(\mathcal{L}(G, N)).$$

Proof. (Sketch) We define a grammar U with the same set of nonterminals as G but with only the following set of unary productions.

$$P_h = \{N \to \iota(M) \mid h(\mathcal{L}(G, N)) = h(\mathcal{L}(G, M))\},$$

where ι is the identity function. Let H be the grammar G with this additional set of productions. Then we can see that $\Phi_H^\iota = \Phi_G^\iota \vee \Phi_U^\iota$. Clearly $\xi_H^\iota \geq \xi_G^\iota$.

- By the definitions we have that $\Phi_U^h(h(\xi_G^\iota)) = h(\xi_G^\iota)$.
- Using Lemma 3, $h(\Phi_U^\iota(\xi_G)) = \Phi_U^h(h(\xi_G^\iota)) = h(\xi_G^\iota)$.
- We can show that if $h(\xi) \leq h(\xi_G^\iota)$ then $h(\Phi_U^\iota(\xi)) \leq h(\xi_G^\iota)$, and furthermore $h(\Phi_G^\iota(\xi)) \leq h(\xi_G^\iota)$ and therefore $h(\Phi_H^\iota(\xi)) \leq h(\xi_G^\iota)$.
- By induction on n we can show that for all n, $h(\Phi_H^{\iota,n}(\xi_\perp)) \leq h(\xi_G^\iota)$.
- Finally we can show that $h(\xi_H^\iota) \leq h(\xi_G^\iota)$ which completes the proof. □

Informally, this says the original grammar's derivations are mapped to the same element that the merged grammar's derivations are mapped to. As a consequence, using the fact that $h^*(h(x)) \geq x$ for all x, we can easily derive the following algebraic bound on the languages derived in the merged grammar: this lemma unifies these two separate strands. On the left we have a grammar which is the result of a morphism; on the right a purely algebraic bound.

Lemma 5. *For any grammar G, nonterminal N and homomorphism h,*

$$\mathcal{L}(\phi_h(G), N) \subseteq h^*(h(\mathcal{L}(G, N))) \, .$$

We now define the natural extension of the classic automata theoretic notion of a monoid recognizing a regular language [4].

Definition 12. *Let A be a PCIS and h a PCIS-homomorphism from $\mathfrak{F}(\Sigma) \to A$, and L some language over Σ. Then we say that A recognizes the language L through h iff*

$$L = h^*(h(L)) \, .$$

By Lemma 5, if G generates L and A recognizes L through h, then ϕ_h is an exact morphism.

Note that if A is the trivial one-element PCIS ($A_1 = \{\bot\}, A_2 = \{\bot \otimes \bot\}$), then $h^*(h(L)) = \Sigma^*$ and so in general, this will not recognize any language apart from Σ^*. In this case the PCIS is too coarse or small to recognize the language.

Clearly $\mathfrak{F}(\Sigma)$ recognizes the language through the identity homomorphism, and $\mathfrak{B}(L)$ recognizes L through the homomorphism $X \to X^{\rhd\lhd}$, since $L = L^{\rhd\lhd}$.

Our main theorem is then immediate.

Theorem 2. *Let G be a 2-MCFG that defines a language L, and define ϕ_L to be the morphism given by $\phi_L(N) = \mathcal{L}(G, N)^{\rhd\lhd}$. Then ϕ_L is an exact morphism: $\mathcal{L}(\phi_L(G)) = L$.*

We will now show that $\mathfrak{B}(L)$ is the smallest PCIS that recognizes the language.

Lemma 6. *Suppose, A is some PCIS that recognizes L through a morphism h. Suppose $x, y \in \mathcal{P}((\Sigma^*)^d)$ are such that $h_d(x) = h_d(y)$; then $x^{\rhd} = y^{\rhd}$.*

Proof. Suppose $l \square r \in x^{\rhd}$ for some $l, r \in \Sigma^*$. That means that $lxr \subseteq L$; so $h(lxr) \leq h(L)$ since h is monotonic. This implies that $h(\{l\}) \circ h(x) \circ h(\{r\}) \leq h(L)$ using the fact that h is a homomorphism. So $h(\{l\}) \circ h(y) \circ h(\{r\}) \leq h(L)$ since $h(x) = h(y)$. Therefore $h(\{l\}y\{r\}) \leq h(L)$ since it is a homomorphism. So $h^*(h(\{l\}y\{r\})) \leq h^*(h(L))$ since h^* is monotonic. Now $h^*(h(L)) = L$ since A recognizes L. Therefore $h^*(h(\{l\}y\{r\})) \leq L$. So using the fact that $h^*(h(x)) \geq x$ we have $\{l\}y\{r\} \leq h^*(h(\{l\}y\{r\})) \leq h^*(h(L)) = L$. So $l \square r \in y^{\rhd}$. The converse argument is identical and so $x^{\rhd} = y^{\rhd}$.

The argument for sort 2 is identical but requires some additional notation so for reasons of space we omit it. □

We now show that $\mathfrak{B}(L)$ is the unique up to isomorphism smallest structure that recognizes the language: a terminal object in category theoretic terms.

Theorem 3. *Suppose A is a PCIS that recognizes L through a surjective homomorphism j. Let h_L be the homomorphism $\mathfrak{F}(\Sigma) \to \mathfrak{B}(L)$ given by $h_L(x) = x^{\rhd\lhd}$. Then there is a homomorphism f from A to $\mathfrak{B}(L)$ such that $h_L(x) = f(j(x))$.*

Proof. (Sketch) We define f as the pair of functions $f_d : A_d \to \mathfrak{B}^d(L)$

$$f_d(x) = j_d^*(x)^{\triangleright\triangleleft}$$

By Lemma 6 for any $x, y \in (\mathcal{P}(\Sigma^*))^d$, if $j_d(x) = j_d(y)$ then $x^{\triangleright} = y^{\triangleright}$. This means that $j_d^*(j_d(x)) \subseteq x^{\triangleright\triangleleft}$, and therefore $(j_d^*(j_d(x)))^{\triangleright\triangleleft} = x^{\triangleright\triangleleft}$; in other words $h_L(x) = f(j(x))$. We can then verify that it is a homomorphism. □

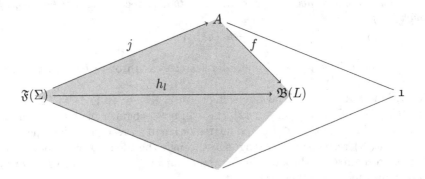

Fig. 2. A diagram illustrating the universal property of the lattice described in Theorem 3. The shaded area consists of those PCIS which recognize L; the unshaded area contains those which do not; on the far right is the trivial single element PCIS, 1. If A recognizes the language there is a unique homomorphism from A to $\mathfrak{B}(L)$.

Theorem 2 means that any grammar for L without mergeable nonterminals will have nonterminals that correspond to elements of $\mathfrak{B}(L)$. Theorem 3 shows that $\mathfrak{B}(L)$ is the smallest structure that has this property.

7 Conclusion

The first important observation is that the set of derivation contexts of nonterminal of dimension 2 in an MCFG correspond exactly to the string contexts of the form $l\square m\square r$. The second observation is that if the family of operations that build up objects bottom up are viewed algebraically, then homomorphisms of an appropriate algebra will induce "nice" morphisms of the grammar, and typically allow a precise characterization of some minimal structure. This general strategy is applicable to a broader range of grammatical formalisms. The extension to MCFGs of higher dimension is we think straightforward; but we feel that this does not exhaust the possibilities of this family of techniques.

From one perspective, this is very natural: each nonterminal in a grammar with context-free derivations defines a decomposition into the set of derivation contexts and the set of yields. The result here shows that we can reverse this process and define nonterminals based on decompositions: the "minimal" grammar will then be based on maximal decompositions.

The results we have presented here imply that we can assume, without loss of generality, that the nonterminals of an MCFG correspond to, or represent, elements of the syntactic concept lattice. Rather than being arbitrary atomic symbols, they have a rich algebraic structure. This implies that it is possible to develop techniques for example for translating between CFGs and MCFGs, for minimizing grammars and so on. This is also an important step towards the structural learning of MCFGs.

References

1. Clark, A.: Learning context free grammars with the syntactic concept lattice. In: Sempere, J.M., García, P. (eds.) ICGI 2010. LNCS, vol. 6339, pp. 38–51. Springer, Heidelberg (2010)
2. Clark, A.: The syntactic concept lattice: Another algebraic theory of the context-free languages? Journal of Logic and Computation (2013)
3. Davey, B.A., Priestley, H.A.: Introduction to Lattices and Order. Cambridge University Press (2002)
4. Eilenberg, S.: Automata, languages, and machines. Academic Press (1974)
5. Ginsburg, S., Rice, H.G.: Two families of languages related to ALGOL. Journal of the ACM (JACM) 9(3), 350–371 (1962)
6. Groenink, A.: Surface without structure: Word Order and Tractability Issues. Ph.D. thesis, University of Utrecht (1997)
7. Morrill, G.: Categorial grammar: Logical syntax, semantics and processing. Oxford University Press (2011)
8. Pereira, F.C.N., Shieber, S.M.: The semantics of grammar formalisms seen as computer languages. In: Proceedings of the 10th International Conference on Computational Linguistics and 22nd Annual Meeting on Association for Computational Linguistics, pp. 123–129. Association for Computational Linguistics (1984)
9. Salvati, S.: MIX is a 2-MCFL and the word problem in $\mathbb{Z}^2$ is solved by a third-order collapsible pushdown automaton. Technical Report Inria-00564552, version 1, INRIA (2011)
10. Seki, H., Matsumura, T., Fujii, M., Kasami, T.: On multiple context-free grammars. Theoretical Computer Science 88(2), 191–229 (1991)
11. Yoshinaka, R.: Efficient learning of multiple context-free languages with multidimensional substitutability from positive data. Theoretical Computer Science 412(19), 1821–1831 (2011)
12. Yoshinaka, R.: Integration of the dual approaches in the distributional learning of context-free grammars. In: Dediu, A.-H., Martín-Vide, C. (eds.) LATA 2012. LNCS, vol. 7183, pp. 538–550. Springer, Heidelberg (2012)

An ACG View on G-TAG and Its g-Derivation[*]

Laurence Danlos[1,2,3], Aleksandre Maskharashvili[4,5,6], and Sylvain Pogodalla[4,5,6]

[1] Université Paris Diderot (Paris 7), Paris, F-75013, France
[2] ALPAGE, INRIA ParisRocquencourt, Paris, F-75013, France
[3] Institut Universitaire de France, Paris, F-75005, France
[4] INRIA, Villers-lès-Nancy, F-54600, France
[5] Université de Lorraine, LORIA, UMR 7503, Vandœuvre-lès-Nancy, F-54500, France
[6] CNRS, LORIA, UMR 7503, Vandœuvre-lès-Nancy, F-54500, France
{laurence.danlos,aleksandre.maskharashvili,
sylvain.pogodalla}@inria.fr

Abstract. G-TAG is a Tree Adjoining Grammar (TAG) based formalism which was specifically designed for the task of text generation. Contrary to TAG, the derivation structure becomes primary, as pivot between the conceptual representation and the surface form. This is a shared feature with the encoding of TAG into Abstract Categorial Grammars. This paper propose to study G-TAG from an ACG perspective. We rely on the reversibility property of ACG that makes both parsing and generation fall within a common morphism inversion process. Doing so, we show how to overcome some limitations of G-TAG regarding predicative adjunction and how to propose alternative approaches to some phenomena.

1 Overview

Tree-adjoining grammar (TAG) [8], [9] is one of the most extensively studied grammatical formalism as it considered to be a formalism that can encode the most of natural languages. The point is that TAGs produce string languages that are not in general context free, but mildly context-sensitive. The latter fact means that the tree language produced by a TAG, called *derived tree language*, is not a regular tree language and thus it might be problematic to deal with it in certain tasks. However, in TAG, together with the notion of derived tree, there is defined the notion of *derivation tree* that encodes the history of the process of the derivation of a derived tree. It turns out that while a TAG derived tree language generally is not regular, TAG derivation tree language is regular. This fact makes possible to explore the useful properties of regular tree languages on TAG derivation trees [7]. Furthermore, a type-logical account was given to TAG in [5], where TAG was represented as second order ACGs.

G-TAG [3], [13] is a formalism designed for text generation, which makes use of the notions defined within TAG. However, in G-TAG the central notion of derivation tree (called *g-derivation* trees) is different from one that is defined in TAG. The goal of the current paper is to show that g-derivation and g-derived trees can be encoded in the ACG framework in the same spirit as TAG is encoded as ACGs, and also to simulate G-TAG text generation process in the confines of the ACG framework.

[*] This work has been supported by the French agency Agence Nationale de la Recherche (ANR-12-CORD-0004).

N. Asher and S. Soloviev (Eds.): LACL 2014, LNCS 8535, pp. 70–82, 2014.
© Springer-Verlag Berlin Heidelberg 2014

2   Tree Adjoining Grammars

Tree adjoining grammars have been widely used in computational linguistics in a number of tasks including parsing and generation (e.g. [12], [7]).

A TAG has two kinds of entries: *initial* and *auxiliary* trees, which are called elementary trees. An initial tree has interior nodes labeled by non-terminal symbol and frontier nodes, i.e. leaves, labeled by the symbols which can be either non-terminal or terminal ones. The non-terminal symbols appearing on the leaves of an initial tree are marked for *substitution*. For instance, γ_{reward}, γ_{John} and γ_{Mary} are initial trees of TAG. Similarly to initial trees, an auxiliary tree has its interior nodes labeled by the non-terminal symbols and frontier nodes labeled by either non-terminal or terminal ones; the frontier non-terminal symbols are marked for substitution as well, *except for one distinguished node* that is called the *foot node* and which has additionally attached an asterisk $*$. The label of the foot node is the same as the root node of the auxiliary tree. For instance, γ_{really} is an auxiliary tree.

A TAG *derived* tree language is produced from elementary trees with the help of *substitution* and *adjunction* operations defined in TAG. In short, TAG substitution is a substitution of frontier non-terminals of an initial tree by other initial trees; TAG adjunction is substitution of a internal node A of an initial tree by an auxiliary tree so that all the daughters of the substituted node become daughters of the node with label A of the substituted auxiliary tree. This process of producing a derived tree is encoded with a *derivation* tree.

For instance, via substituting γ_{Jean} and γ_{Marie} trees in the initial tree γ_{reward} and via adjoining γ_{really} into v node of γ_{reward}, one can get the derived tree given on the figure 1(b) The

$$\gamma_{Jean} = \begin{array}{c} \text{np} \\ \text{Jean} \end{array} \quad \gamma_{reward}= \begin{array}{c} \text{S} \\ \overline{\text{np} \quad \text{v} \quad \text{np}} \\ \text{récompense} \end{array} \quad \gamma_{Marie} = \begin{array}{c} \text{np} \\ \text{Marie} \end{array} \quad \gamma_{really} = \begin{array}{c} \text{v} \\ \overline{\text{v}^* \quad \text{vraiment}} \end{array}$$

process of the production of the derived tree 1(b) is recorded by the corresponding *derivation* tree, which is represented as the tree 1(a).[1]

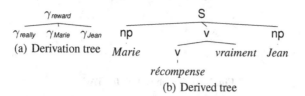

(a) Derivation tree

(b) Derived tree

Fig. 1. *Marie récompense vraiment Jean*

3   ACG Definition

ACGs provide a framework in which several grammatical formalisms may be encoded [6]. ACGs generate languages of linear λ-terms, which generalize both string and tree languages.

---

[1] Here, we omit tree addresses, which are usually used in TAG.

Definition 1. *A* higher-order linear signature *is defined to be a triple* $\Sigma = \langle A, C, \tau \rangle$, *where, A is a finite set of atomic types (also noted A_Σ), C is a finite set of constants (also noted C_Σ), and τ is a mapping from C to $\mathscr{T}_A$ the set of types built on A:* $\mathscr{T}_A ::= A \mid \mathscr{T}_A \multimap \mathscr{T}_A$ *(also noted $\mathscr{T}_\Sigma$). A higher-order linear signature will also be called a* vocabulary. $\Lambda(\Sigma)$ *is the set of λ-terms built on Σ, and for $t \in \Lambda(\Sigma)$ and $\alpha \in \mathscr{T}_\Sigma$ such that t has type α, we note* $t :_\Sigma \alpha$

Definition 2. *An* abstract categorial grammar *is a quadruple* $\mathscr{G} = \langle \Sigma, \Xi, \mathscr{L}, s \rangle$ *where:*
  1. *Σ and Ξ are two higher-order linear signatures, which are called the* abstract vo-cabulary *and the* object vocabulary, *respectively;*
  2. *$\mathscr{L} : \Sigma \longrightarrow \Xi$ is a* lexicon *from the abstract vocabulary to the object vocabulary. An ACG lexicon $\mathscr{L}$ is a homomorphism that maps types and terms built on Σ to types and terms built on Ξ, in the following way:*
     – *If $\alpha \multimap \beta \in \mathscr{T}_\Sigma$ then $\mathscr{L}(\alpha \multimap \beta) = \mathscr{L}(\alpha) \multimap \mathscr{L}(\beta)$.*
     – *If $\lambda x.t, (t\,u) \in \Lambda(\Sigma)$ then $\mathscr{L}(\lambda x.t) = \lambda x.\mathscr{L}(t)$ and $\mathscr{L}(t\,u) = \mathscr{L}(t)\,\mathscr{L}(u)$*
     – *For any constants $c :_\Sigma \alpha$ of Σ we have $\mathscr{L}(c) :_\Xi \mathscr{L}(\alpha)$.*
  3. *$s \in \mathscr{T}_\Sigma$ is a type of the abstract vocabulary, which is called the* distinguished type *of the grammar.*
The abstract language *of an ACG $\mathscr{G} = \langle \Sigma, \Xi, \mathscr{L}, s \rangle$ is $\mathcal{A}(\mathscr{G}) = \{t \in \Lambda(\Sigma) \mid t :_\Sigma s\}$*
The object language *of the grammar $\mathcal{O}(\mathscr{G}) = \{t \in \Lambda(\Xi) \mid \exists u \in \mathcal{A}(\mathscr{G}).\, t = \mathscr{L}_G(u)\}$*

Let us notice that since there is no structural difference between the abstract and the object vocabulary as both of them are higher-order signatures, ACGs can be combined in various ways: either by having a same abstract vocabulary shared by several ACGs in order to make two object terms (for instance a string and a logical formula) share the same underlying structure as $\mathscr{G}_{d\text{-}ed\ trees}$ and $\mathscr{G}_{Log}$ in Fig. 2, or by making the abstract vocabulary of an ACG the object vocabulary of another ACG, allowing the latter to control the admissible structures of the former, as $\mathscr{G}_{yield}$ and $\mathscr{G}_{d\text{-}ed\ trees}$ in Fig. 2.

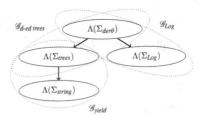

Fig. 2. ACG architecture for TAG

4   TAG as ACG

TAG derivation trees are encoded in a second order signature of an ACG [5]. An attrac-tive side of the ACG encoding of TAG is that the grammars and the algorithms are the same for *parsing* and for *generation* [11].

A TAG derivation tree corresponds to a ground term of the second order signature. The encoding of TAG into ACG uses two ACGs $\mathscr{G}_{d\text{-}ed\ trees} = \langle \Sigma_{der\theta}, \Sigma_{trees}, \mathscr{L}_{d\text{-}ed\ trees}, \mathsf{S} \rangle$

and $\mathcal{G}_{yield} = \langle \Sigma_{trees}, \Sigma_{string}, \mathcal{L}_{yield}, \tau \rangle$. The signature $\Sigma_{der\theta}$ is used to define derivation tree language of TAG. $\Sigma_{der\theta}$ has constants as entries that encode elementary trees of TAG. The notion of derivation tree of TAG corresponds to the terms build on $\Sigma_{der\theta}$ that have distinguished type S. Moreover, in order to model derived trees and surface forms, there are introduced Σ_{trees} and Σ_{string}, respectively, which are defined as follows:

$\Sigma_{der\theta}$: Its atomic types include S, vp, np, S_A, vp_A...where the X types stand for the categories X of the nodes where a substitution can occur while the X_A types stand for the categories X of the nodes where an adjunction can occur. For each elementary tree $\gamma_{lex.\,entry}$ it contains a constant $C_{lex.\,entry}$ whose type is based on the adjunction and substitution sites as Table 1 shows. It additionally contains constants $I_X : X_A$ that are meant to provide a fake auxiliary tree on adjunction sites where no adjunction actually takes place in a TAG derivation.

Σ_{trees}: Its unique atomic type is τ the type of trees. Then, for any X of arity n belonging to the ranked alphabet describing the elementary trees of the TAG, we have a

$$\text{constant } X_n : \overbrace{\tau \multimap \cdots \multimap \tau}^{n \text{ times}} \multimap \tau$$

Σ_{string}: Its unique atomic type is σ the type of strings. The constants are the terminal symbols of the TAG (with type σ), the concatenation $+ : \sigma \multimap \sigma \multimap \sigma$ and the empty string $\varepsilon : \sigma$.

Table 1 illustrates $\mathcal{L}_{d\text{-}ed\,trees}$.[2] $\mathcal{L}_{yield}$ is defined as follows:

- $\mathcal{L}_{yield}(\tau) = \sigma$;
- for $n > 0$, $\mathcal{L}_{yield}(X_n) = \lambda x_1 \cdots x_n.x_1 + \cdots + x_n$;
- for $n = 0$, $X_0 : \tau$ represents a terminal symbol and $\mathcal{L}_{yield}(X_0) = X$.

Table 1. TAG with Semantics as ACGs: $\mathcal{L}_{d\text{-}ed\,trees}$ and $\mathcal{L}_{log.sem}$ lexicons

Abstract constants $\Sigma_{der\theta}$	Their images by $\mathcal{L}_{d\text{-}ed\,trees}$	The corresponding TAG trees
$C_{Jean} : np$	$c_{Jean} \begin{array}{l} : \tau \\ = np_1\, Jean \end{array}$	$\gamma_{Jean} = \begin{array}{c} np \\ \mid \\ Jean \end{array}$
$C^v_{really} : v_A \multimap v_A$	$c^v_{really} \begin{array}{l} : (\tau \multimap \tau) \multimap (\tau \multimap \tau) \\ = \lambda^o v x.v \,(v_2\, x\; vraiment) \end{array}$	$\gamma_{really} = \begin{array}{c} v \\ \overline{v^*\quad vraiment} \end{array}$
$C_{reward} : \begin{array}{l} S_A \multimap v_A \multimap np \\ \multimap np \multimap S \end{array}$	$c_{reward} \begin{array}{l} : \begin{array}{c} (\tau \multimap \tau) \multimap (\tau \multimap \tau) \\ \multimap \tau \multimap \tau \multimap \tau \end{array} \\ = \lambda^o a v s o.\, a \\ \;(S_3\, s\,(v\,(v_1\; r\acute{e}compense))\, o) \end{array}$	$\gamma_{reward} = \begin{array}{c} S \\ \overline{np \quad v \quad np} \\ r\acute{e}compense \end{array}$
$I_X : X_A$	$\lambda x.x : \tau \multimap \tau$	

We exemplify the encoding[3] of a TAG by analyzing the sentence (1), whose corresponding derivation and derived trees are given on Fig. 1.[4]

---

[2] With $\mathcal{L}_{d\text{-}ed\,trees}(X_A) = \tau \multimap \tau$ and for any other type X, $\mathcal{L}_{d\text{-}ed\,trees}(X_A) = \tau$.
[3] We refer the reader to [14] for the details.
[4] We follow the grammar of [1].

(1) *Marie récompense vraiment Jean*
     Mary rewards   really   John

The term α corresponds to the derivation tree on Fig. 1; while, the image of α by $\mathscr{L}_{d\text{-}ed\ trees}$ corresponds to the derived tree from Fig. 1. Finally, applying $\mathscr{L}_{yield}$ to the derived tree produces the string representation.

$$\alpha = C_{reward}\ I_{\mathsf{S}}\ (C^{\mathsf{V}}_{really}\ I_{\mathsf{S}})\ C_{Marie}\ C_{Jean}$$
$$\mathscr{L}_{d\text{-}ed\ trees}(\alpha) = \mathsf{S}_3\ (\mathsf{np}_1\ Marie)(\mathsf{v}_2\ (\mathsf{v}_1\ récompense)\ vraiment)\ (\mathsf{np}_1\ Jean)$$
$$\mathscr{L}_{yield}(\mathscr{L}_{d\text{-}ed\ trees}(\alpha)) = Marie + récompense + vraiment + Jean$$

5 Introduction G-TAG

G-TAG produces texts given a semantic input. In the text production task, G-TAG makes use of TAG elementary trees and G-TAG notions of *g-derivation* and *g-derived* trees.

G-Derivation Trees. A TAG derivation tree can be seen as a record of the substitutions and adjunction occurring during a TAG analysis. The same is true for g-derivation tree. However, while TAG derivation trees are considered as a by-product,[5] with inflected anchors, G-TAG derivation trees are first class structures that are combined in order to reflect the conceptual input. To abstract from the surface form and from the derived tree they can relate to, they don't correspond to inflected forms but bear features that are used in a post-processing step. Complex g-derivation trees are built by going through the dynamic selection process of a lexical item from the set of appropriate candidates for a given concept. So contrary to TAG derivation trees, they are not fully instantiated trees: their arguments are represented by variables whose lexicalization are not carried out yet.

G-Derived Trees. A g-derivation tree defines a unique g-derived tree corresponding to it. This correspondence is maintained all along the production process and a post-processing module outputs the surface representation (text) from the g-derived tree. In addition to inflecting forms using the feature values the post-processing module can perform some rewriting to propose *different versions* of the initial text. In this particular sense, g-derived tree corresponds to possible multiply text outputs generated by the post-processing module.

A Conceptual Representation: G-TAG Input. G-TAG conceptual representation language is a sublanguage of LOGIN defined in [2][6] G-TAG conceptual representation makes use of notions as *second order relation*, *first order relation* and *thing*. So, they are divided into two categories: RELATION and THING. Second order relations have two arguments which are from RELATION category (either first or second order ones), whereas first order relations have THING as their arguments.

---

[5] Despite that TAG derivation trees were considered as good candidates for extracting semantics, it was possible to straightforwardly use them, because of which there were proposed several modifications of the formalism [15], [10].

[6] LOGIN is more expressive than Prolog, and at the same time as LOGIN uses unification rather than the resolution used in Prolog, LOGIN is more efficient from computational points of view.

On the table 2 is presented a G-TAG input that is given in [3], and which will be further used in the paper. For instance, E_0 is an input, where SUCCESSION is a second order relation having two arguments, which are relations themselves.

Table 2. G-TAG conceptual representation input

```
E0  =: SUCCESSION [1st-EVENT ⇒ E1, 2ND-EVENT ⇒ E2]
E1  =: GOAL [Action ⇒ E11, Purpose ⇒ E12]
E2  =: NAPPING [NAPPER ⇒ H1]
E11 =: VACUUMING [VACUUMER ⇒ H1]
E12 =: REWARDING [REWARDER ⇒ H2, REWARDEE ⇒ H1]
H1  =: HUMAN [NAME ⇒ "Jean", gender ⇒ masc]
H2  =: HUMAN [NAME ⇒ "Marie", gender ⇒ fem]
```

5.1 G-TAG Generation Process

Let us assume the input of Table 2. The G-TAG process starts by lexicalizing relations that have the widest scope in the conceptual representation: typically second order relations, then first order relations, and finally, things.[7] Back to the example, we first lexicalize the second order relation of E_0: SUCCESSION. Several items are associated to this relation: après (after), avant (before), ensuite (afterwards), auparavant (beforehand), puis (then), etc. Each of them has two arguments, however, some of them produce texts comprising from two or more sentences, like ensuite(afterwards); some of them can produce either two sentence texts or one sentence text, while others produce only one sentence. For instance, *Jean a passé l'aspirateur. Ensuite, il a fait une sieste* (John has vacuumed. Afterwards, he took a nap) is a two sentence text while *John a fait une sieste après avoir passé l'aspirateur* (John took a nap after having vacuumed) is a one sentence text. For this reason, items describing the arguments or the result of second order relations have features expressing the following constraints: $(+T, +S)$ indicates it is a text (two ore more sentences); $(+S)$ indicates it is either a single sentence or a text; $(-T, +S)$ indicates it is a sentence (not a text). Every second order relation has three features: one for output, and two for inputs.[8]

Let us assume that the G-TAG g-derivation tree ensuite$(+T, +S)$ belonging to the lexical database associated with the concept SUCCESSION is chosen so that the result is a text rather than a sentence (illustrated by the leftmost g-derivation tree of Figure 3 . The process then tries to realize E_1 and E_2, the arguments of E_0. E_1 involves the GOAL relation that can be realized either by pour (in order to) or by pour que (so that), as exemplified by the rightmost g-derivation trees of Figure 3. Both have features $(-T, +S)$ for the inputs (i.e. arguments) and return a tree labeled at the root by $(-T, +S)$.

---

[7] Correctness of the process is ensured because the grammars do not contain auxiliary trees that would invert the predication order. [3] argues such cases do not occur in technical texts, the first target of G-TAG. We do not elaborate on this point since the ACG approach we propose remove this constraint for free.

[8] In G-TAG, any discourse connective has exactly two arguments. A discussion about this point is provided in [3].

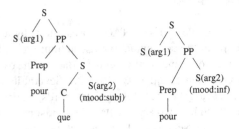

Fig. 3. G-derivation trees samples

Despite pour and pour que bear the same features, the syntactic trees corresponding to pour and pour que are quite different. For pour que S substitution nodes can be substituted by two tensed sentences, while pour takes a finite sentence and a "sentence" in the infinitive form without any nominal subject. Selecting one or the other during the generation process restricts the possible realizations for the arguments. This is enforced by a feature associated to the elementary tree, namely the (+reduc-subj) feature as shown in Fig. 4.

Fig. 4. TAG elementary trees corresponding pour que and pour

Again, we may assume that G-TAG selects pour, which will enforce, because of the associated elementary trees, that the subject of the first and the second arguments are the same. Afterwards, we need to lexicalize E_{11} and E_{12}. Since we chose pour, it means that E_{11} has to have H_1 as its subject that is the same subject that E_{12} has. From a semantic point of view, NAPPER (the agent) of E_{11} has to be REWARDEE (the beneficiary) of E_{12}. E_{11} can only be lexicalized as passer-l'aspirateur (run-the-vacuum-cleaner), while there are several lexicalization options for E_{12}. The REWARDING relation can be lexicalized by the following entries: récompenser (to reward), donner-récompense (to give-reward), and recevoir-récompense (to receive-reward). Let us notice that donner-récompense does not meet the constraint on a shared subject as it cannot have REWARDEE as its subject[9]. The remaining options are: recevoir-récompense, whose canonical representation has REWARDEE as the subject; and récompense whose passive construction has REWARDEE as the subject. Assuming a choice of récompenser[+passive],[10] we have lexicalized all the *relations*.

The last step of the lexicalization process, and consequently g-derivation building process is to lexicalize THING relations. So at this step, we have partially lexicalized

---

[9] It lacks passivation in French and there is no form equivalent to: John was given a reward by Mary.

[10] Of course, all these branching points offer several realizations of the same entry. But for explanatory purposes, we describe only one at each step.

g-derivation tree, whose the nodes that correspond to RELATION category are already lexicalized, while instead of the lexical items corresponding to *Jean* and *Marie*, H_1 and H_2 variables are used in the tree.

Let us notice that in the input (given on Table 2) H_2 occurs only once and it is in the subject position. Therefore H_2 can only be lexicalized as <u>Marie</u>. On the other hand, H_1 occurs three times: as arguments of E_{12} and of E_2, and as an argument of E_{11}, for which it is already lexicalized as ϵ. So, it remains to lexicalize H_1 in E_{12} and of E_2: H_1 can be either lexicalized in both of the cases as <u>Jean</u>, or <u>Jean</u> and the pronoun <u>il</u> (*he*). Thus, this step can be regarded as referring expression generation step. G-TAG has post-processing rules that take care of the generation of referring expressions, but we omit their formulations here. We assume that H_1 is lexicalized as <u>Jean</u> in E_{12} and as <u>il</u> in E_2. Figure 5 shows the g-derivation tree associated with the input of Table. 2 and Fig. 5 shows the unique resulting (non-inflected) derived tree as well. Afterwards, the post-processing module computes morphological information of the g-derived and outputs:

(2) *Jean a   passé l'aspirateur pour être récompensé par Marie.*
     John vacuumed in   order   to   be   rewarded   by Mary.
     Ensuite,   il   a   fait une sieste.
     Afterwards, he   took a   nap.

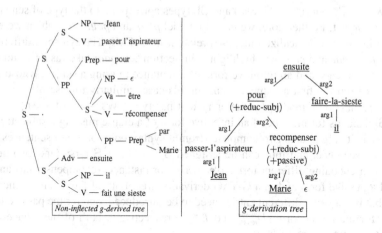

Fig. 5. g-derived and g-derivation trees of G-TAG

6 G-TAG as ACG

In order to model G-TAG in ACG, one needs to design the abstract signature $\Sigma_{g\text{-}derivations}$ whose members will reflect the ideology of G-TAG. For instance, in G-TAG a discourse level word like *ensuite* (then), which is a lexicalization of SUCCESSION relation, can take as its arguments texts and sentences and produces text. In order to model this, we introduce types S and T. Then, we can define D^{SS}_{then}: S $\multimap$ S $\multimap$ T, which means that

D_{then}^{SS} has takes two arguments of type S and returns a result of type T. As in G-TAG, *ensuite* can take two texts as arguments and return text as well, we need to do have another entry for modeling this fact. This makes us to introduce another constant D_{then}^{TT}: T $\multimap$ T $\multimap$ T. For the same kind of reason, we introduce following constants: D_{then}^{ST}: S $\multimap$ T $\multimap$ T, D_{then}^{TS} and T $\multimap$ S $\multimap$ T. Other relations, like *auparavant* are modeled in the same way as *ensuite* in $\Sigma_{g\text{-}derivations}$.

Moreover, there are other connectives such as *avant* (before) and *après* (after) that can be used in lexicalization of SUCCESSION as well, but must be modeled differently from *ensuite*. While, *ensuite* results in a text, placing side by side a text and a sentence separated with a period, in the French language, *avant* and *après* combine in a single sentence a (full) clause and an infinitive clause with an implicit subject: the one of the first clause. It is clear that in order to type *avant* and *après* in the $\Sigma_{g\text{-}derivations}$ signature, one should use a type which schematically looks as ... $\multimap$ S. On the other hand, one needs to give the exact type to them. Despite that in TAG and G-TAG *avant* and *après* take two sentential arguments (labeled by S), the second argument bears a feature indicating it lacks the subject and that the latter has to be shared with the first sentence. For instance: *Jean a fait une sieste après avoir passé l'aspirateur* (John took a nap after having vacuumed), here the subject of *avoir passé l'aspirateur* (having vacuumed) is *Jean*, which comes from the sentence *Jean a fait une sieste* (John took a nap). So, *Jean a fait une sieste* (John took a nap) can be seen as a sentence whose subject is shared by another sentence as well. In order to model this point, we use following type: Sws $\multimap$ Sh $\multimap$ np $\multimap$ S. Sws and Sh types correspond to the type of sentences missing a subject. Furthermore, we need to model *pour* and *pour que*, which were introduced in order to lexicalize the GOAL relation in G-TAG. The syntactic difference between *pour que* and *pour* was highlighted in Section 5.1: *pour* takes as its arguments a complete sentence and an infinitive form of a sentence missing a subject whose subject comes from the first argument. Thus, in this case, similarly to case of *avant* and *après*, *pour* has to be modeled as an entry that has type Sws $\multimap$ Sinf $\multimap$ np $\multimap$ S, where Sinf stands for the type of an infinitive form of a clause missing a subject; *pour que* takes as its arguments two complete (from a syntax point of view) sentences and produces a sentence, and thus can be assigned S $\multimap$ S $\multimap$ S type. One also needs to deal with encoding different forms of a verb. For instance, récompenser has an active and a passive form and in a G-TAG derivation tree, both of them can be encountered. That is why, two different entries need to be introduced, one for the passive form and one for the active form: $D_{reward}^{passive}$ and D_{reward}^{active}, respectively; both of them have type $S_A \multimap v_A \multimap np \multimap np \multimap S$.

The problem of giving compositional account of v adjunction of the discourse connective was faced in G-TAG. For instance, the following text *Jean a passé l'aspirateur. Il a ensuite fait une sieste* (John vacuumed. Afterwards, he took a nap) can only be obtained with the help of post processing module that is able to convert the sentence [*ensuite, il a fait une sieste*] into the sentence [*il a ensuite fait une sieste*]. Using ACG approach, we can handle this by introducing a constant $D_{ensuite}^{V}$ of type: S $\multimap$ (v_A $\multimap$ S) $\multimap$ T, that models the fact that $D_{ensuite}^{V}$ is applied to two sentences from which one needs to take adjunction on v.

Encoding Referring Expressions in $\Sigma_{g\text{-}derivations}$: Let us recall that in G-TAG derivation process H_1 can be substituted by different values, like Jean, il or ϵ. In order to give
account to this fact, three different constants are introduced in $\Sigma_{g\text{-}derivations}$: $D_{Jean}{}^1$, $D_{Jean}{}^2$
and $D_{Jean}{}^3$, all of which have type np. This allows us to generate terms as follows:

$$D_{then}^{SS} \left(D_{vac} I_S I_v D_{Jean}{}^1 \right) \left(D_{reward} I_S I_v D_{marie} D_{Jean}{}^2 \right)$$

There are two different constants at derivation step corresponding to *Jean*: $D_{Jean}{}^1$ and
$D_{Jean}{}^2$. Thus, as already in the derivation level G-TAG has differantiated between Jean
and il, we also do that by introducing different constants of the same type.

From G-TAG g-derivation Trees to TAG Derivation Trees : We translate terms of
$\Sigma_{g\text{-}derivations}$, which correspond to g-derivation trees, into the TAG derivation tree language defined on $\Sigma_{der\theta}$ using the lexicon $\mathscr{L}_{der\text{-}der}$ as follows:
$\mathscr{L}_{der\text{-}der}(\mathsf{S}) = \mathscr{L}_{der\text{-}der}(\mathsf{T}) = \mathscr{L}_{der\text{-}der}(\mathsf{Sws}) = \mathscr{L}_{der\text{-}der}(\mathsf{Sinf}) = \mathscr{L}_{der\text{-}der}(\mathsf{Sh}) = \mathsf{S};$
$\mathscr{L}_{der\text{-}der}(\mathsf{np}) = \mathsf{np}$ and $\mathscr{L}_{der\text{-}der}(I_X) = I_X, X = \mathsf{S}, \mathsf{v}.$
   Moreover, the different constants introduced for modeling referring expressions as
$D_{Jean}{}^1$, $D_{Jean}{}^2$ and $D_{Jean}{}^3$, are translated to the different constants of $\Sigma_{der\theta}$ signature:
$\mathscr{L}_{der\text{-}der}(D_{Jean}{}^1) = C_{Jean}{}^1$, $\mathscr{L}_{der\text{-}der}(D_{Jean}{}^2) = C_{Jean}{}^2$ and $\mathscr{L}_{der\text{-}der}(D_{Jean}{}^1) = C_{Jean}{}^1$.

G-Derived Trees as Interpretation of g-Derivation Trees : As soon as g-derivation
trees as terms built on $\Sigma_{g\text{-}derivations}$ are interpreted as terms built on $\Sigma_{der\theta}$, we can map
them to derived trees. Thus, by composing the two lexicons $\mathscr{L}_{der\text{-}der}$ and $\mathscr{L}_{d\text{-}ed\ trees}$ we
can get directly from g-derivation trees of G-TAG into TAG derived trees.
   Now we can translate constants $C_{Jean}{}^1$, $C_{Jean}{}^2$ and $C_{jean}{}^3$ to different trees of Σ_{trees}
from which surface realization is produced via applying $\mathscr{L}_{yield}$. For instance, in order to produce the g-derived tree from Fig. 5, we translate: $\mathscr{L}_{d\text{-}ed\ trees}(C_{Jean}{}^1) = \gamma_{John}$,
$\mathscr{L}_{d\text{-}ed\ trees}(C_{Jean}{}^2) = \gamma_{il}$, and $\mathscr{L}_{d\text{-}ed\ trees}(C_{Jean}{}^3) = \gamma_{\epsilon}$.

6.1   From G-TAG to Montague Style Semantics Using ACGs

In [14] is defined a signature $\Sigma_{semantics}$ and a lexicon $\mathscr{L}_{Log}$ from $\Sigma_{der\theta}$ to $\Sigma_{semantics}$.
The entries in $\Sigma_{semantics}$ have Montague like semantics. Below, we sketch the signature
Σ_{conrep}, where the formulas of G-TAG conceptual representations are build,[11] and the
lexicon $\mathscr{L}_{der\text{-}con}$ from $\Sigma_{g\text{-}derivations}$ to Σ_{conrep}, which gives Montague style translations to
the entries of $\Sigma_{g\text{-}derivations}$. In Σ_{conrep}, there are two atomic types e and t and constants
such as: **j, m** ... of type e, the constant **VAC**, **NAP** of type $e \multimap t$; **REWARD** of type
$e \multimap e \multimap t$, and **SUCC**, **GOAL** of type $t \multimap t \multimap t$.
   $\mathscr{L}_{der\text{-}con}$ interprets both T and S as t. np is interpreted as $[\![\mathsf{np}]\!] = (e \rightarrow t) \multimap t$, using
a non-linear implication. This illustrates that semantic terms usually are not linear, but
we do not elaborate on this here. [12] Typically, the sharing of the subject by two clauses
related by *pour* or *avant* induces non linearity. Furthermore, Sinf, Sh, and Sws types

---

[11] Let us notice that a formula of Σ_{conrep} signature is a higher-order logic formula that can be
seen as a approximation of an conceptual representation input used in [3].

[12] It's enough to say that as long as the non-linear variables are of atomic type and are not erased,
the computational complexity of inverting the morphism (ACG parsing) is unchanged.

all are interpreted as $[\![np]\!] \multimap [\![S]\!] = ((e \to t) \multimap t) \multimap t$ as they denote clauses lacking a subject. Then the constants of $\Sigma_{g\text{-}derivations}$ are translated as follows:

$$\mathscr{L}_{der\text{-}con}(D_{rewards}) = \lambda^\circ s\ a\ O\ S.s(S(a(\lambda x.O(\lambda y.(\textbf{REWARD}\ x\ y))))$$

$$\mathscr{L}_{der\text{-}con}(D_{pour}) = \lambda^\circ s_1.\lambda^\circ s_2.\lambda^\circ N.N(\lambda x.(\textbf{GOAL}(s_1(\lambda P.P\ x))(s_2(\lambda P.P\ x))))$$

$$\mathscr{L}_{der\text{-}con}(D_{apres}) = \lambda^\circ s_1.\lambda^\circ s_2.\lambda^\circ N.N(\lambda x.(\textbf{SUCC}(s_1(\lambda P.P\ x))(s_2(\lambda P.P\ x))))$$

$$\mathscr{L}_{der\text{-}con}(D_{then}^{SS}) = \mathscr{L}_{der\text{-}con}(D_{then}^{ST}) = \cdots = \mathscr{L}_{der\text{-}con}(D_{then}^{TS}) = \lambda^\circ\ s_1 s_2.\textbf{SUCC}\ s_2\ s_1$$

Encoding Referring Expressions in Σ_{conrep} : The different constants that were added to model referring expressions are translated as the same term of Σ_{conrep}. For example, we have added constants $D_{Jean}{}^1$, $D_{Jean}{}^2$ and $D_{Jean}{}^3$ in order to have different expressions referring to *Jean*. In other words, our aim was to produce text, where at some places instead of *Jean* there *il* (he) or for instance, nothing, i.e. ϵ (in passive sentences). Nevertheless, the conceptual representation of all these different constants $D_{Jean}{}^i$ for $i = 1, 2, 3$ are translated as $\lambda^\circ P.P.(\mathbf{j})$, because they are different referring expressions of one and the same semantic object.

6.2   G-TAG Generation Process as ACG Morphism Composition

Given a formula F in Σ_{conrep} that corresponds to a conceptual input of G-TAG, taking into account ACG reversibility property, we can produce texts that correspond to F. This will be ACG account to G-TAG text production process that begins with accepting a conceptual representation input and ends up with outputting a corresponding surface realization. So, in order to produce a surface realization from F formula, we first have to invert the morphism $\mathscr{L}_{der\text{-}con}$, which gives the set of terms of $\Sigma_{g\text{-}derivations}$:

$$\mathscr{L}_{der\text{-}con}{}^{-1}(F) = \{t_1, \ldots, t_n\}$$

Then we compute $\mathscr{L}_{der\text{-}der}(t_i)$ for $i = 1, 2, \ldots, n$. Further mapping of these terms (corresponding to g-derivation trees) $\mathscr{L}_{der\text{-}der}(t_i)$ for $i = 1, 2, \ldots, n$ via $\mathscr{L}_{d\text{-}ed\ trees}$ results in n different derived trees; after that by mapping the received derived trees via $\mathscr{L}_{yield}$, there are produced n different texts. For instance, the preimage of a formula $F_0 = \textbf{SUCC}(\textbf{VAC}(\mathbf{j}), \textbf{NAP}(\mathbf{j}))$ under $\mathscr{L}_{der\text{-}con}$ is the set of terms given on Fig.6. [13]

Thus, ACG composition of morphisms $\mathscr{L}_{yield}(\mathscr{L}_{d\text{-}ed\ trees}(\mathscr{L}_{der\text{-}der}(\mathscr{L}_{der\text{-}con}{}^{-1})))$ models G-TAG text production process within ACG framework. On the other hand, G-TAG outputs only one text, whereas using a composition of morphisms, from one formula we produce all the texts that correspond to it. This can be regarded as an advantage, as all the possible surface realizations are produced, but it has its disadvantages. Namely, among produced texts, there can be such which is comprised from valid sentences, but from discourse point of view, it is incoherent. For instance, the text produced from t_{20}, i.e. $\mathscr{L}_{yield}(\mathscr{L}_{d\text{-}ed\ trees}(\mathscr{L}_{der\text{-}der}(t_{20})))$ is following: *Il a passé l'aspirateur. Ensuite, il a fait une sieste.* (He vacuumed. Afterwards, he took a nap.) This text (comprised from syntactically correct sentences) fails to be coherent from anaphoric reference point of view.

---

[13] Note that there are 20 possibilities using D_{jean}^1 and D_{jean}^2 as lexicalization of *Jean*.

$$t_1 = D_{then}^{SS}(D_{vac}I_SI_vD_{jean}^1)(D_{sleep}I_SI_vD_{jean}^1)$$
$$t_2 = D_{bef.}^{SS}(D_{sleep}I_SI_vD_{jean}^1)(D_{vac}I_SI_vD_{jean}^1)$$
$$t_3 = D_{ensuite}^V(D_{vac}I_SI_vD_{jean}^1)(\lambda^0 a.D_{sleep}I_S a D_{jean}^1)$$
$$t_4 = D_{avant}(D_{vac}^{ews}I_SI_v)(D_{sleep}I_SI_v)D_{jean}^1$$
$$t_5 = D_{apres}(D_{sleep}^{ews}I_SI_v)(D_{vac}I_SI_v)D_{jean}^1$$
$$t_6 = D_{then}^{SS}(D_{vac}I_SI_vD_{jean}^1)(D_{sleep}I_SI_vD_{jean}^2)$$
$$\vdots$$
$$t_{20} = D_{then}^{SS}(D_{vac}I_SI_vD_{jean}^2)(D_{sleep}I_SI_vD_{jean}^2)$$

Fig. 6. The Preimage of F_0 by $\mathcal{L}_{der\text{-}con}$

7 Conclusion

This paper makes shows how G-TAG can be encoded as ACG. It relies on the fact that both G-TAG and TAG encodings as ACGs make the derivation tree a primary notion. Moreover, we can benefit from the polynomial reversibility of the ACG framework. It also offers a generalization of the process to all kinds of adjunctions, including the predicative ones. As a general framework, it also allows for natural more powerful models of some linguistic attachment. This shows for instance in the compositional treatment of the v adjunction model of the *ensuite* (afterwards) adverb. The type-theoretical foundations also offers an interesting link to more evolved theories of discourse relations using, in particular higher-order types [4]. The clarification of g-derivation tree status also suggests to study in a more principled way the relations between G-TAG and other approaches of generation using TAG such as [12, 7]. Note, however, that contrary to an important part of G-TAG that offers a way (based on a semantic and linguistic analysis) to rank the different realizations of a conceptual representation, we do not deal here with such kind of preferences. As syntactic ambiguity treatment is usually not part of the syntactic formalism, we prefer the "realization ambiguity" treatment not to be part of the generation formalism. Finally, a crucial perspective is to integrate a theory of generation of referring expressions.

Acknowledgement. We would like to thank two anonymous referees for their thorough review and useful comments on the paper.

References

[1] Abeillé, A.: Une grammaire électronique du français. Sciences du langage. CNRS Éditions (2002)

[2] Aït-Kaci, H., Nasr, R.: Login: A logic programming language with built-in inheritance. J. Log. Program. 3(3), 185–215 (1986)

[3] Danlos, L.: G-tag: A lexicalized formalism for text generation inspired by tree adjoining grammar. In: Abeillé, A., Rambow, O. (eds.) Tree Adjoining Grammars: Formalisms, Linguistic Analysis, and Processing, pp. 343–370. CSLI Publications (2000)

[4] Danlos, L.: D-STAG: A formalism for discourse analysis based on SDRT and using synchronous TAG. In: de Groote, P., Egg, M., Kallmeyer, L. (eds.) Formal Grammar. LNCS, vol. 5591, pp. 64–84. Springer, Heidelberg (2011)

[5] de Groote, P.: Tree-adjoining grammars as abstract categorial grammars. In: Proceedings of TAG+6, pp. 145–150 (2002)

[6] de Groote, P., Pogodalla, S.: On the expressive power of Abstract Categorial Grammars: Representing context-free formalisms. Journal of Logic, Language and Information 13(4), 421–438 (2004)

[7] Gardent, C., Perez-Beltrachini, L.: RTG based surface realisation for TAG. In: Proceedings of the 23rd International Conference on Computational Linguistics (COLING 2010), Beijing, China, pp. 367–375. Coling 2010 Organizing Committee (August 2010)

[8] Joshi, A.K., Levy, L.S., Takahashi, M.: Tree adjunct grammars. Journal of Computer and System Sciences 10(1), 136–163 (1975)

[9] Joshi, A.K., Schabes, Y.: Tree-adjoining grammars. In: Rozenberg, G., Salomaa, A. (eds.) Handbook of Formal languages, ch. 2, vol. 3. Springer (1997)

[10] Kallmeyer, L.: Using an enriched tag derivation structure as basis for semantics. In: Proceedings of TAG+6 (2002)

[11] Kanazawa, M.: Parsing and generation as datalog queries. In: Proceedings of the 45th Annual Meeting of the Association of Computational Linguistics (ACL), pp. 176–183 (2007), http://www.aclweb.org/anthology/P/P07/P07-1023

[12] Koller, A., Striegnitz, K.: Generation as dependency parsing. In: ACL, pp. 17–24 (2002)

[13] Meunier, F.: Implantation du formalisme de génération G-TAG. Ph.D. thesis, Université Paris 7 — Denis Diderot (1997)

[14] Pogodalla, S.: Advances in Abstract Categorial Grammars: Language Theory and Linguistic Modeling. ESSLLI 2009 Lecture Notes, Part II (2009), http://hal.inria.fr/hal-00749297

[15] Rambow, O., Vijay-Shanker, K., Weir, D.: D-Substitution Grammars. Computational Linguistics (2001)

On Harmonic CCG and Pregroup Grammars

Annie Foret

IRISA, University of Rennes 1
Campus de Beaulieu, 35042 Rennes cedex, France
foret@irisa.fr

Abstract. This paper studies mappings between CCG and pregroup grammars, to allow a transfer of linguistic resources from one formalism to the other. We focus on mappings that preserve the binary structures, we also discuss some possible alternatives in the underlying formalisms, with some experiments.

Keywords: categorial grammars, formal language theory for natural language processing, acquiring linguistic resources.

1 Introduction

We consider in parallel two families of categorial formalisms, with a view to providing some convergence both at the formal level and at the level of ressources (via formally rooted transfers, and some hypotheses that can be experimentically tested).

These families are on one side (1) the family of combinatory categorial grammars (CCG) [19,18] and on the other side (2) a family of Lambek-like grammars, focussing on pregroups (PG) [16] that have been introduced as a simplification of Lambek calculus [15].

The article mainly addresses classes weakly equivalent to context-free grammars, with some insight into connections for larger classes. We focus on methods for preserving parse structure, using pregroup rules as in [2].

The CCG formalism shares some properties with type-logical grammars [1]. See also [10,8] for some kinds of connections between these frameworks.

The paper is organized as follows: Section 2 gives some background on the grammar formalisms. In section 3 we consider mappings from CCG to PG, and show connections in particular at the structure levels. In section 4 we propose and discuss some variants, in order to get stronger correspondences.

2 Background on Categorial Formalisms

2.1 Categorial Combinatory Grammars (CCG)

Several versions of categorial combinatory grammars (CCG) have been considered. See [19,18] or [1] for details. The definition below is close to the presentation in [11].

N. Asher and S. Soloviev (Eds.): LACL 2014, LNCS 8535, pp. 83–95, 2014.
© Springer-Verlag Berlin Heidelberg 2014

Definition 1. *A CCG grammar is a tuple* $G = \langle V_T, V_N, S, I, R \rangle$, *where*

- V_T *is the set of lexical items*
- V_N *is the set of atomic types, with a distinguished element* S
- I *is the lexicon, with types constructed from* V_N *and[1] binary* $|_i \in \{ \,|_< \,, \,|_> \,\}$
- R *is a finite set of combinatory rules*

$$
\begin{array}{ll}
(_>B^n) \ (\mathbf{x} \,|_> \mathbf{y}) \ (...(\mathbf{y}|_{i_1} z_1)...|_{i_n} z_n) & \to (...(\mathbf{x}|_{i_1} z_1)...|_{i_n} z_n) \\
(_<B^n) \ (...(\mathbf{y}|_{i_1} z_1)...|_{i_n} z_n) \ (\mathbf{x} \,|_< \mathbf{y}) & \to (...(\mathbf{x}|_{i_1} z_1)...|_{i_n} z_n)
\end{array}
$$

we consider a version with type-raising[2] rules

$$
\begin{array}{lll}
(_>T) & \mathbf{x} \to y \,|_> (y \,|_< \mathbf{x}) & \textit{(forward)} \\
(_<T) & \mathbf{x} \to y \,|_< (y \,|_> \mathbf{x}) & \textit{(backward)}
\end{array}
$$

In the binary rules: $(\mathbf{x}|_i \mathbf{y})$ is called the *primary* component, the other part is the *secondary* component ; the number n in the secondary component is called the *degree* of the rule, it is 1 when omitted in the name of the rule $(_>B, _<B)$. *Application rules* are the special cases of degree 0:

$$
\begin{array}{lll}
(_>) & (\mathbf{x} \,|_> \mathbf{y}) \ \mathbf{y} \to \mathbf{x} & \textit{(forward)} \\
(_<) & \mathbf{y} \ (\mathbf{x} \,|_< \mathbf{y}) \to \mathbf{x} & \textit{(backward)}
\end{array}
$$

Harmonic rules. For a type of the form $(x|_i y)$, $|_i$ is the *main type-constructor*. When the composition degree is 1, the composition rules are said *harmonic* when both components have the same main type-constructor. In this article, we shall later extend this notion to other composition degrees.

The language of $G = \langle V_T, V_N, S, I, R \rangle$ *is* $L(G) = \{w_1...w_n \,|\, c_1...c_n \to S$ *for some* $c_i \in I(w_i), 1 \leq i \leq n\}$ (by successive applications of the rules).

A tiny example. Let $CCG_1 = \{Mary, John \mapsto N \,; \, likes \mapsto (S \,|_< N) \,|_> N\}$, the sentence "Mary likes Johns" belongs to the language, because (by application) $N \ (S \,|_< N) \,|_> N \ N \to N \ (S \,|_< N) \to S$.

Restrictions and pure CCG. The definition of a grammar may also include restrictions associated with some combinatory rules, expressed as constraints on variable instantiations in the use of a rule. See also [14] for a formal discussion.

When type-raising is a rule in $G = \langle V_T, V_N, S, I, R \rangle$, a common restriction is that only arguments in the lexicon are type-raised, i.e. elements of $\mathcal{C}_{arg}$ where:
$$\mathcal{C}_{arg} = \{\mathbf{y} \text{ such that } (((...(\mathbf{x}|_{i1}\mathbf{y})|_{i_2} y_2)...)|_{i_n} y_n) \in \bigcup\{I(a_i) \,|\, a_i \in V_T\}\}$$
Pure CCG usually refers to a version of CCG without restrictions (the grammar rules are universal).

---

[1] $A \,|_< B$ stands for $B \setminus A$ in Lambek's notation, for $A \setminus B$ in Steedman's notation, whereas $A \,|_> B$ is $A \,/\, B$ in both.

[2] in some common variants, type-raising is assumed to take place in the lexicon, and not taken as grammatical rule.

An alternative is multi-modal CCG [13] defined with different modes for slashes but universal rules. We do not explore connections with this variant here, we only mention [12] as a pregroup alternative.

2.2   Pregroups Grammars (PG)

Definition 2 (A *pregroup*). *is a structure* $(P, \leq, \cdot, l, r, 1)$ *such that* $(P, \leq, \cdot, 1)$ *is a partially ordered monoid* [3] *and* l, r *are two unary operations on* P *that satisfy for all element* $x \in P$:
   $x^l x \leq 1 \leq x x^l$ *and* $x x^r \leq 1 \leq x^r x.$

Notation. Iterated left and right adjoints are also written using integers as exponents, by $(p^{(n)})^l = p^{(n-1)}$, $(p^{(n)})^r = p^{(n+1)}$, $(XY)^l = Y^l X^l$ and $(XY)^r = Y^r X^r$. We write X for $X^{(0)}$.
The product symbol (.) will often be omitted.

Definition 3 (*Free Pregroup Calculus.*). *Let* $(P, \leq)$ *be a partially ordered set of basic types,* $P^{(\mathbb{Z})} = \{p^{(i)} \mid p \in P, i \in \mathbb{Z}\}$ *be the set of simple types and* $T_{(P, \leq)} = (P^{(\mathbb{Z})})^* = \{p_1^{(i_1)} \cdots p_n^{(i_n)} \mid 0 \leq k \leq n, p_k \in P \text{ and } i_k \in \mathbb{Z}\}$ *be the set of types. The empty sequence in* $T_{(P, \leq)}$ *is denoted by* 1. *For* X *and* $Y \in T_{(P, \leq)}$, $X \leq Y$ *iff this relation is derivable in the following system where* $p, q \in P$, $n, k \in \mathbb{Z}$ *and* $X, Y, Z \in T_{(P, \leq)}$:

Axiom rule	Cut rule
$X \leq X$ (Id)	$\dfrac{X \leq Y \qquad Y \leq Z}{X \leq Z}$ (Cut)
Adjoints steps	
$\dfrac{XY \leq Z}{X p^{(n)} p^{(n+1)} Y \leq Z}$ (A_L)	$\dfrac{X \leq YZ}{X \leq Y p^{(n+1)} p^{(n)} Z}$ (A_R)
Induced steps	
$\dfrac{X p^{(k)} Y \leq Z}{X q^{(k)} Y \leq Z}$ (IND_L)	$\dfrac{X \leq Y q^{(k)} Z}{X \leq Y p^{(k)} Z}$ (IND_R)
$q \leq p$ if k is even, and $p \leq q$ if k is odd	

This construction, proposed by [5], defines a pregroup that extends $\leq$ on basic types P to $T_{(P, \leq)}$.

The cut rule in the Free Pregroup calculus can be eliminated: every derivable inequality has a cut-free derivation.

Let FP denote the free pregroup with equality as preorder on primitive types.

We only illustrate the notion of pregroup grammar and languages, on a short example.

---

[3] We briefly recall that a *monoid* is a structure $< M, \cdot, 1 >$, such that $\cdot$ is associative and has a neutral element 1 ($\forall x \in M : 1 \cdot x = x \cdot 1 = x$). A partially ordered monoid is a monoid $< M, \cdot, 1 >$ with a partial order $\leq$ that satisfies $\forall a, b, c : a \leq b \Rightarrow c \cdot a \leq c \cdot b$ and $a \cdot c \leq b \cdot c$.

A tiny example. Let $PG_1 = \{Mary, John \mapsto N \; ; \; likes \mapsto N^{(1)}.S.N^{(-1)}\}$. The sentence "Mary likes Johns" belongs to the pregroup language of PG_1, because $N.N^{(1)}.S.N^{(-1)}.N \leq S$

Extensions. The pregroup formalism has been extended in several ways, in particular for iteration types [4], used in section 4.3. See also [12] and [17,9] for alternatives beyond context-freeness.

3   Pregroups as Models

3.1   At the Calculus Level

One may define the following interpretation, that translates valid sequents in Lambek calculus (with products) into valid sequents in the free pregroup [5].

Definition 4 (Pregroup interpretation Φ). *Φ is a morphism from types constructed with* $|_>$, $|_<$ *to pregroup types (written with integer exponents), such that:*

$\Phi(\mathbf{x} |_> \mathbf{y}) = \Phi(\mathbf{x}).\Phi(\mathbf{y})^{(-1)}$

$\Phi(\mathbf{x} |_< \mathbf{y}) = \Phi(\mathbf{y})^{(1)}.\Phi(\mathbf{x})$

$\Phi(p) = p$ *(in the primitive case)*

this Φ interpretation is extended to sequences by:

$\Phi(\mathbf{x_1}, \ldots \mathbf{x_n}) = \Phi(\mathbf{x_1}). \; \ldots \; .\Phi(\mathbf{x_n})$

The next property can easily be shown (by cases and induction on a derivation length), it also follows from the fact that application, harmonic composition of degree 1 and type-raising are derivable in the associative Lambek Calculus.

Notation. R_{h1} will denote the set of rules containing the application rules and harmonic composition rules of degree 1. Tr will denote type-raising rules.

Proposition 1 (R_{h1} models). *Let R be a subset of $R_{h1} \cup Tr$, then:*

if $\Gamma \to C$ by rules in R then $\Phi(\Gamma) \leq \Phi(C)$

Remarks.
(i) In particular, backward type-raising translates as:

$\Phi(x |_< (x |_> y)) = \Phi(y).\Phi(x)^{(1)}.\Phi(x)$

where $\Phi(x) \leq \Phi(x |_< (x |_> y))$ is obtained from the axiom $\Phi(y) \leq \Phi(y)$ and the adjoint step corresponding to $1 \leq \Phi(x)^{(1)}.\Phi(x)$.
(ii) Observe that the translation is not an equivalence, as illustrated by *argument lowering*, that holds in Lambek calculus and pregroups but not in CCG :

$\Phi(z |_> (x |_< (x |_> y))) \; \leq \; \Phi(z |_> y)$

that is $zx^{(-1)}x^{(-2)}y^{(-1)} \; \leq \; zy^{(-1)}$ for atoms.
(iii) The proposition is stated for pure CCG but also applies to rule restrictions.

3.2   At the Parse Level, Using [C], [I].

CCG parse structures. Let R be a set of CCG rules, the set of *full R-parse structures*, with types as leaves, is denoted by $\mathcal{T}_R$ and may consist in binary nodes as well as unary nodes.

CCG binary structures. For a CCG parse structure T, $Bin(T)$ will denote the structure obtained by erasing all unary parts in T.

Pregroup parse structures. We consider two rules for pregroups: partial composition [C] and internal reduction [I] that give a parsing method [2] used in a pregroup parser [4], called *PPQ*. One interest of this method is to generate binary trees on words.

The set of pregroup parses using [C] and [I], with pregroup types as leaves, is denoted by $\mathcal{T}'_{R'}$, for $R' \subseteq \{[C], [I]\}$ and may consist in binary nodes (using [C] as well as unary nodes using [I]).

Notation. The width of a type X, $width(X)$, is n_k for $X = p_1^{(n_1)}...p_k^{(n_k)}$.
Below Γ, Δ range over sequences of pregroup types, $X, Y, ...$ range over pregroup types.

Definition 5 (partial composition). *The* partial composition *rule [C] applies to pairs of words, whose types are separated with* ","; *it is defined by :*
$$\Gamma , Xp_1^{(n_1)}...p_k^{(n_k)} , q_k^{(n_k+1)}...q_1^{(n_1+1)}Y , \Delta \to \Gamma , XY , \Delta$$
such that for $1 \leq i \leq k$: ($p_i \leq q_i$ and n_i is even) or ($q_i \leq p_i$ and n_i is odd)

PPQ parser. The *PPQ* pregroup parser uses a refinement of *partial composition,* referred to as *majority composition,* with the additional requirement that:
$$width(XY) \leq max(width(XX'), width(Y'Y))$$
The parser has also been adapted for dealing with *iteration types* [4].

Definition 6 (internal). *The* internal *rule [I] applies to a type, (or a word with a type) that is reducible as follows: $\Gamma , Xp^{(n)}q^{(n+1)}Y , \Delta \to \Gamma , XY , \Delta$ such that : ($p \leq q$ and n is even) or ($q \leq p$ and n is odd)*

Parsing with [C],[I]. As shown in [2], when the right hand-side s of a pregroup sequent $X \leq s$ is primitive, parsing can be based on these two rules [C],[I]:
$X \leq s$ iff $\exists q$ primitive such that $q \leq s$ and $X \to^* q$ using [C], [I]
Note that a derivation for a non-primitive right-hand-side, may involve an *expansion rule* (EXP):
$$\Gamma, XY, \Delta \to \Gamma, Xp^{(n+1)}q^{(n)}Y, \Delta, \text{ for } (p \leq q \text{ and } n \text{ even}) \text{ or } (q \leq p \text{ and } n \text{ odd})$$

Tree mapping. We now provide a mapping involving essentially [C], [I], at the parse level. We consider two cases, depending on the use of type-raising. We also focus on binary structures, and use the same notation $Bin(T')$ on CCG and PG, for the structure obtained by erasing all unary parts in T'.

Definition 7 (Tree interpretation Φ_t). *The pregroup interpretation Φ, induces a tree homomorphism written Φ_t such that each node $\mathbf{x}$ is mapped to $\Phi_t(\mathbf{x})$.*

Proposition 2 (Binary structure images).
   (1) Let R be a subset of R_{h1}, the tree homomorphism Φ_t induced by Φ maps a CCG parse $T \in \mathcal{T}_R$ to an isomorphic pregroup parse $T' \in \mathcal{T}'_{[C]}$.

(2) Let R be a subset of $R_{h1} \cup Tr$, the tree homomorphism Φ_t induced by Φ maps a CCG parse T in $\mathcal{T}_R$ to a pregroup parse, such that if T has no two successive applications of Tr, then $\Phi_t(T)$ can be transformed to a parse T' in $\mathcal{T}'_{[C],[I]}$, with isomorphic binary structures: $Bin(T)$ is isomorphic to $Bin(T')$.

In other words, each such CCG parse is associated with a similar pregroup parse tree using partial composition $[C]$.

Proof (1). The justification of this property is pictured as follows (in the forward case) :

$$\frac{(\mathbf{x} \mid_> \mathbf{y}) \qquad \mathbf{y}}{\mathbf{x}}(>) \qquad \mapsto \qquad \frac{xy^{(-1)} \qquad y}{x}[C]$$

$$\frac{(\mathbf{x} \mid_> \mathbf{y}) \qquad (\mathbf{y} \mid_> \mathbf{z_1})}{\mathbf{x} \mid_> \mathbf{z_1}}(_>B^1) \quad \mapsto \quad \frac{xy^{(-1)} \qquad yz_1^{(-1)}}{xz_1^{(-1)}}[C]$$

Where $x = \phi(\mathbf{x})$, etc. and if $\mathbf{y}$ is a complex type, $y^{(-1)}$ is rewritten accordingly as a sequence of atoms with their exponent.

Type-raising. We now explain how Proposition2 holds, in the case of CCG with type-raising. For a type-raising (unary) step, the parallel could be as follows:

$$\frac{\mathbf{y}}{(\mathbf{x} \mid_> (\mathbf{x} \mid_< \mathbf{y}))}(_>T) \qquad \mapsto \qquad \frac{\mathbf{y}}{xx^{(-1)}y}$$

Note that the rule on the right is an expansion, not produced by $\{[C], [I]\}$. However, in a CCG parse, a type-raised type is later combined by composition. We consider theses cases below and how to map them using only $\{[C], [I]\}$.

Proof (2). We get two cases (we consider one direction, the other one is similar): (below, each [t] on the right indicates an image by Φ, but it is dropped in the final pregroup structure in $\mathcal{T}'_{[C],[I]}$).
   (i) if the type-raised category is a functor, a unary simplification is possible

$$\frac{\dfrac{\mathbf{y}}{(\mathbf{x} \mid_> (\mathbf{x} \mid_< \mathbf{y}))}(_>T) \qquad (\mathbf{x} \mid_< \mathbf{y})}{x}(>) \qquad \mapsto \qquad \frac{\dfrac{y}{\cancel{xx^{(-1)}y}} \qquad y^{(1)}x}{x}(C)$$

$$\frac{\dfrac{\mathbf{y}}{(\mathbf{x} \mid_> (\mathbf{x} \mid_< \mathbf{y}))}(_>T) \qquad (\mathbf{x} \mid_< \mathbf{y}) \mid_> \mathbf{z}}{\mathbf{x} \mid_> \mathbf{z}}(_>B^1) \quad \mapsto \quad \frac{\dfrac{y}{\cancel{xx^{(-1)}y}} \qquad y^{(1)}xz^{(-1)}}{xz^{(-1)}}(C)$$

if $\mathbf{y}$ was infered by Tr from $\mathbf{y_1}$, then $y^{(1)}xz^{(-1)}$ yields $y_1^{(1)}xz^{(-1)}$ by [I]

(ii) if the type-raised category is an argument, an internal rule [I] is possible:

$$\frac{(\mathbf{u}\mid_> \mathbf{v}) \quad \dfrac{\mathbf{y}}{\mathbf{v} = (\mathbf{x}\mid_> (\mathbf{x}\mid_< \mathbf{y}))}\ (_>T)}{\mathbf{u}}\ (>) \quad\mapsto\quad \frac{uv^{(-1)}}{uy^{(-1)}}\ (I) \quad \frac{y \quad \cancel{[xx^{(-1)}y]}}{u}\ (C)$$

$$\text{(similarly for the other direction of type-raise)}$$

$$\frac{(\mathbf{u}\mid_> \mathbf{x}) \quad \dfrac{\mathbf{y}}{(\mathbf{x}\mid_> (\mathbf{x}\mid_< \mathbf{y}))}\ (_>T)}{\mathbf{u}\mid_> (\mathbf{x}\mid_< \mathbf{y})}\ (_>B^1) \quad\mapsto\quad \frac{ux^{(-1)} \quad \dfrac{y \quad \cancel{[xx^{(-1)}y]}}{}}{ux^{(-1)}y}\ (C)$$

however, in the $(_>B^1)$ *case above, if* y *was again infered by* Tr *from* y_1, *then* $ux^{(-1)}y$ *is infered from* $ux^{(-1)}$ *and* y_1, *using an expansion rule.*

As a result, considering [C],[I] only : if no two successive type-raising occur in a secondary branch, we get an isomorphic PG image of the binary CCG structure (obtained by erasing the unary branches in a parse), where each node labelled with a CCG type x_i , is associated with a node labelled by its PG image $\Phi(x_i)$.

Example. The sentence in Figures 1 and 2 is taken from the "universal declaration of human rights". These figures illustrate the *tree homomorphism* Φ_t.

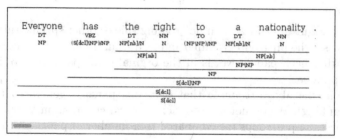

Fig. 1. C&C parse

Pregroup nets and Φ. We give an example, illustrating a quotient at the level of pregroup structures:

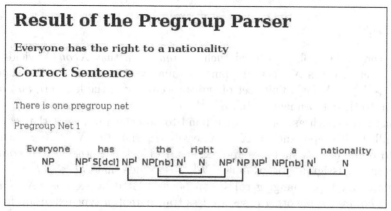

Fig. 2. Pregroup parse, with a grammar induced from C&C

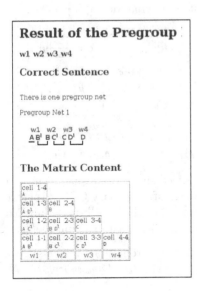

This PG is a mapping of a CCG lexicon:

$$w1 := A \mid_> B$$
$$w2 := B \mid_> C$$
$$w3 := C \mid_> D$$
$$w4 := D$$

There is one pregroup net for $w1w2w3w4$, when D is the selected type, which represents several CCG parse trees for the same sentence (depending on the order of compositions).

Remarks.

(i) As seen in Figures 1 and 2 when no crossing rule or other specific rule is used in a C&C parse, the pregroup grammar induced from C&C , generates a similar parse, such that each pair of words in the orginal C&C parse is also linked in the pregroup parse.

(ii) We see in the above example that only one parse is generated (without statistical ranking). We do not address here general criterion on the number of potential parses in pregroups (as compared to a number of parses in the source grammar).

3.3   At the Practical Level

In practice a CCG has some specific rules [6]. We consider some of them below.

Specific rules.

- the *conj* rule applies to word such as *and*, such that $XconjX$ yields X, for a set of types X. In a mapping, we may view *conj* as a set of types : $(X \mid_< X) \mid_> X$ for a finite set of types (occurring in the lexicon), and map them to their PG image $X^{(1)}XX^{(-1)}$;
- ponctuation such as comma correspond to absorbing schemas, that can be handled with types such as $X \mid_< X$, easily translated as $X^{(-1)}X$. A variant is to refine it with subtypes and axioms, to block patterns such as comma repetition, assigning for example $NP^{(-1)}\overline{NP}$ such that $NP \leq \overline{NP}$;
- some unary type-changing rules, can be translated by axioms : $N \leq NP$ etc. ; however some other cases are less transparent, a type-extension in the lexicon may be preferable for those cases.

Refining the interpretation. We may refine Φ as an interpretation Φ_c, where c expresses some context information, such that an atomic type p is translated depending on c_i, and axioms may be chosen differently for different p_{c_i} (c_i could also encode position information). A refinement of atomic types complies with the view in [7] of pregroups as a logical functor and composed calculi. The context part and axiom part could also integrate statistical information in the resulting pregroup grammar.

4   Investigating Variants of CCG

This section addresses frameworks variants expected to be compatible with previous mappings (at the level of parses as well).

4.1   Generalized Harmonic Composition

When pregroups are viewed as models, in fact more CCG rules can be considered and constitute what we call the (generalized) harmonic composition rules.

Definition 8. *We extend the definition of harmonic rule to any degree as follows:*
$$(_>B^n) \ (\mathbf{x} \mid_> \mathbf{y}) \ (...(\mathbf{y}\mid_{i_1} z_1)...\mid_{i_n} z_n) \to (...(\mathbf{x}\mid_{i_1} z_1)...\mid_{i_n} z_n)$$
is said harmonic, iff $\mid_> \mid_{i_1}...\mid_{i_n}$ are all the same operator. Similarly :
$$(_<B^n) \ (...(\mathbf{y}\mid_{i_1} z_1)...\mid_{i_n} z_n) \ (\mathbf{x} \mid_< \mathbf{y}) \to (...(\mathbf{x}\mid_{i_1} z_1)...\mid_{i_n} z_n)$$
is said harmonic, iff $\mid_< \mid_{i_1}...\mid_{i_n}$ are all the same operator.

Notation. R_h will denote the set of rules containing the harmonic composition rules of any degree $n \geq 0$. To distinguish between the basic notion and the extended one, we may use the term "generalized harmonic composition" for harmonic composition at a degree greater than 1.

One interest of this generalization is that it induces a tree homomorphism property between CCG and PG binary parse trees:

Proposition 3 (R_h models and structures)
(0) Let R be a subset of $R_h \cup Tr$, then if $\Gamma \to C$ by rules in R then $\Phi(\Gamma) \leq \Phi(C)$
(1) Let R be a subset of R_h, the tree homomorphism Φ_t induced by Φ maps a CCG parse $T \in \mathcal{T}_R$ to an isomorphic pregroup parse in $T' \in \mathcal{T}'_{[C]}$.

Proof. The proof of (0) is straightforward. The proof of (1) is sketched as follows:

$$
\frac{(\mathbf{x} \mid_> \mathbf{y}) \quad (...(\mathbf{y} \mid_> \mathbf{z_1})... \mid_> \mathbf{z_n})}{(...(\mathbf{x} \mid_> \mathbf{z_1})... \mid_> \mathbf{z_n})} \ (_>B^n) \quad \mapsto \quad \frac{xy^{(-1)} \quad yz_1^{(-1)}...z_n^{(-1)}}{xz_1^{(-1)}...z_n^{(-1)}} \ [C]
$$

Where if $\mathbf{y}$ is a complex type, $y^{(-1)}$ is rewritten accordingly as a sequence of atoms with their exponent.

Remark. For $R_h \cup Tr$, the mapping may involve an expansion rule, we do not detail this variant here.

Open question. Instead of defining classes of CCG by a uniform bound on the composition degree, we propose to split the set of rules in two sets with different degree constraints: the first set is R_h (that is an unbound degree for harmonic rules), with application (and possibly type-raising), the second set consists in the remaining rules, with a given bound degree N_B. This raises both the question of the complexity and of the generative capacity of such classes CC_{N_B}.

4.2   A Partial Preorder in CCG

We propose to include a partial preorder in CCG, in a way compatible with previous mappings.

Definition 9. *Given a preorder $\leq_P$ on atoms, we consider a natural extension of $\leq_P$ to CCG types taking into account contravariance (or polarity) as follows:*
$$\mathbf{x_1} \mid_i \mathbf{y_1} \leq_p \mathbf{x_2} \mid_i \mathbf{y_2} \text{ iff } \mathbf{x_1} \leq_p \mathbf{x_2} \text{ and } \mathbf{y_2} \leq_p \mathbf{y_1}$$

We get the following fact:

Proposition 4 (Preorder and Φ). *Let $\mathbf{y}, \mathbf{y'}$ be CCG types: if $\mathbf{y} \leq_P \mathbf{y'}$ then $\Phi(\mathbf{y}) \leq \Phi(\mathbf{y'})$ in the free pregroup calculus over $(P, \leq_P)$*

Proof. This can be easily shown by structural induction:

- this is clear for atoms ;
- if $\mathbf{x_1} \mid_> \mathbf{y_1} \leq_p \mathbf{x_2} \mid_> \mathbf{y_2}$ then (by def.) $\mathbf{x_1} \leq_p \mathbf{x_2}$ and $\mathbf{y_2} \leq_p \mathbf{y_1}$, therefore (by rec.) $\Phi(\mathbf{x_1}) \leq \Phi(\mathbf{x_2})$ and $\Phi(\mathbf{y_2}) \leq \Phi(\mathbf{y_1})$, then $\Phi(\mathbf{y_1})^{(-1)} \leq \Phi(\mathbf{y_2})^{(-1)}$ (in pregroups: $x \leq y$ entails $y^{(-1)} \leq y^{(-1)}.x.x^{(-1)} \leq y^{(-1)}.y.x^{(-1)} \leq x^{(-1)}$) and $\Phi(\mathbf{x_1} \mid_> \mathbf{y_1}) \leq_p \Phi(\mathbf{x_2} \mid_> \mathbf{y_2})$. The other direction is similar.

On the CCG side, an expected outcome of this proposal is to express in a more compact and elegant way some unary type-changing rules, as well as a form of control for the coverage of the initial assignment of types to words. Another expected outcome is to facilitate transfer between PG and CCG, in both ways.

Rule adaptation. An option is to add unary rules. We choose below to adapt the composition rules as follows:

$(_>B'^n)$ if $\mathbf{y'} \leq_p \mathbf{y}$ $(\mathbf{x} \mid_> \mathbf{y})$ $(...(\mathbf{y'} \mid_{i_1} z_1)... \mid_{i_n} z_n)$	$\rightarrow (...(\mathbf{x} \mid_{i_1} z_1)... \mid_{i_n} z_n)$
$(_<B'^n)$ if $\mathbf{y'} \leq_p \mathbf{y}$ $(...(\mathbf{y'} \mid_{i_1} z_1)... \mid_{i_n} z_n)$ $(\mathbf{x} \mid_< \mathbf{y})$	$\rightarrow (...(\mathbf{x} \mid_{i_1} z_1)... \mid_{i_n} z_n)$

Notation. For a given preorder $\leq_P$, $R_{h'1, \leq_P}$ will denote "R_{h_1} adapted with $\leq_P$", the set containing $(_>B'^0)$, $(_<B'^0)$ and the harmonic rules $(_>B'^1)$ and $(_<B'^1)$ (both components have the same main type-constructor), using only $\leq_P$.

Proposition 5 (R_{h_1} adapted with $\leq_P$: models and structures).
(0) Let R be a subset of $R_{h'_1, \leq_P} \cup Tr$ then
    if $\Gamma \to C$ by rules in R then: $\Phi(\Gamma) \leq \Phi(C)$ using $\leq_P$ on atoms
(1) Let R be a subset of $R_{h'_1, \leq_P}$, the tree homomorphism Φ_t induced by Φ maps a CCG parse $T \in \mathcal{T}_R$ to an isomorphic pregroup parse in $T' \in \mathcal{T}'_{[C]}$.

Proof. This proposition is similar to the case of R_{h1}, the key point is that if $\mathbf{y} \leq_P \mathbf{y}'$ then $\Phi(\mathbf{y}) \leq \Phi(\mathbf{y}')$ in the free pregroup calculus over $(P, \leq_P)$.

Experiments. In this experiment, we use a lexicon from the C&C parser for English, written $Lex_{C\&C}$ for short, that has 74671 assignments (of a type to a word). The atomic categories are S, NP, N and PP. An atomic category X may be specified by a feature f, encoded as $X[f]$. For example $S[dcl]$ stands for declarative sentences[4]. We have tested a possible impact of a preorder on the lexicon.

Preorder. We take $\leq_P$ induced from the following set of axioms:
    $\{N \leq NP\} \cup \{X[f] \leq X$ such that X is atomic$\}$
    We have conducted experiments based on $Lex_{C\&C}$ that we have imported in postgresql. We have implemented several modules/mappings using postgresql with its xml capabilities (also pl/sql and xpath).
    We get for 1287 distinct assigned types 44035 distinct words, and 74671 assignments in the lexicon:
    - 349 pairs $(c1, c2)$ such that $c_1 \leq_P c_2$, and the two types are distinct
    - 442 occurrences of the form $(w, c1, c2)$ where $c_1 \leq_P c_2$ and $c_1 \neq c_2$ and both types are assigned to w ;
    for example, we get:

```
would   | (S[dcl]\NP)/(S[b]\NP)   | 2089 | (S[dcl]\NP[expl])/(S[b]\NP)  |  25
would   | (S[dcl]\NP)/(S[b]\NP)   | 2089 | (S[dcl]\NP[thr])/(S[b]\NP)   |   9
would   | (S[q]/(S[b]\NP))/NP     |   14 | (S[q]/(S[b]\NP))/NP[expl]    |   1
```

From this test we could get a reduced lexicon and use $\leq_P$, in CCG and PG.

4.3   Repeated Argument Types

Repeating type constructs have been mainly studied for categorial dependency grammars with a dependency typing mode. They have also been introduced for pregroups, theoretically and practically [3,4]. We refer to these papers for details. Informally, iteration, that also corresponds to an exponential in linear logic, is introduced there for atomic types allowing their repetition as successive arguments.
    We checked this feature on linguistic data available for CCG: whether successive arguments in a given direction are the same, at the main level (for types of order 1). The atomic types that are repeated are : NP, N, PP, S[dcl]. Only few

---

[4] http://svn.ask.it.usyd.edu.au/trac/candc/wiki/Grammar

cases of repeating patterns are not atomic (of the form $S[.] \setminus NP$). This observation complies with the hypotheses underlying the pregroup calculus extended with iterated types.

We found that 77 assigned atomic types have such a repeating pattern (and 8 non atomic), among which only one has an argument repeated more than two times.

```
(N/N)/N                                  | /N

((S[dcl]\S[dcl])\S[dcl])/NP              | \S[dcl]
(((S\NP)\(S\NP))/S[dcl])/S[dcl]          | /S[dcl]

((((NP\NP)/NP)/NP)/NP)/NP                | /NP,/NP,/NP
```

From this test, we propose (1) to take apart NP (and N) that may correspond to arguments, (2) for other X such as PP or possibly $S[dcl]$, repetitions of successive arguments X, could be generalized during translation to X^+ (as PP^+ or $S[dcl]^+$). If X^* is an allowed construct, but not X^+, then X^+ can be rewritten as $X.X^*$.

CCG version. On the CCG side, such an iteration construct could also be integrated, rewriting for example (C&C slashes notation):
$$((S[dcl] \setminus NP)/PP)/PP \mapsto (S[dcl] \setminus NP)/PP^*$$
for example, in an actual CCG, "wrote" has several types with this pattern:

```
wrote   | ((S[dcl]\NP)/PP)/PP
wrote   | (S[dcl]\NP)/PP
wrote   | S[dcl]\NP                ...
```

However, we do not detail such a CCG variant here.

5   Conclusion and Further Questions

We have considered connections between CCG and PG, and shown how similarity also holds at the level of binary parse structures, in the context-free case. This can serve as a basis for a reliable induction of grammars and linguistic resources. It would be interesting to further investigate this relation beyond context-freeness. This paper also raises proposals for variants of CCG, preserving the similarity, with questions on both the formal and the practical side.

References

1. Baldridge, J., Hoyt, F.: Categorial grammar. To appear in Kiss, T., Alexiadou, A. (eds.) Handbook of Syntax. de Gruyter, Berlin (2014)
2. Béchet, D.: Parsing pregroup grammars and Lambek calculus using partial composition. Studia Logica 87(2-3), 199–224 (2007)
3. Béchet, D., Dikovsky, A.J., Foret, A., Garel, E.: Optional and iterated types for pregroup grammars. In: Martín-Vide, C., Otto, F., Fernau, H. (eds.) LATA 2008. LNCS, vol. 5196, pp. 88–100. Springer, Heidelberg (2008)

4. Béchet, D., Foret, A.: A pregroup toolbox for parsing and building grammars of natural languages. Linguistic Analysis Journal 36 (2010)
5. Buszkowski, W.: Lambek grammars based on pregroups. In: de Groote, P., Morrill, G., Retoré, C. (eds.) LACL 2001. LNCS (LNAI), vol. 2099, pp. 95–109. Springer, Heidelberg (2001)
6. Clark, S., Curran, J.R.: Wide-coverage efficient statistical parsing with ccg and log-linear models. Computational Linguistics 33(4), 493–552 (2007)
7. Foret, A.: A modular and parameterized presentation of pregroup calculus. Inf. Comput. 208(5), 510–520 (2010)
8. Fowler, T.: Parsing CCGbank with the Lambek calculus. In: Proc. Parsing with Categorial Grammars, ESSLLI Workshop, in Bordeaux, France (2009)
9. Francez, N., Kaminski, M.: Commutation-augmented pregroup grammars and mildly context-sensitive languages. Studia Logica 87(2-3), 295–321 (2007)
10. Jäger, G.: Lambek grammars as combinatory categorial grammars. Logic Journal of the IGPL 9(6), 781–792 (2001)
11. Joshi, A., Vijay-Shanker, K., Weir, D.: The convergence of mildly context-sensitive grammar formalisms. In: Wasow, T., Sells, P. (eds.) The Processing of Linguistic Structure, pp. 31–81. MIT Press (1991)
12. Kislak-Malinowska, A.: On the logic of beta -pregroups. Studia Logica 87(2-3), 323–342 (2007)
13. Kruijff, G.J.M., Baldridge, J.: Multi-modal combinatory categorial grammar. In: EACL, pp. 211–218. The Association for Computer Linguistics (2003)
14. Kuhlmann, M., Koller, A., Satta, G.: The importance of rule restrictions in ccg. In: Hajic, J., Carberry, S., Clark, S. (eds.) ACL, pp. 534–543. The Association for Computer Linguistics (2010)
15. Lambek, J.: The mathematics of sentence structure. American Mathematical Monthly 65 (1958)
16. Lambek, J.: Type grammar revisited. In: Lecomte, A., Perrier, G., Lamarche, F. (eds.) LACL 1997. LNCS (LNAI), vol. 1582, pp. 1–27. Springer, Heidelberg (1999)
17. Stabler, E.: Tupled pregroup grammars. Polimetrica Computational Algebraic Approaches to Morphology and Syntax (2-3), 23–52 (2004)
18. Steedman, M.: The Syntactic Process. MIT Press, Cambridge (2000)
19. Steedman, M.: Taking Scope - The Natural Semantics of Quantifiers. MIT Press (2012)

The Granularity of Meaning in Proof-Theoretic Semantics

Nissim Francez

Computer Science Dept., Technion-IIT, Haifa, Israel
francez@cs.technion.ac.il

Abstract. The paper compares two conceptions of meaning both for logic and for natural language:

- Model-theoretic semantics (MTS), basing meaning on reference and truth conditions (in arbitrary models).
- Proof-theoretic semantics (PTS), basing meaning on canonical derivations in meaning-conferring natural-deduction proof-systems.

It is shown that PTS induces a much finer granularity on meanings, in particular distinguishing the meanings of logically equivalent sentences. A certain coarsening by means of equating meanings based on identical grounds for assertion is proposed, useful in certain contexts.

Keywords: proof-theoretic semantics, granularity of meaning, grounds for assertion.

1 Introduction

When applying logic for the definition of a theory of meaning for a formal or natural language, there are two main approaches.

model-theoretic: This is the dominant approach, basing meaning on *truth* (in arbitrary models) as its central concept.

proof-theoretic: This is an alternative approach, basing meaning on *proof* (or, more generally, on derivation via proof-rules) as its central concept.

The main claim in this paper is that Proof-Theoretic Semantics (PTS – explained below) provides a more adequate granularity of meanings than model-theoretic semantics (MTS) does. It does so by imposing a finer granularity on meanings, not identifying logically equivalent propositions. In particular, not all logically true propositions have identical meaning. While this point was briefly mentioned by me previously, in this paper I am highlighting it by expanding more some of the details.

No attempt is made here to motivate and justify PTS as a theory of meaning. There is a vast literature on that. See [7] and [5] for brief summaries of the motivation.

N. Asher and S. Soloviev (Eds.): LACL 2014, LNCS 8535, pp. 96–106, 2014.

2 The PTS Programme in a Nutshell

In a nutshell, the PTS programme can be described as follows.

- *For sentences, replace the received approach of taking their meanings as* **truth-Conditions** *(in arbitrary models) by an approach taking meanings to consist of* **canonical derivability conditions** *(from suitable assumptions).* Canonicity is explained below. For logic, the usual natural-deduction (ND) proof systems are used. For natural language, a "dedicated" natural-deduction proof-system needs to be developed – on which the derivability conditions are based. In a sense, the proof system should reflect the "use" of the sentences in the considered fragments, and should allow recovering pre-theoretic properties of the meanings of these sentences such as entailment, assertability conditions and consequence drawing.
- For *subsentential phrases*, down to lexical units (logical constants in logic, words in natural language), replace taking their denotations (extensions in arbitrary models) as meanings, by taking their **contributions** to the meanings (in our explication, derivability conditions) of sentences in which they occur. This adheres to Frege's *context principle* [9], made more specific by the incorporation into a Type-Logical Grammar (see Moortgat [13]).

Dummett introduces ([1], p. 48) an important distinction between *content* and *ingredient sense*. The content of an (affirmative) sentence S is the meaning of S "in isolation", on its own. The ingredient sense of S is what S contributes to the meaning of any S' in which S occurs as a sub-expression, a component. A grasp of the ingredient sense always includes a grasp of the meaning, but not necessarily vice versa. This distinction is propagated to sub-sentential phrases too.

I will be concerned here with the contents of sentences only. For the definition of meanings for sub-sentential phrases and for ingredient senses of sentences and of sub-sentential phrases, the reader is referred to [6] (for logic) and [8] (for natural language).

3 Canonical Derivations

Consider an object language L (either formal or natural), and suppose a meaning-conferring ND-system[1] $\mathcal{N}$ for L is given, containing introduction rules (I-rules) and elimination rules (E-rules) for the various constructs in the language. For a fragment of English, such systems were presented in [7] and [5]. For logic, such systems are standard. *Derivations* (in tree-like form), ranged over by $\mathcal{D}$, are defined recursively in a standard way. There is a class of derivations, the canonical ones, that play a central role in the definition of the proof-theoretic meaning (see [3] for a discussion).

---

[1] I assume familiarity of the reader with the basics of ND-systems.

Definition 1 (canonical derivation from open assumptions). *A $\mathcal{N}$-derivation $\mathcal{D}$ for deriving a conclusion ψ from (open) assumptions Γ (called a context) is canonical iff it satisfies one of the following two conditions.*

- *The last rule applied in $\mathcal{D}$ is an I-rule (for the main operator of ψ).*
- *The last rule applied in $\mathcal{D}$ is an assumption-discharging E-rule, the major premise of which is some φ in Γ, and its encompassed sub-derivations $\mathcal{D}_1, \cdots, \mathcal{D}_n$ are all canonical derivations of ψ.*

Denote by $\vdash^c_{\mathcal{N}}$ canonical derivability in $\mathcal{N}$ and by $[\![\varphi]\!]^c_{\Gamma}$ the collection of all (if any) canonical derivations of φ from Γ.

The important observation regarding the recursion in the definition is that it always terminates via the first clause, namely by an application of an I-rule. In particular, the attribute of canonical proofs that there are none for an *atomic* sentence is preserved by the definition of canonical derivations from open assumptions too. The above mentioned observation justifies the definition of canonicity for derivations from open assumptions Γ by preserving the *directness* of the inference, but the conclusion ψ, inferred via an I-rule, needs to be *propagated* through application of E-rules to open assumptions in Γ. This also justifies viewing Γ as grounds for assertion of ψ (Definition 4 below).

To see the need for the second clause, consider the meaning of disjunction in minimal propositional logic. The standard I/E-rules for disjunction in this logic are the following.

$$\frac{\varphi}{\varphi \vee \psi}\ (\vee I_1) \qquad \frac{\psi}{\varphi \vee \psi}\ (\vee I_2) \qquad \frac{\varphi \vee \psi \quad \overset{[\varphi]_i}{\overset{\vdots}{\chi}} \quad \overset{[\psi]_j}{\overset{\vdots}{\chi}}}{\chi}\ (\vee E^{i,j}) \tag{1}$$

Here $[\varphi]_i, [\psi]_j$ are assumptions discharged by applying the $(\vee E)$ rule.

Pre-theoretically, one might wish to say that the *commutativity* and *associativity* of disjunction, as expressed by the derivability claims $(\varphi \vee \psi) \vdash (\psi \vee \varphi)$ and $(\varphi \vee (\psi \vee \chi)) \vdash ((\varphi \vee \psi) \vee \chi)$, are parts of the meaning of disjunction, and therefore there should be canonical derivations establishing them. However, the standard derivations of the sequents expressing commutativity and associativity are, respectively,

$$\frac{(\varphi \vee \psi) \quad \dfrac{[\varphi]_1}{(\psi \vee \varphi)}\ (\vee_2 I) \quad \dfrac{[\psi]_2}{(\psi \vee \varphi)}\ (\vee_1 I)}{(\psi \vee \varphi)}\ (\vee E^{1,2}) \tag{2}$$

and

$$\frac{(\varphi \vee (\psi \vee \chi)) \quad \dfrac{\dfrac{[\varphi]_1}{(\varphi \vee \psi)}\ (\vee I_1)}{((\varphi \vee \psi) \vee \chi)}\ (\vee I_1) \quad \dfrac{[(\psi \vee \chi)]_2 \quad \dfrac{\dfrac{[\psi]_3}{(\varphi \vee \psi)}\ (\vee I_2)}{((\varphi \vee \psi) \vee \chi)}\ (\vee I_1) \quad \dfrac{[\chi]_4}{((\varphi \vee \psi) \vee \chi)}\ (\vee I_2)}{((\varphi \vee \psi) \vee \chi)}\ (\vee E^{3,4})}{((\varphi \vee \psi) \vee \chi)}\ (\vee E^{1,2}) \tag{3}$$

By the conception of canonicity of derivations from open assumptions as based on 'the last rule applied', these derivations are *not* canonical, as the last rule applied in each one of them is $(\vee E)$. Furthermore, *there are no* derivations for the above sequents ending with an application of one of the $(\vee I)$-rules.

Note that a derivation of φ from itself by means of the *identity axiom* in every ND-system, namely $\varphi \vdash \varphi$ (or more generally $\Gamma, \varphi \vdash \varphi$) *is not* canonical, and does not derive φ according to its meaning.

4   The Reification of Meaning

According to the main PTS school, called inferentialism, I-rules[2] are taken, to *determine* the meanings of the introduced construct (such as logical constants or determiner phrases), but they do not *constitute* those meanings. Thus, the general conception in the inferentialism literature is that PTS provides an *implicit definition* of the meanings of the introduced expressions. However, when approaching meaning from a computational point of view (which is my own point of view), rather than from a philosophical one, an *explicit* definition is needed, something of the form

$$[\![\xi]\!] = \cdots \qquad (4)$$

where 'ξ' is any expression the meaning of which is proof-theoretically determined. I refer to such meanings, explicitly defined, as '*reified meanings*'. Reified meanings do not "hang in the air" but reside (as abstract entities) within a grammar.

There are several reasons why such an explicit definition of a reified meaning is needed. For example:

- facilitating a discussion of the compositionality of the meaning of formulas having the defined operator (e.g., a logical constant or an NL expression such as a determiner) as their main operator as determined by the rules at hand.
- designing a *lexicon* for a grammar (specifying both syntax and semantics) for a (logical or natural) language of which the defined expression is a part, for computational purposes. This fits smoothly the approach of Type-Logical Grammar (TLG) [13], my preferred tool for grammar specification.
- allowing a definition of synonymity (sameness of meaning) and translation from one language to another (more important for natural language, though).
- in the case of NL sentences, having their reified meanings to serve as arguments for *propositional attitudes*.

But what exactly is explicitly defined as the result of the determination of meaning via the meaning-conferring rules?

According to one prevailing view of what is being determined by the meaning conferring rules (e.g., [2], [12], [10]) PTS is viewed as the ability to reconstruct (or recover) the truth-tables (or general truth-conditions) from the ND-rules. Thus, we are back to truth in a model as the meaning determined – actually back

---

[2] For other views of PTS see [4].

to MTS. I consider this approach as beating the purpose of PTS and therefore
be rejected by PTS proponents, and am not going to relate to it any further.

Rather, I present an alternative answer to the question what *does* constitute
those reified meanings. In [6] and [8], such a definition is provided, for two strata
of meaning. A central claim there, adopted here too, is that it is the explicit
definition of *sentential* meaning of compound sentences that is determined directly by the ND-rules; the meanings of the operators themselves are *derived*
from the sentential meanings of sentences formed using those operators. This
contrasts the usual MTS compositional approach (especially as manifested in
TLG tradition) where lexical meanings are assumed to be given, and sentential
meanings are generated compositionally from those word meanings. Note that
in spite of viewing meanings as reified, seemingly being denotations (a feature
usually attributed to MTS), this view *does not* contradict PTS! The denotations
(i.e., semantic values) are proof-theoretic objects (collections of canonical derivations), and there is no notion of satisfaction in a model, the main characteristic
of MTS. The main line of presentation follows the I-based inferentialism PTS,
with occasional indications about the other approaches.

The *reification* of meaning, referred to as a (proof-theoretic) *semantic value*,
is obtained by adhering to the following principles. There is a distinction here
between atomic and compound sentences.

Atomic sentences: Meanings of atomic sentences are usually viewed in PTS
as *given* (possibly from outside the meaning-conferring ND-system), and the
meaning of compound sentences are obtained *relatively* to the given meanings
of atomic sentences, and, hence, may *vary* with the meanings of atomic sentences. Atomic meanings can be conceived as obtained by direct observation,
or by methods as in [14].

Compound sentences: For compound sentences, sentential meanings are defined as the *collection of canonical derivations*. This is very much in the spirit
of the modern approach "propositions as types" (see, for example, [11]), the
inhabitants of a type being the proofs of the proposition. For logic, a reification of (proof-theoretic) meanings is presented in [8], and is reproduced
below. The approach was applied also to natural language in [6].

A possible reification of sentential meanings in MTS is via the truth (of a
formula, in a model) denoted by $\mathcal{M}\models\varphi$. This leads to the following definition.

Definition 2 (model-theoretic sentential semantic values). *For any $\varphi\in L$,
its model-theoretic meanings $[\![\varphi]\!]^m$ is given as follows.*

$$[\![\varphi]\!]^m = \{\mathcal{M} \mid \mathcal{M}\models\varphi\} \tag{5}$$

Namely, the (reified) meaning of a sentence is the collection of all its models (of
the appropriate kind), i.e., all models in which it is true. This definition, however, does not let itself to a natural generalization of meanings of subsentential
phrases, which are of crucial importance for grammars. For example, in 1st-order
logic, we do not have anything to qualify as the meaning of the universal quanti-
fier, namely $[\![\forall]\!]$, so that $[\![\forall]\!](x)([\![\varphi]\!]) = [\![\forall x.\varphi]\!]$. See [6] for such a proof-theoretic
meaning for '$\forall$'.

Below is the definition of the analogous notion, the reified proof-theoretic sentential meaning.

Definition 3. (proof-theoretic sentential semantic values). *For a compound $\varphi \in L$, its* proof-theoretic meanings $[\![\varphi]\!]^P$ *is given as follows.*

$$[\![\varphi]\!]^P = \lambda \Gamma.[\![\varphi]\!]^c_\Gamma \tag{6}$$

Note that the denotational meaning of φ is *a proof-theoretic object*, a contextualized function from contexts to the collection of canonical derivations of φ from that context, not to be confused with model-theoretic denotations (of truth-values, in the propositional logic case).

To realize the role of canonicity in the definition of reified proof-theoretic meanings, consider the following example derivation in propositional logic.

$$\frac{\alpha \quad (\alpha \rightarrow (\varphi \wedge \psi))}{\varphi \wedge \psi} \, (\rightarrow E) \tag{7}$$

This is a derivation of a conjunction – but not a canonical one, as it does not end with an application of $(\wedge I)$. Thus, the conjunction here was *not* derived according to its meaning! As far as this derivation is concerned, it could mean anything, e.g., disjunction. On the other hand, the following example derivation *is* according to the conjunction's meaning, being canonical.

$$\frac{\dfrac{\alpha \quad \alpha \rightarrow \varphi}{\varphi} \, (\rightarrow E) \quad \dfrac{\beta \quad \beta \rightarrow \psi}{\psi} \, (\rightarrow E)}{\varphi \wedge \psi} \, (\wedge I) \tag{8}$$

Similar examples can be seen in natural language. The following rules (from [7]) are I/E rules for intersective adjectives. The rules capture adjectival modification by such adjectives as a "silent" implicit conjunction. In the rule, X ranges over verbs and A ranges over (intersective) adjectives. I am avoiding here the use of proper names for a certain technical complication. See [7] for their PTS treatment.

$$\frac{\Gamma \vdash j \text{ isa } X \quad \Gamma \vdash j \text{ is } A}{\Gamma \vdash j \text{ isa } A \, X} \, (adjI) \qquad \frac{\Gamma \vdash j \text{ isa } A \, X}{\Gamma \vdash j \text{ isa } X} \, (adjE_1) \qquad \frac{\Gamma \vdash j \text{ isa } A \, X}{\Gamma \vdash j \text{ is } A} \, (adjE^{1,2}) \tag{9}$$

An instance of $(adjI)$ is

$$\frac{\Gamma \vdash j \text{ isa girl} \quad \Gamma \vdash j \text{ is beautiful}}{\Gamma \vdash j \text{ isa beautiful girl}} \, (adjI)$$

The conclusion of $(adjI)$ can be obtained non-canonically by applying the E-rule for elimination of universal quantification (in (15) below), not appealing at all to the conjunctive meaning of adjectival modification.

$$\frac{\Gamma \vdash j \text{ isa girl} \quad \Gamma \vdash \text{every girl isa beautiful girl}}{\Gamma \vdash j \text{ isa beautiful girl}} \, (eE)$$

To realise the impact of the different conception of meaning between MTS and
PTS, consider the following simple example. In propositional Classical Logic, we
have the equivalence

$$\varphi \wedge \psi \equiv \neg(\neg\varphi \vee \neg\psi) \tag{10}$$

Both sides of the equivalence are assigned the same meaning by MTS (here,
same truth-table). However, those two propositions do differ in several aspects
involving meaning, most notable in inference. While it is fairly natural to re-
gard a transition from $\varphi \wedge \psi$ to φ as some kind of an "elementary" transition, a
transition from $\neg(\neg\varphi \vee \neg\psi)$ to φ, while model-theoretically valid, cannot count
as elementary, and its validity needs explanation by means of decomposition to
more elementary steps.

5   Granularity of Meaning

In this section, I compare the granularities of meaning resulting from the MTS
reified meaning definition in (5) and the PTS definition in (6). Clearly, the PTS
reified meaning obtained as above are very *fine-grained*.

Logic: Under the MTS reification, logically equivalent sentences have the *same*
class of models. Thus, in classical propositional logic, basing meaning on
truth-tables, the following equalities of meaning hold.

$$[\![\varphi \wedge \varphi]\!]^m = [\![\varphi]\!]^m, \quad [\![\varphi \wedge \psi]\!]^m = [\![\psi \wedge \varphi]\!]^m, \quad [\![((\varphi \wedge \psi) \wedge \xi)]\!]^m = [\![(\varphi \wedge (\psi \wedge \xi))]\!]^m \tag{11}$$

Both sides of each equality have the same truth-table, i.e., are true in the
same models (assignment to propositional variables). Similarly,

$$[\![\varphi \rightarrow \varphi]\!]^m = [\![\varphi \vee \neg\varphi]\!]^m = [\![\text{any other tautology}]\!]^m \tag{12}$$

each tautology is true under every assignment.
On the other hand, under the PTS definition, we have

$$[\![\varphi \wedge \varphi]\!]^p \neq [\![\varphi]\!]^p, \quad [\![\varphi \wedge \psi]\!]^p \neq [\![\psi \wedge \varphi]\!]^p, \quad [\![((\varphi \wedge \psi) \wedge \xi)]\!]^p \neq [\![(\varphi \wedge (\psi \wedge \xi))]\!]^p \tag{13}$$

The first inequality, for example, obtains because every canonical derivation
which is a member of $[\![\varphi \wedge \varphi]\!]^p$ ends with an application of $(\wedge I)$, while canonical derivations in $[\![\varphi]\!]^p$ end with an application of the I-rule of the main
operator of φ.

   In particular, note that it is not the case that all tautologies (or all con-
tradictions) share the same meaning like in MTS. For example,

$$[\![\varphi \rightarrow \varphi]\!]^p \neq [\![(\varphi \rightarrow (\psi \rightarrow \varphi))]\!]^p \tag{14}$$

For every Γ, all canonical derivations for $\Gamma \vdash^c \varphi \rightarrow \varphi$ have the form

$$\frac{[\varphi]_i}{\varphi \rightarrow \varphi} \ (\rightarrow I^i)$$

(not using Γ), while canonical derivations for $\Gamma \vdash (\varphi \to (\psi \to \varphi))$ have the form

$$\frac{\dfrac{[\varphi]_i}{\psi \to \varphi} \ (\to I^j)}{(\varphi \to (\psi \to \varphi))} \ (\to I^i)$$

vacuously disgorging an assumption ψ (also not using Γ); hence the inequality of meanings.

Natural Language: Consider the following I/E-rules for determiner-phrases with the determiner every, a simplified version of the corresponding rules in [7]. For example, the issue of scope is ignore in these rules. In the rules, X ranges over verbs, $\mathbf{j}$ is an *individual parameter*, and $S[\mathbf{j}]$ is a sentence S with $\mathbf{j}$ occupying some designated position. Then, $S[\text{every } X]$ is the same sentence S with the determiner phrase every X occupying the same designated position.

$$\frac{\Gamma, \mathbf{j} \text{ isa } X \vdash S[\mathbf{j}]}{\Gamma \vdash S[(\text{every } X)]} \ (eI) \qquad \frac{\Gamma \vdash S[(\text{every } X)] \quad \Gamma \vdash \mathbf{j} \text{ isa } X}{\Gamma \vdash S[\mathbf{j}]} \ (eE) \qquad (15)$$

where $\mathbf{j}$ is fresh for $\Gamma, S[\text{every } X]$ in (eI). The rule expresses the idea that if $S[\mathbf{j}]$ is derivable from a dischargeable assumption $\mathbf{j}$ isa X for an *arbitrary* $\mathbf{j}$ (expressed by freshness of $\mathbf{j}$, not being mentioned in Γ), then $S[\text{every } X]$ is derivable. For example, the following is an instance of (eI).

$$\frac{\Gamma, \mathbf{j} \text{ isa girl} \vdash \mathbf{j} \text{ smiles}}{\Gamma \vdash \text{every girl smiles}} \ (eI) \qquad (16)$$

By those rules,

$$\llbracket \text{every girl isa girl} \rrbracket^p \neq \llbracket \text{every boy isa boy} \rrbracket^p \qquad (17)$$

In $\llbracket \text{every girl isa girl} \rrbracket^p$ we have a canonical derivations of the form

$$\frac{\Gamma, \mathbf{j} \text{ isa girl} \vdash \mathbf{j} \text{ isa girl}}{\Gamma \vdash \text{every girl isa girl}} \ (eI)$$

while in $\llbracket \text{every boy isa boy} \rrbracket^p$ we have *different* canonical derivations of the form

$$\frac{\Gamma, \mathbf{j} \text{ isa boy} \vdash \mathbf{j} \text{ isa boy}}{\Gamma \vdash \text{every boy isa boy}} \ (eI)$$

To see that the reified proof-theoretic meaning does not necessarily distinguish between the meanings of *every* two different sentences, consider the following example employing passivisation.

Suppose that for a binary relation R (representing an active transitive verb) we denote by R^{-1} its passivisation. Thus, $\text{love}^{-1} = \text{is loved by}$.

Recall that meanings of compound sentences are defined by the ND-rules modulo some externally given meaning assignment to atomic sentences. Suppose that on the atomic level we have

$$\llbracket \mathbf{j} \ R \ \mathbf{k} \rrbracket = \llbracket \mathbf{k} \ R^{-1} \ \mathbf{j} \rrbracket$$

Under this assumption, we can show that

$$[\![(\text{every } X)_2 \; R \; (\text{some } Y)_1]\!] = [\![(\text{some } Y)_1 \; R^{-1} \; (\text{every } X)_2]\!]$$

The canonical derivations (from identical open assumptions) are:

$$\cfrac{\cfrac{[\text{j isa } X]_1 \quad \text{j } R \text{ k} \quad \text{k isa } Y}{\text{j } R \; (\text{some } Y)_1)_1} \; (sI)}{(\text{every } X)_2 \; R \; (\text{some } Y)_1} \; (eI^1) \qquad \cfrac{\cfrac{[\text{j isa } X]_1 \quad \text{k } R^{-1} \text{ j} \quad \text{k isa } Y}{(\text{some } Y)_1)_1 \; R^{-1} \; \text{j}} \; (sI)}{(\text{some } Y)_1 \; R^{-1} \; (\text{every } X)_2} \; (eI^1)$$

The indices on *dps* indicate scope level of the quantifiers. The exact specification how quantifier scope is treated by the rules can be found in [7].

The ultimate evaluation of the level of granularity of reified meaning is by appealing to the entailment relation it supports. Otherwise, one could use "brute force" and let $[\![\varphi]\!] = \varphi$, which is certainly very fine grained ... I defer the discussion of the entailment induced by the reified meaning I propose to a separate paper.

6   Coarsening the Reified Proof-Theoretic Meaning

The fine-grainedness of proof-theoretic meanings can be somewhat relaxed by imposing equivalence relations on meanings, and identifying sameness of meaning with such an equivalence.

As an example, I base an equivalence of sentences on *sameness of grounds* to obtain coarser reified meanings. Let φ be a compound sentence of L.

Definition 4 (grounds for assertion).

$$GA[\![\varphi]\!] = \{\Gamma \mid \Gamma \vdash^c \varphi\} \tag{18}$$

A context Γ from which φ can be canonically derived (i.e., according to its meaning) serves as a grounds for asserting φ, a central concept in the philosophy underlying PTS.

Definition 5 (G-equivalence). *For two sentences* φ, ψ, $\varphi \equiv_G \psi$ *iff* $GA[\![\varphi]\!] = GA[\![\psi]\!]$.

Thus, the meanings of two sentences having the same grounds (i.e., assertable under the same condition) are equated.

Let us return to the examples mentioned above in (11). Note that

$$GA[\![\varphi \wedge \psi]\!] = GA[\![\psi \wedge \varphi]\!] = GA[\![\varphi]\!] \cup GA[\![\psi]\!] \tag{19}$$

it is easy to see that '$\equiv_G$' "forgets" the difference in meaning between φ and $\varphi \wedge \varphi$, namely

$$GA[\![\varphi \wedge \varphi]\!] = GA[\![\varphi]\!] \tag{20}$$

hence

$$\varphi \wedge \varphi \equiv_G \varphi \tag{21}$$

and similarly

$$\varphi \wedge \psi \equiv_G \psi \wedge \varphi \tag{22}$$

Finally, since

$$GA([((\varphi \wedge \psi) \wedge \xi)]]) = GA([(\varphi \wedge (\psi \wedge \xi))]]) = GA \; [\![\varphi]\!] \cup GA \; [\![\psi]\!] \cup GA \; [\![\xi]\!] \tag{23}$$

we get

$$((\varphi \wedge \psi) \wedge \xi) \equiv_G (\varphi \wedge (\psi \wedge \xi)) \tag{24}$$

The last equivalence justifies the common view of conjunction as having an arbitrary arity, based on its associativity. The grounds for asserting such a general conjunctive sentence are the union of the grounds for assertion of the separate conjunct. This situation is analogous to the situation in MTS, where the truth-condition of conjunction, conceived as having *arbitrary* arity (due to its associativity), is the truth (in the same model) of all conjuncts. For example,

However, not *all* boolean equivalences are restored. For example,

$$\varphi \wedge \psi \not\equiv_G \neg(\neg \varphi \vee \neg \psi) \tag{25}$$

since the grounds of the r.h.s. are not simply $GA[\![\varphi]\!] \cup GA[\![\psi]\!]$.

7 Conclusion

The paper presented MTS and PTS, two approaches to meaning via logic, and compared and contrasted them w.r.t. the granularity of meaning. PTS emerges as inducing a much finer granularity on meanings than MTS does; in particular, PTS does not identify meanings of of logically equivalent sentences, a step that might be helpful for defining the meaning of propositional attitudes reports. I propose a certain possible natural relaxation of the fine-graindness of PTS meanings, based on identifying the meanings having the same grounds for assertion.

References

[1] Dummett, M.: The Logical Basis of Metaphysics. Harvard University Press, Cambridge (1993), (paperback). Hard copy 1991

[2] Engel, P.: Logic, reasoning and the logical constants. Croatian Journal of Philosophical VI(17), 219–235 (2006)

[3] Francez, N.: On the notion of canonical derivations from open assumptions and its role in proof-theoretic semantics. Review of Symbolic Logic (2014) (under refereeing)

[4] Francez, N.: Views of proof-theoretic semantics: Reified proof-theoretic meanings. Journal of Computational Logic (to appear, 2014), Special issue in honour of Roy Dyckhoff

[5] Francez, N., Ben-Avi, G.: A proof-theoretic reconstruction of generalized quantifiers. Journal of Semantics (to appear, 2014)

[6] Francez, N., Ben-Avi, G.: Proof-theoretic semantic values for logical operators. Review of Symbolic Logic 4(3), 337–485 (2011)

[7] Francez, N., Dyckhoff, R.: Proof-theoretic semantics for a natural language fragment. Linguistics and Philosophy 33(6), 447–477 (2010)

[8] Francez, N., Dyckhoff, R., Ben-Avi, G.: Proof-theoretic semantics for subsentential phrases. Studia Logica 94, 381–401 (2010)

[9] Frege, G.: Die Grundlagen der Arithmetik. Georg Olms (1884)

[10] Garson, J.W.: Natural semantics: Why natural deduction is intuitionistic. Theoria LXVII, 114–139 (2001)

[11] Girard, J.-Y., Lafont, Y., Taylor, P.: Proofs and Types. Cambridge Tracts in Theoretical Computer Science, vol. 7. Cambridge University Press, Cambridge (1989)

[12] Hjortland, O.T.: The Structure of Logical Consequence: Proof-Theoretic Conceptions. PhD thesis, University of St Andrews (2009)

[13] Moortgat, M.: Categorial type logics. In: van Benthem, J., ter Meulen, A. (eds.) Handbook of Logic and Language, pp. 93–178. North-Holland (1997)

[14] Wieckowski, B.: Rules for subatomic derivation. Review of Symbolic Logic 4(2) (2011)

Late Merge as Lowering Movement in Minimalist Grammars

Thomas Graf

Department of Linguistics
Stony Brook University
mail@thomasgraf.net
http://thomasgraf.net

Abstract. Minimalist grammars can be specified in terms of their derivation tree languages and a mapping from derivations to derived trees, each of which is definable in monadic second-order logic (MSO). It has been shown that the linguistically motivated operation Late Merge can push either component past the threshold of MSO-definability. However, Late Merge as used in the syntactic literature can be elegantly recast in terms of Lowering movement within the framework of Movement-generalized Minimalist grammars. As the latter are MSO-definable, the linguistically relevant fragment of Late Merge is too.

Keywords: Minimalist grammars, countercyclic operations, late merge, lowering movement, monadic second-order logic.

Introduction

Minimalist grammars (MGs; [24, 25]) were conceived as a formalization of the currently dominant framework in theoretical syntax [1], so it is hardly surprising that they have frequently been used as a testbed for the ideas and mechanisms entertained by linguists. In recent years, a lot of work has focused on countercyclic operations, in particular Late Merge [4, 10, 14]. Under a derivational conception of syntax, an operation is countercyclic iff any new material it introduces is not added to the top of the structure built so far but instead inserted at a lower position.

Countercyclic operations are intriguing from the perspective of a resource-sensitive formalism like MGs, where every lexical item has a finite number of features that must be checked. For one thing, feature checking — i.e. Minimalist resource consumption — is no longer linked to structure-building in a one-to-one fashion because the feature triggering a countercyclic operation may actually license the insertion of new structure at a very different position. More importantly, though, the material introduced by a countercyclic operation might itself contain features that need to be checked, so that a substructure that already had all of its features checked may suddenly be in need of feature checking again.

Both possibilities add a lot of complexity to the formalism. It is already known that Late Merge can increase weak generative capacity [14], and even when

N. Asher and S. Soloviev (Eds.): LACL 2014, LNCS 8535, pp. 107–121, 2014.

Late Merge is sufficiently constrained to preserve strong generative capacity it requires a more powerful mapping from derivations to derived trees [4, 10, 18]. MGs can be specified in terms of their derivation tree languages and a mapping from derivation to derived tree languages [5, 8, 15]. For standard MGs, both components are definable in monadic second-order logic (MSO). Neither holds for MGs with unrestricted Late Merge [10].

While the formal underpinnings of unrestricted Late Merge are certainly interesting and provide deep insights into the inner workings of MGs, the loss of MSO-definability and the computational advantages that come with it should be avoided unless absolutely necessary. I argue in this paper that for the cases discussed so far in the linguistic literature, Late Merge can be easily reduced to the more standard operation of Lowering movement [6]. Since Lowering is MSO-definable, so must be Late Merge. In a certain sense, the reduction provides a normal form theorem for MGs — results on Lowering immediately carry over to Late Merge. For example, if the MG parser in [26, 27] is enriched with inference rules for Lowering, it will also work for grammars with Late Merge.

The paper is laid out as follows: Section 1.1 provides an intuitive introduction to MGs, which is subsequently expanded in Sec. 1.2 to Movement-generalized MGs, a weakly equivalent variant of MGs where grammars may have multiple types of movement, including Lowering. Section 1.3 then discusses Late Merge from a linguistic perspective. The reduction of Late Merge to Lowering is presented in Sec. 2. This is followed by technical observations on generative capacity and derivational complexity (3.1), limitations of the reduction (3.2), and the interaction of Late Merge and movement (3.3).

1   Preliminaries

1.1   Standard Minimalist Grammars

MGs [24, 25] are a lexicalized grammar formalism where every lexical item has an ordered list of features that must be checked in this specific order by the operations Merge and Move, which in turn combine these lexical items into tree structures.

For instance, the DP *the boy* would be built by merging the lexical item *the* with *boy*. In order to license this application of Merge, *the* has a *selector feature* N^+ indicating that it selects a noun, and the noun *boy* has a matching *category feature* N^-. Moreover, since the entire phrase is a DP and *the* is the head of the DP, *the* also has a category feature D^-. The selector feature N^+ on *the* precedes the category feature D^- because *the* must select its argument before it can project a DP. The structure-building process can be depicted as a derivation tree, which closely mirrors the structure of the derived tree.

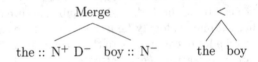

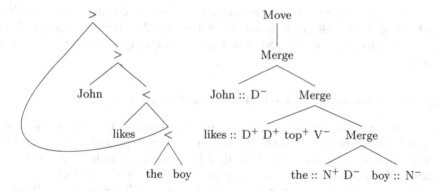

Fig. 1. Multi-dominance tree with movement and its corresponding derivation tree

The main difference is the absence of features in the derived tree as well as the new label for the interior node, which points in the direction of the projecting head. This is always the head that had one of its positive polarity features (i.e. a feature with superscript $+$) checked by the operation in question.

In the sentence *the boy John likes*, the object DP *the boy* has been topicalized, which is analyzed as movement from the position where it was merged to a higher landing site. A simplified derived tree and its derivation are given in Fig. 1. Here *the boy* is assumed to move to a specifier of the verb *likes*. This is licensed by the *licensor feature* top$^+$ on *likes* and the *licensee feature* top$^-$ on *the*. A few things are worth pointing out explicitly:

- Movement in the derived tree is indicated by adding branches. This yields what is called a *multi-dominance tree*. This format of representing movement is formally simpler than the standard trace-based mechanism.
- Once again the derivation tree is very similar to the derived tree. The latter can be obtained from the former as before by relabeling interior nodes and removing features, except that this time one must also add movement branches.
- Even though the licensee feature triggering topicalization is hosted by *the*, it isn't just the determiner that undergoes movement but the entire DP it projects.

Movement is subject to the Shortest Move Constraint (SMC), which blocks all configurations with two LIs that have the same licensee feature as their first unchecked feature. For example, if *John* in the derivation above actually had the feature specification D$^-$ top$^-$, then the derivation would be aborted after *John* is merged because then both *John* and *the* would have the licensee feature top$^-$ as their first unchecked feature.

The SMC grants MGs a variety of appealing properties. Their derivation tree languages are regular tree languages and thus definable in MSO [5, 15, 17].

The mapping from derivation trees to derived trees is also definable in MSO, which entails that MGs generate mildly context-sensitive string languages [6, 8, 15, 18, 19]. This result can be sharpened: MGs are weakly equivalent to MCFGs [9, 17].

1.2   Movement-Generalized Minimalist Grammars

Movement-generalized MGs (MGMGs) were introduced by Graf in [6] and allow for new types of movement instead of just upward movement of a phrase to a c-commanding position. Crucially, though, all movement types must be definable in MSO, which implies via a battery of previously known theorems that MGs and MGMGs are weakly (but not strongly) equivalent. A full definition of MGMGs is rather laborious and unnecessary for the purposes of this paper, so I restrict myself to an abridged version here; the interested reader is referred to [6].

MGMGs build on the insight that the MG feature calculus driving Move can be recast in tree-geometric terms. Basically, one has to ensure that every Move node is targeted by exactly one moving phrase, and every licensee feature on every LI is checked by exactly one Move operation. This amounts to regulating the distribution of Move nodes in the derivation.

The essential notion is that of *occurrences*. Given a lexical item l and node m in the derivation, m is the i-th occurrence of l iff it checks l's $(i+1)$-th negative polarity feature. Hence the *zero occurrence* of a lexical item l is the Merge node that checks its category feature and thus introduces it into the derivation. *Positive occurrences* (for which $i > 0$) are the Move nodes that check one of l's licensee features. The requirements of MG feature calculus with respect to Move can then be enforced as constraints on the distribution of occurrences. For every derivation tree t, node m of t, and lexical item l with licensee features $f_1^- \cdots f_n^-$, $n \geq 0$:

Move there exist distinct nodes $m_1, \ldots, m_n$ such that m_i (and no other node of t) is the ith occurrence of l, $1 \leq i \leq n$.

SMC if m is a Move node, there is exactly one lexical item that m is an occurrence of.

But how does one determine whether a Move node is an occurrence for a lexical item? In the case of standard MGs, there is a simple algorithm that depends only on proper dominance.

Occurrence. A Move node m is the i-th occurrence of a lexical item l with licensee features $f_1^- \cdots f_n^-$ iff
 - m is associated to the matching licensor feature f_i^+, and
 - m properly dominates the $(i-1)$-th occurrence of l,
 - there is no Move node z such that m properly dominates z and z satisfies the previous two clauses.

Intuitively, the i-th occurrence of l is found by moving upwards from the $(i-1)$-th occurrence until one encounters a Move node that can check f_i^- on l.

Graf notes that new movement types can be created by replacing proper dominance by a different relation over trees. For example, the inverse of proper dominance gives rise to downward movement since now the i-th occurrence is dominated by the $(i-1)$-th occurrence rather than the other way round. Since the constraints **Move** and **SMC** make no assumptions as to which nodes may count as occurrences, they restrict this kind of movement in the same fashion as standard movement. Thus new types of movement can be introduced without altering the spirit of movement regarding the MG feature calculus.

As long as the relation connecting occurrences is MSO-definable, **Move** and **SMC** will be, too, which implies that MGMGs still have regular — that is, MSO-definable — derivation tree languages. The mapping from derivations to derived also is built over the notion of occurrences, so it need not be altered either. Graf allows for every feature to specify whether the moving phrase should be linearized to the left or to the right of the landing site, but this is a technically innocent change without negative repercussions. The weak generative capacity of MGMGs therefore does not exceed that of standard MGs, yet they provide a simple mechanism for adding new movement types that can generate more complex tree languages.

Building on the MGMG system, I will use two types of movement in this paper. *Raising* is the standard kind of MG movement. That is to say, the phrase targets a c-commanding position in the derived tree, which corresponds to using proper dominance for determining occurrences. *Lowering* is the inverse of raising: a phrase moves to a c-commanded position, and occurrences are determined by the inverse of proper dominance. Raising and Lowering will be indicated by the prefixed subscripts $\uparrow$ and $\downarrow$, respectively. Moreover, the prefixed superscripts λ and ρ indicate whether a mover is linearized to the left or the right. So ${}_{\downarrow}^{\rho}f^{-}$, for instance, is a licensee feature triggering rightward Lowering. A (linguistically implausible) example derivation is given in Fig. 2.

1.3   Late Merge

In the Minimalist literature, *Late Merge* refers to cases where a tree s is merged with a tree t at some point after t has already been merged with another tree u. The best known instance of this is in Lebeaux's analysis of Principle C exceptions [16].

(1)   a.   * He$_i$ believed the argument that John$_i$ made.

       b.   Which argument that John$_i$ made did he$_i$ believe?

In the ungrammatical (1a) the R-expression *John* is c-commanded by the co-indexed DP *he*, which constitutes a Principle C violation. This part is expected; the puzzle is why (1b) is grammatical. Since *which argument that John$_i$ made* started out as the object of *believe*, *John* was c-commanded by a co-indexed DP at some point during this derivation, too, so a Principle C violation should obtain as before. Lebeaux contends that the violation can be avoided because the relative clause *that John made* does not have to merge with *which argument* until

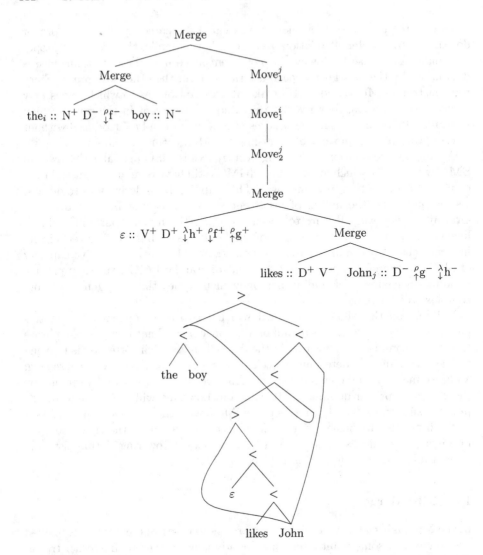

Fig. 2. An implausible derivation of *John likes the boy* with Raising and Lowering; occurrences are distinguished by superscripts i and j and numbered with subscripts

the latter has moved out of the c-command domain of *he*. Lebeaux's derivation can be roughly sketched as follows:

$$\text{did he}_i \text{ believe [which argument]} \tag{1}$$

$$\text{[which argument] did he}_i \text{ believe} \tag{2}$$

$$\text{[which argument [that John}_i \text{ made]] did he}_i \text{ believe} \tag{3}$$

No derivation resembling the one above is compatible with standard MGs. Combining the relative clause with *which argument* must involve a feature on *which* or *argument*. But after *which argument* undergoes movement, all its features have been discharged, it has become completely opaque as far as the formalism is concerned. Any implementation of Late Merge thus has to modify the way resources are handled in MGs, and the modification has to work for a variety of cases.

Lebeaux's account is just one of many where Late Merge is used to factor some subtree out of a domain where its presence would cause problems. Ochi [22] posits that VP-adjuncts undergo Late Merge because they would otherwise act as an intervener between a verb and the inflectional head T, which would incorrectly predict under his proposal that *John quickly left* is always realized as *John did quickly leave*. Nissenbaum [21] also has to assume that VP-adjuncts are merged late in order to avoid a type conflict which can only arise before the subject undergoes movement. And Stepanov [28] proposes that the phrase *to Mary* in *John$_i$ seems to Mary [t$_i$ to be smart]* must be merged countercyclically in order to avoid a subjacency violation.

In all the cases above, only adjuncts undergo Late Merge, which is why the operation is also called *Late Adjoin* or *Late Adjunction*. However, there are accounts that extend Late Merge to arguments, too [29]. For instance, the LF-derivation for *every spy sneezed* could proceed along the following lines:

$$[\text{every}]_i \text{ sneezed} \tag{1}$$
$$[\text{every}]_i \ t_i \text{ sneezed} \tag{2}$$
$$[\text{every spy}] \ t_i \text{ sneezed} \tag{3}$$

For this little toy example, Late Merger of the NP *spy* serves little purpose. The real motivation for Late Merge in this case stems from Principle C exceptions that are similar to the ones noted by Lebeaux for adjuncts, except that they now arise with the NP-argument of a quantified DP.

(2)   a.   * Which argument that John$_i$ is a genius seems to him$_i$ to be true?

   b.   Every argument that John$_i$ is a genius seems to him$_i$ to be true

Takahashi and Hulsey [29] argue that (2b) is well-formed because the presence of quantifier allows for the argument to be late-merged. The derivation proceeds roughly as follows:

$$[\text{every}]_i \text{ true} \tag{1}$$
$$[\text{every}]_i \text{ seems to him}_i \ [t_i \text{ to be } [t_i \text{ true}]] \tag{2}$$
$$[[\text{every}] \ [\text{argument that John}_i \text{ is a genius }]] \text{ seems to him}_i \ [t_i \text{ to be } [t_i \text{ true}]] \tag{3}$$

Since this example involves a lot of structure and intermediate movement steps, the toy example *every spy sneezed* will be used in the next section for the sake of simplicity.

Even though we omitted many technical details, it should be clear that none of the cases above require something like Late Merge. In each case, it would be sufficient to modify the mechanism that conflicts with the subtree, rather than have the subtree be merged in a countercyclic fashion. Principle C could ignore adjuncts of a moving DP, Ochi's account of English inflection could stipulate that adjuncts do not count as interveners, and so on. Readers familiar with model-theoretic approaches such as the formalization of Government-and-Binding theory in terms of MSO [23] will also realize that making such modifications is easier than adding a completely new operation and restricting its application domain. So from a purely formal perspective, there is no compelling argument for Late Merge. Both weak and strong generative capacity of the standard formalisms are already sufficient for the phenomena above, and bringing in Late Merge in a controlled fashion such that the computational properties of the formalism are preserved just means extra work.

Crucially, though, weak and strong generation of natural languages is but one of many duties of a grammar formalism. The formalism also has to be capable of stating structural generalizations. This isn't just a matter of scientific methodology — the fewer generalizations the formalism makes, the greater the number of stipulations it requires, which implies a bigger grammar size. Small grammars show better parsing performance and are easier to maintain; so even if one only cares about the engineering aspects of a formalism, a mechanism that unifies a range of empirical phenomena is worth studying regardless of whether it is vacuous with respect to generative capacity.

2   Late Merge as Lowering

2.1   Late Merger of Arguments

A maximally faithful implementation of how linguists think about Late Merge in sentences like *every spy sneezed* would arguably involve an MG derivation like the one in Fig. 3. This derivation is ill-formed in three respects: *every* cannot be merged directly with *sneezed* given its feature make-up, *spy* cannot be merged with the empty C-head, and no Merge operation combines *every* and *spy*.

However, if one uses MGMGs as defined in [6], then the minimally different derivation in Fig. 4 is well-formed and produces the intended string *every spy sneezed*. The selector feature N^+ on *every* has been replaced by a rightward lowering licensor feature $^\rho_\downarrow 1^+$, and a corresponding Move node has been added in the derivation. The matching licensee feature $^\rho_\downarrow 1^-$ occurs on *spy*. Hence *spy* will lower down to *every*, where it is linearized to its right. The other minor change is the presence of a second empty C-head, with the first C-head as its complement and *spy* as a specifier. This head only serves as a means for introducing *spy* into the derivation — there are many viable alternatives, for instance adjunction of *spy* to the first C-head using one of the many MG implementations of adjunction [2, 3]. The important point is that the countercyclic behavior of Late Merge is emulated by countercyclic movement, i.e. Lowering.

```
                Merge
          _____
spy :: N⁻          Merge
              _____
      ε :: T⁺ C⁻              Move
                              |
                            Merge
                    _____
            ε :: V⁺ nom⁺ T⁻        Merge
                          _____
                    every :: N⁺ D⁻ nom⁻   sneezed :: D⁺ V⁻
```

Fig. 3. A faithful candidate for a Late Merge derivation

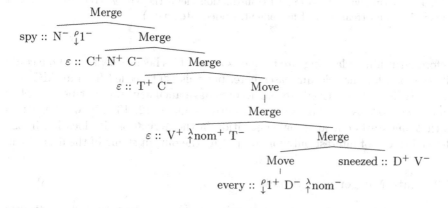

Fig. 4. A Lowering derivation for Late Merge

However, Lowering does not produce the intended structure under the standard MSO-transduction from derivation to multi-dominance trees given in [6, 8], as is evidenced by Fig. 5. Since movement is invariably linked to the introduction of movement branches in the standard transduction, Lowering gives rise to a structure where *spy* originates in a high position. This is at odds with linguists' intuitions, according to which *spy* has not been part of the structure at all before being merged in its surface position. An easy solution is at hand, though: a return to the original MG conception of movement in which one does not keep track of where a mover originated from. It is an easy task to modify the MSO transduction such that Lowering does not introduce branches or leave behind traces. As a matter of fact, once could even delete the empty head that introduced the late-merged phrase into the derivation via a simple modification of the transduction defined in Sec. B.4.6 of [8].

Another point where the Lowering implementation differs slightly from linguistic intuition is that *spy* lowers before *every* moves into subject position. This is due to an explicit ban against licensee features preceding licensor features in [6], wherefore *every* cannot move on its own to check one of its licensee features

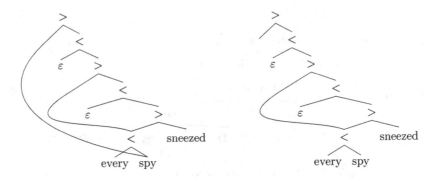

Fig. 5. Lowering with the standard transduction yields the wrong structure (left), but the original MG treatment of movement is adequate (right)

before furnishing a landing site for *spy* via one of its licensor features. One could lift this ban for the relevant cases here, but this isn't needed from an MG perspective. Since the derived tree structures have ancillary status at best in MGs and most work is done directly over derivations [8, 12, 13, 15], what matters is that *spy* starts out at a higher position in the derivation. Its location in the derived tree is of interest only for computing the output string of the derivation.

2.2   Late Merger of Adjuncts

The strategy of emulating Late Merge via Lowering can be extended to adjuncts without much trouble. If only one adjunct is being late-merged, the corresponding derivation perfectly matches the one outlined in the previous section.

In principle, however, a phrase p may have an unbounded number of adjuncts, so one would expect that an unbounded number of adjuncts can be late-merged with p. But due to the SMC, the number of moving elements at any given step of the derivation is finitely bounded, so it seems that only a bounded number of adjuncts can be late-merged with p.

This issue has some linguistic relevance for if one follows Ochi and Nissenbaum [21, 22], then all VP adjuncts — of which there can be unboundedly many — are introduced by Late Merge. Crucially, though, VP adjuncts fall into two major categories determined by whether they are linearized to the left or to the right of the phrase they adjoin to. Suppose, then, that there are two empty heads h_l and h_r with Lowering licensee features $\overset{\lambda}{\downarrow}1^-$ and $\overset{\rho}{\downarrow}1^+$, respectively. Left adjuncts adjoin to h_l, whereas right adjuncts adjoin to h_r (this can be enforced with an MSO-constraint). Then h_l and h_r both lower to positions furnished by the phrase the adjuncts are supposed to late-merge with; an example with Frey and Gärnter adjunction [3] is given in Fig. 6.

The kind of "piggybacking" proposal advocated here captures the spirit of Late Merge while producing the right surface string. The derived tree it produces deviates from standard assumptions in that the adjuncts no longer c-command

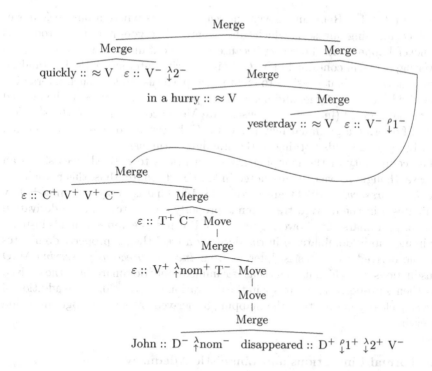

Fig. 6. Derivation (left) and derived tree (right) for Late Merge of multiple adjuncts

the phrase they are late-merged with. However, there are few cases where c-command matters for adjuncts. If for some reason adjunct *a* must c-command the phrase it adjoins to, a minor variant of Lowering may be added to the grammar that allows the adjunct to move to the landing site on its own even though the former does not c-command the latter. Alternatively, one could also switch the adjunction feature of *a* to a category feature and have the empty head select *a* directly. In this case lowering of *a* would proceed exactly as for late-merged arguments.

3 Technical Remarks

3.1 Generative Capacity and Derivational Complexity

The reduction of Late Merge to Lowering immediately entails the definability of the former in MSO and, by extension, that Late Merge does not increase the weak generative capacity of standard MGs. Their strong generative capacity is not increased, either, even though MGs with raising and lowering movement are more powerful than standard MGs in this respect (a corollary of [7]).

Generative capacity is preserved because Lowering movement by itself only generates regular tree languages, which is due to the impossibility of *remnant lowering* (cf. [11]). Remnant movement refers to cases where a phrase X moves out of a containing phrase Y, which subsequently undergoes movement, too. This can never happen with Lowering because if X is contained in Y and undergoes Lowering, it is still contained in Y. Only if Lowering interacts with the standard raising movement is it possible to create such patterns. But no such interaction is required for Late Merge, and hence the dependencies it creates in the derived tree are all regular (in a certain sense, Late Merge corresponds to the simplest kind of Lowering a grammar may possess). With respect to generative capacity, then, Late Merge adds nothing to the standard formalism.

The complexity of the mapping from derivations to derived trees shows an increase, though, as was already noted in [4]. For standard MGs, this mapping is a *direction preserving* MSO transduction [18, 19]. That is to say, if x immediately dominates y in the derived tree, then x properly dominates y in the derivation tree. For grammars with Lowering instead of Raising, the opposite holds instead: if x immediately dominates y in the derivation tree, then x properly dominates y in the derived tree (this is different from *inverse direction preserving* MSO transductions, for which it holds that if x immediately dominates y in the derived tree, then y properly dominates x in the derivation tree [18, 20]). The addition of Lowering clearly entails that the mapping to derived trees is no longer direction preserving.

3.2   Formal Limitations and Linguistic Adequacy

It is important to keep in mind that only a subpart of Late Merge is emulated by Lowering. A completely unrestricted version of Late Merge is capable of increasing the weak generative capacity of MGs [14]. The strategy provided here inherits the major limitation of movement in MGs: only a finitely bounded number of items can undergo Late Merge at the same time.

Yet the limitation to a bounded number of Late Mergers does not seem to be problematic for linguistic applications. Late Merge is not delayed indefinitely but usually takes place within the smallest domain that properly subsumes the application domain of the constraint that the late-merged material has to escape, usually a CP. Given this assumption the only scenarios where one could possibly have an unbounded number of Late Merge operations involve adjuncts or recursion inside an argument, e.g. a DP whose NP selects a DP. But we have already seen that adjuncts can be limited to two instances of Late Merge, and there are no cases in the literature where, say, every NP of a recursive DP has some late-merged adjunct such that all of them originate outside the DP. As a matter of fact, there aren't even any cases of Late Merger with a late-merged phrase. Overall, then, linguists use only a fraction of the power a maximally general version of Late Merge could provide, and this fragment is easily recast in terms of Lowering.

3.3   Movement of Late-Merged Phrases

An unrestricted version of Late Merge increases the generative capacity of MGs as it makes it possible to introduce new licensee features into the derivation without violating the SMC. For example, if both a and b have a licensee feature f^- and they both are merged before the first f^+ occurs, the derivation is aborted due to the SMC. But if a is late-merged after f^- on b has been checked, then no SMC violation obtains and a can undergo movement once another f^+ has been introduced. Among other things, this grants MGs the power to generate tree languages with context-free path languages.

I have not said anything about the interaction of Late Merge with movement, for two reasons: I) the syntactic literature discusses no such cases, and II) once Late Merge is reduced to Lowering, movement of a late-merged phrase is regulated by the constraints MGMGs impose on Move [cf. 6]. In particular, the SMC holds for all movement types in MGMGs, so any configuration like the one above will always be blocked.

Conclusion

Emulating Late Merge via Lowering movement reduces an operation that is still not particularly well understood to the familiar MG mechanism of movement. Lowering is not powerful enough to handle everything that Late Merge is in principle capable of, but it is more than sufficient for the cases discussed in the syntactic literature. So even though a lot of work remains to be done on Late Merge from a technical perspective, the reduction to Lowering shows that Late Merge as used by syntacticians is easily accommodated by MGs. Therefore a linguistically adequate treatment of Late Merge can be reconciled with MSO-definability in a straightforward fashion. Moreover, as we learn more about Lowering and its effects on MGs, our grasp of the linguistically relevant fragment of Late Merge will improve, too.

References

[1] Chomsky, N.: The Minimalist Program. MIT Press, Cambridge (1995)
[2] Fowlie, M.: Order and optionality: Minimalist grammars with adjunction. In: Proceedings of MOL 2013 (2013) (to appear)
[3] Frey, W., Gärtner, H.M.: On the treatment of scrambling and adjunction in minimalist grammars. In: Proceedings of the Conference on Formal Grammar (FGTrento), Trento, pp. 41–52 (2002)
[4] Gärtner, H.M., Michaelis, J.: A note on countercyclicity and minimalist grammars. In: Penn, G. (ed.) Proceedings of Formal Grammar 2003, pp. 95–109. CSLI-Online, Stanford (2008)
[5] Graf, T.: Locality and the complexity of minimalist derivation tree languages. In: de Groote, P., Nederhof, M.-J. (eds.) Formal Grammar 2010/2011. LNCS, vol. 7395, pp. 208–227. Springer, Heidelberg (2012)

[6] Graf, T.: Movement-generalized minimalist grammars. In: Béchet, D., Dikovsky, A. (eds.) LACL 2012. LNCS, vol. 7351, pp. 58–73. Springer, Heidelberg (2012)

[7] Graf, T.: Tree adjunction as minimalist lowering. In: Proceedings of the 11th International Workshop on Tree Adjoining Grammars and Related Formalisms (TAG+11), pp. 19–27 (2012)

[8] Graf, T.: Local and Transderivational Constraints in Syntax and Semantics. Ph.D. thesis, UCLA (2013)

[9] Harkema, H.: A characterization of minimalist languages. In: de Groote, P., Morrill, G., Retoré, C. (eds.) LACL 2001. LNCS (LNAI), vol. 2099, pp. 193–211. Springer, Heidelberg (2001)

[10] Kobele, G.M.: On late adjunction in minimalist grammars (2010), slides for a talk given at MCFG+ 2010

[11] Kobele, G.M.: Without remnant movement, MGs are context-free. In: Ebert, C., Jäger, G., Michaelis, J. (eds.) MOL 10/11. LNCS, vol. 6149, pp. 160–173. Springer, Heidelberg (2010)

[12] Kobele, G.M.: Idioms and extended transducers. In: Proceedings of the 11th International Workshop on Tree Adjoining Grammars and Related Formalisms (TAG+11), Paris, France, September 2012, pp. 153–161 (2012), http://www.aclweb.org/anthology-new/W/W12/W12-4618

[13] Kobele, G.M.: Importing montagovian dynamics into minimalism. In: Béchet, D., Dikovsky, A. (eds.) LACL 2012. LNCS, vol. 7351, pp. 103–118. Springer, Heidelberg (2012)

[14] Kobele, G.M., Michaelis, J.: Disentangling notions of specifier impenetrability: Late adjunction, islands, and expressive power. In: Kanazawa, M., Kornai, A., Kracht, M., Seki, H. (eds.) MOL 12. LNCS (LNAI), vol. 6878, pp. 126–142. Springer, Heidelberg (2011)

[15] Kobele, G.M., Retoré, C., Salvati, S.: An automata-theoretic approach to minimalism. In: Rogers, J., Kepser, S. (eds.) Model Theoretic Syntax at 10, pp. 71–80 (2007)

[16] Lebeaux, D.: Language Acquisition and the Form of the Grammar. Ph.D. thesis, University of Massachusetts, Amherst (1988)

[17] Michaelis, J.: Transforming linear context-free rewriting systems into minimalist grammars. In: de Groote, P., Morrill, G., Retoré, C. (eds.) LACL 2001. LNCS (LNAI), vol. 2099, pp. 228–244. Springer, Heidelberg (2001)

[18] Mönnich, U.: Grammar morphisms (2006), ms. University of Tübingen

[19] Mönnich, U.: Minimalist syntax, multiple regular tree grammars and direction preserving tree transductions. In: Rogers, J., Kepser, S. (eds.) Model Theoretic Syntax at 10, pp. 83–87 (2007)

[20] Mönnich, U.: A logical characterization of extended TAGs. In: Proceedings of the 11th International Workshop on Tree Adjoining Grammars and Related Formalisms (TAG+11), Paris, France, pp. 37–45 (September 2012), http://www.aclweb.org/anthology-new/W/W12/W12-4605

[21] Nissenbaum, J.: Covert movement and parasitic gaps. Proceedings of North Eastern Linguistic Society 30 (2000)

[22] Ochi, M.: Multiple spell-out and PF adjacency. Proceedings of the North Eastern Linguistic Society 29 (1999)

[23] Rogers, J.: A Descriptive Approach to Language-Theoretic Complexity. CSLI, Stanford (1998)

[24] Stabler, E.P.: Derivational minimalism. In: Retoré, C. (ed.) LACL 1996. LNCS (LNAI), vol. 1328, pp. 68–95. Springer, Heidelberg (1997)

[25] Stabler, E.P.: Computational perspectives on minimalism. In: Boeckx, C. (ed.) Oxford Handbook of Linguistic Minimalism, pp. 617–643. Oxford University Press, Oxford (2011)

[26] Stabler, E.P.: Top-down recognizers for MCFGs and MGs. In: Proceedings of the 2011 Workshop on Cognitive Modeling and Computational Linguistics (2011) (to appear)

[27] Stabler, E.P.: Bayesian, minimalist, incremental syntactic analysis. Topics in Cognitive Science 5, 611–633 (2012)

[28] Stepanov, A.: Late adjunction and minimalist phrase structure. Syntax 4, 94–125 (2001)

[29] Takahashi, S., Hulsey, S.: Wholesale Late Merger: Beyond the A/$\overline{\text{A}}$ distinction. Linguistc Inquiry 40, 387–426 (2009)

Pseudogapping as Pseudo-VP Ellipsis

Yusuke Kubota[1] and Robert Levine[2]

[1] Ohio State University, JSPS
kubota.7@osu.edu
[2] Ohio State University
levine@ling.ohio-state.edu

Abstract. In this paper, we propose an analysis of pseudogapping in Hybrid Type-Logical Categorial Grammar (Hybrid TLCG; Kubota 2010, Kubota and Levine 2012). Pseudogapping poses a particularly challenging problem for previous analyses in both the transformational and nontransformational literature. The flexible notion of constituency countenanced in categorial grammar in general (including Hybrid TLCG) enables a simple analysis of pseudogapping that overcomes the problems for previous approaches. In addition, we show that Hybrid TLCG offers a useful platform for comparing different types of CG (and analytic ideas embodied in them) within a single framework with a linguist-friendly notation. In the context of an analysis of pseudogapping, this enables us to compare the adequacies of two types of treatments of discontinuous pseudogapping. We believe that this type of cross-framework comparison of different analytic ideas is useful for the purpose of testing the predictions of different types of analyses that can respectively be formulated in only one or the other of the more conservative types of CG.

Keywords: pseudogapping, VP ellipsis, anaphora, Hybrid Type-Logical Categorial Grammar, discontinuous constituency.

1 Introduction

Pseudogapping is a somewhat odd instance of ellipsis in which a lexical verb embedded under an auxiliary is deleted, leaving behind its own complement(s).

(1) Mary hasn't dated Bill, but she has ∅ Harry.

The proper analysis of this phenomenon has long been a problem in the syntactic literature (see Gengel (2013) and references therein).[1] We argue in this paper that a simple analysis of pseudogapping becomes possible in categorial grammar (CG). The flexible notion of constituency that CG countenances plays a key role in enabling an analysis in which both the syntactic category and the semantic content of the missing material (which is often, but not necessarily, a lexical verb) is explicitly represented as a constituent in the derivation of the antecedent clause, which we show is exactly the information that is needed to license pseudogapping. We formulate our analysis in a variant of CG called Hybrid TLCG

---

[1] Due to space limitations, we do not discuss the problems for these previous approaches in this paper. This is left for another occasion.

N. Asher and S. Soloviev (Eds.): LACL 2014, LNCS 8535, pp. 122–137, 2014.

(Kubota 2010, Kubota and Levine 2012), a framework that can be thought to combine the Lambek-based tradition in TLCG with an order-insensitive calculus of linguistic composition pioneered in Oehrle (1994). Though there are now several analyses of ellipsis phenomena in the literature of TLCG (Hendriks 1995, Morrill and Merenciano 1996, Jäger 2005, Barker 2013), so far as we are aware, this is the first analysis of pseudogapping in CG.

It should be noted at the outset that our choice of framework here should *not* be taken as an attempt to demonstrate the advantage of Hybrid TLCG over its many alternatives. In fact, so far as we can see, the core underlying idea of our proposal can be expressed in almost any of the contemporary variants of CG, including Multi-Modal Categorial Type Logics (Moortgat 1997, Bernardi 2002), the Displacement Calculus (Morrill 2010, Morrill et al. 2011) and the family of 'Linear Categorial Grammars' (LCGs) (Oehrle 1994, de Groote 2001, Muskens 2003, Mihaliček and Pollard 2012).[2] However, formulating the analysis in Hybrid TLCG enables us to compare two types of treatments of discontinuous constituency that are respectively associated with the 'standard' TLCG tradition (especially the so-called 'multi-modal' variants thereof) and LCGs (which are equipped with λ-binding in the prosodic component). So far as we are aware, the literature remains utterly silent as to which of the two types of approaches to discontinuity is empirically (as opposed to purely theoretically or computationally) superior, or whether they are largely notational variants of each other as far as empirical coverage is concerned.[3] However, as we discuss below, even in the small domain of pseudogapping, the choice between the two alternative approaches to discontinuous constituency has a nontrivial consequence for the range of sentences that are predicted to be grammatical. For this reason, we believe that a general framework like ours which accomodates different analytic techniques originally developed in different traditions is useful for the purpose of cross-framework comparison. Our hope is that such a cross-framework comparison will ultimately lead us to a better understanding of what kinds of formal techniques are most optimal for the analysis of natural language syntax.

2 Pseudogapping in Type-Logical Categorial Grammar

2.1 Hybrid Type-Logical Categorial Grammar

(Non-modalized) Hybrid TLCG is essentially an extension of the Lambek calculus (Lambek 1958) with one additional, non-directional mode of implication.[4]

---

[2] An empirical argument for our approach over the theoretically more spartan LCGs comes from a different empirical domain, one involving coordination. See Kubota (2010: section 3.2.1) and Kubota and Levine (2013a: section 3.6) for the relevant discussion. See also Worth (2014) for some initial attempts at simulating a Hybrid TLCG analysis of coordination in an LCG.

[3] But see Kubota (2010, 2014), which argue for the (potentially controversial) position that both of these two techniques are needed for the analysis of complex interactions between coordination, scope-taking operators and complex predicates in Japanese.

[4] We sketch a multi-modal version below, which goes beyond this characterization.

Since Hybrid TLCG utilizes both the directional slashes (/ and \) from the Lambek calculus and a non-directional slash (notated as |) from LCGs, we start from the definition of syntactic types.[5]

(2)   Atomic types include (at least) NP, N and S.

(3)   Directional types
     a.   An atomic type is a directional type.
     b.   If A and B are directional types, then A/B is a directional type.
     c.   If A and B are directional types, then $B\backslash A$ is a directional type.
     d.   Nothing else is a directional type.

(4)   Syntactic types
     a.   A directional type is a syntactic type.
     b.   If A and B are syntactic types, then $A|B$ is a syntactic type.
     c.   Nothing else is a syntactic type.

We then define the functions Sem and Pros which map syntactic types to semantic and prosodic types. The definition for semantic types is a standard one.

(5)   a.   For atomic syntactic types,
        $\mathsf{Sem}(NP) = e$, $\mathsf{Sem}(S) = t$, $\mathsf{Sem}(N) = e \to t$
     b.   For complex syntactic types,
        $\mathsf{Sem}(A/B) = \mathsf{Sem}(B\backslash A) = \mathsf{Sem}(A|B) = \mathsf{Sem}(B) \to \mathsf{Sem}(A)$.

(6)   a.   For any directional type A, $\mathsf{Pros}(A) = \mathbf{st}$ (with $\mathbf{st}$ for 'strings').
     b.   For any complex syntactic type $A|B$ involving the vertical slash |,
        $\mathsf{Pros}(A|B) = \mathsf{Pros}(B) \to \mathsf{Pros}(A)$.

One thing that one immediately notices from the above definition of syntactic types is that although we have three connectives /, \ and |, the algebra of syntactic types is not a free algebra generated over the set of atomic types with these three binary connectives. We take this to be a feature, not a bug. For example, in Hybrid TLCG, a vertical slash cannot occur 'under' a directional slash.[6] Thus, an expression like S/(S|NP) is not a well-formed syntactic type according to (4). The intuition behind this is that such a type is ill-formed since directional slashes make sense only when the argument of the functor has a string phonology. Another thing to note is that there is an asymmetry between Sem and Pros as to how they treat the directional slashes / and \. The semantic types are 'read off' from syntactic types by taking all of /, \, | to be type constructors for functions (as expected), but for the mapping from syntactic types to prosodic

---

[5] We omit parentheses for a sequence of the same type of slash, assuming that / and | are left associative, and \ right associative. Thus, S/NP/NP, NP\NP\S and S|NP|NP are abbreviations of (S/NP)/NP, NP\(NP\S) and (S|NP)|NP, respectively.

[6] Note that in this respect, our calculus differs from the closely related Discontinuous Calculus of Morrill (2010) and Morrill et al. (2011).

types, only the vertical slash $|$ is effectively interpreted as functional. Thus, for example, $\mathsf{Sem}(S|(S/NP)) = (e \to t) \to t$ whereas $\mathsf{Pros}(S|(S/NP)) = \mathbf{st} \to \mathbf{st}$. Again, this is a feature, not a bug, one which we take to be motivated by linguistic considerations rather than meta-logical ones.

With this definition of syntactic types, we can formulate the syntactic rules of the calculus. Following Oehrle (1994) and Morrill (1994), we utilize the labelled deduction notation for writing syntactic rules. The total set of logical inference rules (formulated in the natural deduction format) are given in (7).[7]

(7) **Connective**   **Introduction**   **Elimination**

$$
/ \qquad
\frac{\begin{array}{ccc} \vdots & \vdots & \vdots \quad [\varphi;\, x;\, A]^n \quad \vdots & \vdots & \vdots \\ \hline \vdots \; \vdots & \vdots \; \vdots & \vdots \; \vdots \\ \hline b \circ \varphi;\, \mathscr{F};\, B \end{array}}{b;\, \lambda x.\mathscr{F};\, B/A}\, /\mathrm{I}^n
\qquad\qquad
\frac{a;\, \mathscr{F};\, A/B \quad b;\, \mathscr{G};\, B}{a \circ b;\, \mathscr{F}(\mathscr{G});\, A}\, /\mathrm{E}
$$

$$
\backslash \qquad
\frac{\begin{array}{ccc} \vdots & \vdots & \vdots \quad [\varphi;\, x;\, A]^n \quad \vdots & \vdots & \vdots \\ \hline \vdots \; \vdots & \vdots \; \vdots & \vdots \; \vdots \\ \hline \varphi \circ b;\, \mathscr{F};\, B \end{array}}{b;\, \lambda x.\mathscr{F};\, A\backslash B}\, \backslash \mathrm{I}^n
\qquad\qquad
\frac{b;\, \mathscr{G};\, B \quad a;\, \mathscr{F};\, B\backslash A}{b \circ a;\, \mathscr{F}(\mathscr{G});\, A}\, \backslash \mathrm{E}
$$

$$
| \qquad
\frac{\begin{array}{ccc} \vdots & \vdots & \vdots \quad [\varphi;\, x;\, A]^n \quad \vdots & \vdots & \vdots \\ \hline \vdots \; \vdots & \vdots \; \vdots & \vdots \; \vdots \\ \hline b;\, \mathscr{F};\, B \end{array}}{\lambda \varphi.b;\, \lambda x.\mathscr{F};\, B|A}\, |\mathrm{I}^n
\qquad\qquad
\frac{a;\, \mathscr{F};\, A|B \quad b;\, \mathscr{G};\, B}{a(b);\, \mathscr{F}(\mathscr{G});\, A}\, |\mathrm{E}
$$

The binary connective $\circ$ in the prosodic component designates the string concatenation operation and is associative in both directions (i.e. $(\varphi_1 \circ \varphi_2) \circ \varphi_3 \equiv \varphi_1 \circ (\varphi_2 \circ \varphi_3)$). Note also that, following Oehrle (1994), we admit functional phonological expressions in addition to simple strings (such expressions are manipulated by the Introduction and Elimination rules for $|$, whose prosodic 'effects' are lambda abstraction and function application, respectively).

The rules in (7) are the logical rules. There is also one non-logical rule called the P(rosodic)-interface rule, which replaces the prosodic labelling with an equivalent term in the calculus of prosodic objects, which is a type of lambda calculus:[8]

(8) P-interface rule

$$
\frac{\varphi_0;\, \mathscr{F};\, A}{\varphi_1;\, \mathscr{F};\, A}\, \mathrm{PI}
$$

(where φ_0 and φ_1 are equivalent terms in the prosodic calculus)

---

[7] For phonological variables we use Greek letters $\varphi_1, \varphi_2, \ldots$ (type $\mathbf{st}$); $\sigma_1, \sigma_2, \ldots$ (type $\mathbf{st} \to \mathbf{st}$, $\mathbf{st} \to \mathbf{st} \to \mathbf{st}$, etc.); $\tau_1, \tau_2, \ldots$ (type $(\mathbf{st} \to \mathbf{st}) \to \mathbf{st}$, etc.).

[8] See Kubota (2010) and Kubota and Pollard (2010) for formal details.

There are a couple of points worth noting. First, the prosodic labelling is used here for the purpose of narrowing down the set of possible derivations. In particular, it should be noted that word order is represented in the prosodic labelling in this system rather than the linear order of the premises, and that the applicability of (some of) the rules are constrained by the forms of these prosodic labels.[9] (This in turn means that the order of the premises in the three Elimination rules is immaterial.) Specifically, the Introduction rule for / (\) is applicable only when the variable φ that occurs in the phonology of the premise is on the right (left) periphery. In this sense, the labelling system makes a contribution on its own rather than being isomorphic to the structures of derivations. Note also that there is an asymmetry between | and /, \ in this respect too. Unlike the Introduction rules for / and \, the applicability of the Introduction rule for | is not restricted by the phonological labelling of the premise.

Second, the P-interface rule is the analog of the structural rules (or interaction postulates) in the more standard variants of TLCG (Morrill 1994, Moortgat 1997). This point becomes clearer when we extend the system by incorporating a multi-modal morpho-phonological component below. In a non-modalized system that we work with (except in section 2.3), the role of the P-interface rule is quite limited: it is used only for the purpose of replacing the prosodic labelling with a beta-equivalent term or rebracketing the structure (the latter of which is freely available since ∘ is associative in both directions). For the readability of proofs, we assume the application of this rule implicitly, leaving out all brackets from the prosodic terms and directly writing beta-reduced terms for the prosodic labelling (as well as for semantic labelling).

Third, although we do not attempt to provide an explicit translation, it should be intuitively clear that the present system without the rules for | is equivalent to the Lambek calculus **L** (Lambek 1958); if we instead remove the P-interface rule and retain only the rules for | from the set of logical rules, the system is essentially equivalent to ACG and Lambda grammar.[10] Note also that in this latter case, the prosodic labelling becomes isomorphic to the structure of the derivations (and this is true for semantic labelling too, on the condition that one doesn't allow for beta reduction of semantic translations in the derivations).

We now highlight some interesting properties of Hybrid TLCG. First, in Hybrid TLCG, LCG-type lexical entries for verbs with functional phonologies and Lambek-type lexical entries for verbs with string phonologies are interderivable. The proofs are shown in (9) and (10).

---

[9] We follow Morrill (1994) in this respect. As far as we are aware, Morrill (1994) was the first to recast the Lambek calculus in this labelled deduction format.

[10] Linear Grammar (Mihaliček and Pollard 2012, Worth 2014) is different from its kin in the family of LCGs in that it does not assume a functional mapping from syntactic types to either semantic types or prosodic types. Instead the mapping is relational (see in particular Worth (2014: section 1.1) for an explicit statement of this point). We could relax our definitions of Sem and Pros to make our framework compatible with this assumption.

(9)

$$\cfrac{\cfrac{\lambda\varphi_3\lambda\varphi_4.\ \varphi_4\circ\text{met}\circ\varphi_3;\ \textbf{meet};(S|NP)|NP \qquad \begin{bmatrix}\varphi_1;\\x;\\NP\end{bmatrix}^1}{\begin{bmatrix}\varphi_2;\\y;\\NP\end{bmatrix}^2 \qquad \cfrac{\lambda\varphi_4.\varphi_4\circ\text{met}\circ\varphi_1;\ \textbf{meet}(x);S|NP}{}|E}}{\cfrac{\cfrac{\varphi_2\circ\text{met}\circ\varphi_1;\ \textbf{meet}(x)(y);S}{\text{met}\circ\varphi_1;\ \lambda y.\textbf{meet}(x)(y);NP\backslash S}\backslash I^2}{\text{met};\ \lambda x\lambda y.\textbf{meet}(x)(y);(NP\backslash S)/NP}/I^1}|E$$

(10)

$$\cfrac{\cfrac{\cfrac{\text{met};\ \textbf{meet};\ (NP\backslash S)/NP \qquad \begin{bmatrix}\varphi_1;\\x;NP\end{bmatrix}^1}{\begin{bmatrix}\varphi_2;\\y;NP\end{bmatrix}^2 \qquad \cfrac{\text{met}\circ\varphi_1;\ \textbf{meet}(x);NP\backslash S}{}/E}}{\cfrac{\varphi_2\circ\text{met}\circ\varphi_1;\ \textbf{meet}(x)(y);S}{\lambda\varphi_2.\varphi_2\circ\text{met}\circ\varphi_1;\ \lambda y.\textbf{meet}(x)(y);S|NP}|I^2}\backslash E}{\lambda\varphi_1\lambda\varphi_2.\varphi_2\circ\text{met}\circ\varphi_1;\ \lambda x\lambda y.\textbf{meet}(x)(y);(S|NP)|NP}|I^1$$

Note also that a type S/(NP\S) entry for a quantifier (for the subject position) is derivable from the type S|(S|NP) type entry ($\textbf{V}_{\textbf{person}}$ abbreviates the term $\lambda P.\forall x[\textbf{person}(x)\rightarrow P(x)]$):

(11)

$$\cfrac{\lambda\sigma.\sigma(\text{everyone});\ \textbf{V}_{\textbf{person}};S|(S|NP) \qquad \cfrac{\cfrac{\cfrac{[\varphi_1;x;NP]^1 \quad [\varphi_2;P;NP\backslash S]^2}{\varphi_1\circ\varphi_2;P(x);S}\backslash E}{\lambda\varphi_1.\varphi_1\circ\varphi_2;\lambda x.P(x);S|NP}|I^1}{\text{everyone}\circ\varphi_2;\ \textbf{V}_{\textbf{person}}(\lambda x.P(x));S}|E}{\text{everyone};\ \lambda P.\textbf{V}_{\textbf{person}}(\lambda x.P(x));S/(NP\backslash S)}/I^2$$

We call this type of proof *slanting*. Slanting is a general set of theorems. For example, a type (S/NP)\S entry (for the object position) and a type (S/NP/NP)\(S/NP) entry (e.g., for a medial quantifier in a sentence like *Kim showed everyone Felix*) for a quantifier are also derivable from the type S|(S|NP) entry (derivations are omitted due to space limitations).

But importantly, a proof in the other direction doesn't go through.

(12)

$$\cfrac{\text{everyone};\ \textbf{V}_{\textbf{person}};\ S/(NP\backslash S) \qquad \cfrac{\cfrac{[\sigma;P;S|NP]^1 \quad [\varphi;x;NP]^2}{\sigma(\varphi);P(x);S}|E}{???;\lambda x.P(x);NP\backslash S}\backslash I^2}{\text{FAIL}}$$

The proof fails at the step where we try to apply \I to derive the category NP\S. In order for this rule to be applicable, the prosodic variable φ for the hypothesis to be withdrawn needs to occupy the left periphery of the phonology of the premise. But the term $\sigma(\varphi)$ does not tell us where the variable φ occurs inside the whole term. The failure of this proof is intuitively the right result, since a quantifier with syntactic category S/(NP\S) has a more restricted distribution (limited to the subject position) than one with the category S|(S|NP) (which can appear in any argument position).

As discussed in Kubota and Levine (2013a, 2014), slanting has many important empirical consequences, especially in situations where a semantic operator that appears outside of coordination syntactically is semantically distributed to each conjunct.

2.2   The Basic Analysis of Pseudogapping

Our analysis builds on some ideas from the previous literature. In particular, we follow Miller (1990) in assuming that the ellipsis in pseudogapping essentially involves an anaphoric mechanism. But we also borrow from the transformational approaches (whose insight goes back to Kuno (1981)) the idea that pseudogapping and VP ellipsis are derived by essentially the same mechanism.

The key underlying idea is very simple: pseudogapping in examples like (13) is just transitive verb ellipsis. In VP ellipsis as in (14), the whole VP is deleted, and its meaning is resolved by anaphorically referring back to the VP in the antecedent clause. Pseudogapping is different only in that what's missing is not a full VP but just the verb. But the key anaphoric mechanism that retrieves the missing meaning is the same.

(13)   John can eat the pear. Bill can ∅ the fig.

(14)   John can sing. Bill can't ∅.

In this section, we first formulate an analysis of pseudogapping using directional slashes alone, demonstrating that the core analysis of pseudogapping can be formulated in a purely directional calculus. In the next section, we turn to some empirical challenges that this analysis faces in the domain of discontinuous pseudogapping and sketch two alternative solutions for that problem, each building on different types of techniques for handling discontinuous constituency. A comparison of these two alternatives suggests that the two approaches make different predictions as to the range of admissible pseudogapping sentences. We take this conclusion to be suggestive of the kinds of considerations that one should bear in mind in applying formal techniques to the analysis of linguistic data.

We start with an analysis of VP ellipsis, and then extend the analysis to pseudogapping. The basic idea is that VP ellipsis is licensed by an alternative sign for the auxiliary verb that does not subcategorize for a VP but instead anaphorically retrieves the relevant VP meaning in reference to the preceding discourse. For this purpose, we posit the following empty operator that applies to the lexical sign of auxiliaries of the form in (16) and saturates the VP argument slot that it subcategorizes for (here and in what follows, we use VP, TV and DTV as abbreviations for NP\S, (NP\S)/NP and (NP\S)/NP/NP, respectively).

(15) ε; $\lambda \mathscr{F}.\mathscr{F}(P)$; VP/(VP/VP)
         where P is a free variable whose value is identified with the meaning of some linguistic sign in the preceding discourse with category VP

(16)   can; $\lambda P \lambda x.\Diamond P(x)$; VP/VP

With (15), (17) is analyzed as in (18) (here and in what follows, the syntactic category of the sign that antecedes the VP ellipsis is set in boldface).

(17)   John can sing. Bill can't ∅.

(18)

	can; $\lambda P\lambda x.\Diamond P(x);$ VP/VP	sing; sing; **VP**		$\varepsilon;$ $\lambda\mathscr{F}.\mathscr{F}(\textbf{sing});$ VP/(VP/VP)	can't; $\lambda P\lambda x.\neg\Diamond P(x);$ VP/VP
john; j; NP	can ∘ sing; $\lambda x.\Diamond\textbf{sing}(x);$ VP		bill; b; NP	can't; $\lambda x.\neg\Diamond\textbf{sing}(x);$ VP	

john ∘ can ∘ sing;   bill ∘ can't;
$\Diamond\textbf{sing}(\textbf{j});$ S $\neg\Diamond\textbf{sing}(\textbf{b});$ S

Some comments are in order as to our choice of this analysis involving an empty operator. There are at least three alternatives to this approach: (i) an analysis involving binding of a hypothetical VP to an antecedent VP (Morrill et al. 2011); (ii) one that posits an empty VP; and (iii) one that posits an alternative auxiliary entry (identical to the output of our syntactic empty operator) in the lexicon (Jäger 2005). The binding approach does not extend to intersentential anaphora easily; especially problematic are cases where VP ellipsis occurs across speakers. The present approach is superior to an empty VP approach in capturing the generalization that auxiliaries (including the 'infinitive marker' *to*) are the triggers of VP ellipsis.[11] We believe that our approach is superior to a lexical approach (i.e. (iii)) in straightforwardly generalizing to the pseudogapping case (see below). It is not clear whether one can arrive at a general characterization of the set of alternative entries for the auxiliary on a purely lexical approach like Jäger's (2005).

This approach has at least the same empirical coverage as previous analyses of VP ellipsis in TLCG (Morrill and Merenciano 1996, Jäger 2005). Although space limitations preclude a detailed demonstration, it can account for interactions between VP ellipsis and other phenomena such as quantifier scope and strict/sloppy ambiguity exemplified by well-known examples (such as the $\forall >$ **before** reading for *John read every book before Bill did* and the strict/sloppy ambiguity of *John talked to his boss. Bill did, too*).

There is some evidence that English allows for TV ellipsis other than in pseudogapping. Jacobson (1992, 2008) argues that antecedent contained deletion is to be analyzed as TV ellipsis rather than VP ellipsis. The idea is that in (19), what is missing after *had* is just the transitive verb *showed* instead of a full VP.

(19)   John showed Bill every place that Harry already had.

This requires analyzing auxiliaries in the category TV/TV instead of VP/VP and generalizing the entry for the VP ellipsis operator accordingly (see below in (21)). In the present TLCG setup, the TV/TV entry for the auxiliary can be derived from the more basic VP/VP entry as an instance of the Geach theorem:

---

[11] Note in this connection that the entry in (15) is a simplification, since, as it is, it can combine with any VP/VP. We take it that there is an additional constraint on this empty operator that it can only combine with expressions that have the phonologies of auxiliaries (such as *do*, *should* and *will*). This constraint could be stated easily if the operator instead had the syntactic category VP|(VP/VP) (involving the vertical slash) and phonology $\lambda\varphi.\varphi$ (which would take us from the directional fragment we are working with), in which case it could simply be stated as a restriction on the phonology of the linguistic expression that this operator takes as an argument.

(20)

$$\frac{\dfrac{[\varphi_2; f; \mathrm{TV}]^2 \quad [\varphi_3; x; \mathrm{NP}]^3}{\varphi_2 \circ \varphi_3; f(x); \mathrm{VP}}}{\mathrm{had}; \lambda P \lambda y. P(y); \mathrm{VP/VP}}$$

$$\frac{\mathrm{had} \circ \varphi_2 \circ \varphi_3; \lambda y. f(x)(y); \mathrm{VP}}{\dfrac{\mathrm{had} \circ \varphi_2; \lambda x \lambda y. f(x)(y); \mathrm{TV}}{\mathrm{had}; \lambda f \lambda x \lambda y. f(x)(y); \mathrm{TV/TV}} \text{/I}^2} \text{/I}^3$$

For more details of the analysis of antecedent contained deletion, see Jacobson (1992, 2008).

We schematize the ellipsis operator in (15) using Steedman's (2000) $-notation, since pseudogapping is sometimes not just TV ellipsis, but also DTV ellipsis, etc.:

(21) $\varepsilon; \lambda \mathscr{F}.\mathscr{F}(P); (\mathrm{VP/\$})/((\mathrm{VP/\$})/(\mathrm{VP/\$}))$

where P is a free variable whose value is identified with the meaning of some linguistic sign in the preceding discourse with category VP/$

VP/$ is a metavariable notation for a set of categories where any number of arguments (of any category) are sought via / (VP, VP/NP, VP/NP/PP, etc.). The three occurrences of VP/$ in (21) are to be instantiated in the same way.

Basic pseudogapping like (22) can then be analyzed as in (23). The auxiliary is first derived as TV/TV (cf. (20)) before the 'VP ellipsis' operator applies.

(22)   John should eat the pear. Bill should ∅ the fig.

(23)

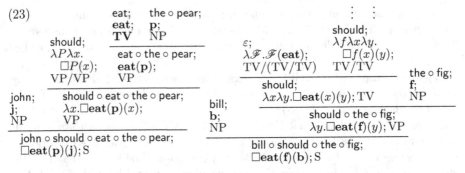

Miller (1990) discusses an interesting type of example of the following form, in which a ditransitive verb instantiates different subcategorization frames (V NP NP vs. V NP PP) in the antecedent clause and the pseudogapping clause:

(24)   I will give Mary my books if YOU will ∅ your records to Ann.

Miller claims that examples like this pose problems for syntactic approaches. Our analysis can accomodate such examples rather straightforwardly, by employing the ∧ connective from Morrill (1994) and Bayer (1996) originally used for the analysis of unlike category coordination. Specifically, by specifying the alternative subcategorization frames for ditransitives with this connective in the lexicon[12] and by assuming that the ellipsis operator can access either of the two category-meaning pairs of such signs, (24) can be analyzed as in (25).

---

[12] See Kubota and Levine (2013b) for independent evidence for this assumption in the context of argument cluster coordination.

(25)

give;
$\langle \lambda x \lambda y \lambda z.\textbf{give}(x)(y)(z),$
$\lambda y \lambda x \lambda z.\textbf{give}(x)(y)(z) \rangle;$
$\dfrac{(VP/PP/NP) \wedge (\textbf{VP}/\textbf{NP}/\textbf{NP})}{\text{give; } \lambda x \lambda y \lambda z.\textbf{give}(x)(y)(z); \text{ VP/PP/NP}}$
my ○ books;
my-bks;
NP

$\dfrac{\text{give ○ my ○ books;}}{\lambda y \lambda z.\textbf{give}(\textbf{my-bks})(y)(z); \text{VP/PP}}$
to ○ mary;
m; PP

will;
$\lambda P \lambda x.$
$\dfrac{P(x);}{\text{VP/VP}}$

i;
i;
NP

$\dfrac{\text{give ○ my ○ books ○ to ○ mary;}}{\lambda z.\textbf{give}(\textbf{my-bks})(\textbf{m})(z); \text{VP}}$

$\dfrac{\text{will ○ give ○ my ○ books ○ to ○ mary; } \lambda z.\textbf{give}(\textbf{my-bks})(\textbf{m})(z); \text{VP}}{\text{i ○ will ○ give ○ my ○ books ○ to ○ mary; } \textbf{give}(\textbf{my-bks})(\textbf{m})(\textbf{i}); \text{S}}$

$\varepsilon;$
$\lambda \mathcal{F}.\mathcal{F}(\lambda y \lambda x \lambda z.$
$\textbf{give}(x)(y)(z));$
DTV/(DTV/DTV)

will;
$\lambda f \lambda x \lambda y \lambda z.f(x)(y)(z);$
(VP/NP/NP)/(VP/NP/NP)

ann;
a;
NP

your ○ records;
your-rcs;
NP

$\dfrac{\text{will; } \lambda x \lambda y \lambda z.\textbf{give}(y)(x)(z); \text{ DTV}}{\text{will ○ ann; } \lambda y \lambda z.\textbf{give}(y)(\textbf{a})(z); \text{ TV}}$

you;
you;
NP

$\dfrac{\text{will ○ ann ○ your ○ records; } \lambda z.\textbf{give}(\textbf{your-rcs})(\textbf{a})(z); \text{ VP}}{\text{you ○ will ○ ann ○ your ○ records; } \textbf{give}(\textbf{your-rcs})(\textbf{a})(\textbf{you}); \text{ S}}$

As the following examples show, the 'deleted' material in pseudogapping is not necessarily a syntactic constituent in the traditional sense:

(26)   a.   You can't **take the lining out of** that coat. You can ∅ this one.

   b.   It [an enema] **leaves some water in** you. At least, it does ∅ me.

   c.   I **expect this idea to be** a problem more than you do ∅ a solution.

In an associative calculus (like the present one), such examples are straightforward. Strings like *take the lining out of* are directly licenseable as constituents, and the ellipsis operator simply refers to such constituents in the antecedent clause for anaphora resolution.[13]

2.3   Discontinuous Pseudogapping

Although a directional calculus is good at handling examples like (26), where the 'nonconstituent' that the ellipsis operator targets is a contiguous string, discontinuous pseudogapping exemplified by data such as the following poses a problem for the purely directional analysis of pseudogapping presented above:

(27)   a.   Although I didn't **give** Bill **the book**, I did ∅ Susan ∅.

   b.   She **found** her co-worker **attractive** but she didn't ∅ her husband ∅.

---

[13] More challenging cases come from examples involving split antecedents (Miller 1990):

(i)   John **saw** Mary and Peter **heard** Ann, but neither did ∅ me.

Here, it seems likely that we would need to relax the condition on anaphora resolution in such a way that the free variable P can be instantiated not just as the meaning of a *single* antecedent verb but a conjunction or disjunction of such antecedent verbs.

An Analysis of Discontinuous Constituency with 'Wrapping'. One way to handle discontinuity is to assume a 'wrapping' operation (Bach 1979, 1984, Dowty 1982), where the elided discontinuous string in examples like those in (27) are units in the combinatoric structure to which the element in the middle is 'infixed'. In the so-called 'multi-modal' variants of TLCG (see, e.g., Morrill (1994), Moortgat and Oehrle (1994), Bernardi (2002)), wrapping is formalized as a string manipulation operation in an algebra that governs surface morpho-phonological realization of linguistic expressions. Here we adopt a particular implementation of this general idea worked out in Kubota (2010) and Kubota and Pollard (2010). In this approach, the prosodic component of a linguistic expression is a term in a preordered algebra, and the ordering relation imposed on this algebra governs the various reordering and restructuring operations pertaining to surface morpho-syntactic constituency.

For our purposes, it suffices to distinguish between two modes of composition in the prosodic algebra: the ordinary concatenation mode ($\circ$) and the infixation mode (which we notate as $\circ$.). Prosodic terms are ordered in the prosodic algebra by the *deducibility* relation between terms (where $\varphi_1 \leq \varphi_2$ is to be read 'φ_2 is deducible from φ_1'), where beta-equivalent terms are inter-deducible and there are mode-specific deducibility relations. In our impoverished fragment (which deals with wrapping in English only), it suffices to posit just one deducibility relation of the following form:

(28) $(A \circ. B) \circ C \leq (A \circ C) \circ B$

The intuition behind this is that when A and B are combined in the infixation mode, an expression C that combines with that unit at a later point in the derivation can be infixed in the middle by a surface morpho-phonological reordering operation. The P-interface rule is slightly revised so that it now refers to the deducibility relation rather than the equivalence relation between the terms.

(29)   P-interface rule
$$\frac{\varphi_0;\ \mathscr{F};\ A}{\varphi_1;\ \mathscr{F};\ A}\ \text{PI}$$
(where $\varphi_0 \leq \varphi_1$ holds in the prosodic calculus)

The syntactic rules of the calculus are also revised to take into account the sensitivity to modes of composition (for space reasons, we only reproduce the rules for /, but the rules for \ are similarly revised; the rules for | remain the same as above):

(30)   **Connective**   **Introduction**   **Elimination**

$$/ \qquad \frac{\begin{array}{c}[\varphi;\ x;\ A]^n \\ \vdots \\ b \circ_i \varphi;\ \mathscr{F};\ B\end{array}}{b;\ \lambda x.\mathscr{F};\ B/_i A}\ /\text{I}^n \qquad \frac{a;\ \mathscr{F};\ A/_i B \quad b;\ \mathscr{G};\ B}{a \circ_i b;\ \mathscr{F}(\mathscr{G});\ A}\ /\text{E}$$

We can then analyze (27a) as follows:[14]

(31)

$$
\begin{array}{c}
\dfrac{\text{give;} \atop \text{give; VP/NP/.NP} \quad \text{thebook;} \atop \text{the-book; NP}}{\text{give } \circ. \text{ thebook; give(the-book); } \textbf{VP/NP}} \\
\end{array}
$$

give;
give; VP/NP/.NP   the-book; NP
───────────────────────────────────
give ∘. thebook; give(the-book); **VP/NP**   bill;
                                                b; NP
───
didn't;   (give ∘. thebook) ∘ bill; **give(the-book)(b); VP**
λPλx.¬P(x);   ─── PI
VP/VP   give ∘ bill ∘ thebook; **give(the-book)(b); VP**
───
i;
i; NP   didn't ∘ give ∘ bill ∘ thebook; λx.¬**give(the-book)(b)(x); VP**
───
   i ∘ didn't ∘ give ∘ bill ∘ thebook; ¬**give(the-book)(b)(i); S**

⋮   ⋮

ε;
λ𝓕.𝓕(**give(the-book)**);   did;
TV/(TV/TV)   λfλxλy.f(x)(y);
                             TV/TV
── susan;
    did; λxλy.**give(the-book)(x)(y); TV**   s; NP
───
i;
i; NP   did ∘ susan; λy.**give(the-book)(s)(y); VP**
───
     i ∘ did ∘ susan; **give(the-book)(s)(i); S**

The point of this derivation is that the (surface) discontinuous string *give __ the book* behaves as a unit in the tectogrammatical derivation (motivation for this assumption comes from patterns of argument structure-sensitive phenomena such as passivization and binding; see, for example, Dowty (1982, 1996)). The pseudogapping operator can then directly refer to the syntactic category and the semantics of this 'underlying constituent' to supply the relevant subcategorization frame and the meaning of the missing TV to the auxiliary, just in the same way as in the non-discontinuous pseudogapping examples above. (27b) can be analyzed in the same way by assuming that the verb-adjective pair *find __ attractive* is a discontinuous constituent that wraps around the direct object *her co-worker*.

Discontinuous Constituency with Prosodic λ-Binding. Another approach to discontinuity is to exploit λ-binding in prosody in LCGs (see also the closely related mechanism involving the 'Lambda' structural postulate in some versions of the Continuation-based Grammar (Barker 2007, Barker and Shan to appear)). In fact, we can formulate the whole analysis of pseudogapping in a subset of Hybrid TLCG involving only the vertical slash (thus simulating a purely LCG analysis). This involves systematically replacing the lexical entries for all lexical items (including the VP ellipsis operator) with ones involving only the vertical slash. The analysis for the basic pseudogapping sentence then goes as follows (here, VP' and TV' respectively abbreviate S|NP and S|NP|NP):

---

[14] We are here ignoring the internal structure of the NP *the book*. For the analysis to properly interact with the wrapping rule in (28), the determiner and the noun need to be combined in a mode that is distinct from the concatenation mode (∘).

(32)

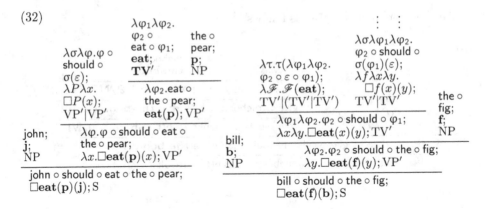

The lexical entry for the pseudogapping operator in (32) already enables us to treat the discontinuous pseudogapping example in (27a). To see this, note that, in this kind of setup, the elided discontinuous constituent *give __ the book* can be analyzed as an expression that has exactly the same syntactic type S|NP|NP as the transitive verb that is elided in the normal pseudogapping example above. This is shown in (33). The pseudogapping clause *I did Susan* can then be analyzed in exactly the same way as in the above example in (32).

(33)

$$\lambda\varphi_1\lambda\varphi_2\lambda\varphi_3.$$
$$\varphi_3 \circ \text{give} \circ \varphi_1 \circ \varphi_2;$$
$$\lambda x\lambda y\lambda z.\text{give}(y)(x)(z);$$
$$\text{DTV}' \qquad \begin{bmatrix} \varphi; \\ x; \\ \text{NP} \end{bmatrix}^1$$

$$\lambda\varphi_2\lambda\varphi_3.\varphi_3 \circ \text{give} \circ \varphi \circ \varphi_2; \qquad \text{the} \circ \text{book};$$
$$\lambda y\lambda z.\text{give}(y)(x)(z); \text{TV}' \qquad \textbf{the-book}; \text{NP}$$

$$\lambda\varphi_3.\varphi_3 \circ \text{give} \circ \varphi \circ \text{the} \circ \text{book};$$
$$\lambda z.\textbf{give}(\textbf{the-book})(x)(z); \text{VP}'$$

$$\lambda\sigma\lambda\varphi. \qquad \lambda\varphi\lambda\varphi_3.\varphi_3 \circ \text{give} \circ \varphi \circ \text{the} \circ \text{book}; \qquad \text{bill};$$
$$\varphi \circ \text{didn't} \circ \sigma(\varepsilon); \qquad \lambda x\lambda z.\textbf{give}(\textbf{the-book})(x)(z); \textbf{TV}' \qquad \text{b}; \text{NP}$$
$$\lambda P\lambda x.\neg P(x);$$
$$(\text{S|NP})|(\text{S|NP}) \qquad \lambda\varphi_3.\varphi_3 \circ \text{give} \circ \text{bill} \circ \text{the} \circ \text{book};$$
i; $\qquad\qquad\qquad \lambda z.\textbf{give}(\textbf{the-book})(\textbf{b})(z); \text{VP}'$
i;
NP $\quad \lambda\varphi.\varphi \circ \text{didn't} \circ \text{give} \circ \text{bill} \circ \text{the} \circ \text{book}; \lambda z.\neg\textbf{give}(\textbf{the-book})(\textbf{b})(z); \text{VP}'$

i $\circ$ didn't $\circ$ give $\circ$ bill $\circ$ the $\circ$ book; $\neg\textbf{give}(\textbf{the-book})(\textbf{b})(\textbf{i}); \text{S}$

Comparison of the Two Approaches to Discontinuity. The question at this point is whether there are any principled grounds for choosing one approach to discontinuity over the other. Since wrapping is lexically-triggered (at least in most proposals), the wrapping-based analysis predicts that discontinuous pseudogapping is possible only when the elided material is a tectogrammatical constituent reflecting the combinatorial property of some lexical item. By contrast, LCGs are equipped with a much more general mechanism for syntactically deriving various sorts of discontinuous constituents. It is then predicted on this latter approach that any discontinuous constituent that can be so derived should in principle be able to undergo pseudogapping. From the (admittedly limited) investigation we have conducted so far, it seems that the 'wrapping'-type approach captures the distribution of pseudogapping in English better than an LCG-type approach. Thus, we tentatively conclude that the former is a more appropriate type of analysis at least so far as pseudogapping is concerned. For example, in addition to the examples above the LCG-type analysis can easily license an example like the following, which however does not seem to be an acceptable instance of pseudogapping:[15]

(34)   *John **laughed when** Bill **arrived**, but he didn't ∅ Sue ∅.

3   Conclusion

There are a couple of useful conclusions to draw from the above analysis of pseudogapping. The first obvious point is that as long as we limit our attention to basic examples such as pseudogapping of a simple transitive verb, we are not likely to arrive at any interesting observations which may potentially distinguish between the predictions of different approaches, since basic examples can be handled in some way or other in any approach. This means that, in order to test the predictions of different approaches (and compare their empirical adequacies), we need to examine more complex cases in which the phenomenon in question interacts with other linguistic phenomena. This is a very basic methodological principle in any scientific domain, but this type of inquiry seems to be significantly underrepresented in the current literature of CG. We have demonstrated in this paper that, in the case of pseudogapping, data that enable this type of potential theory comparison come from interactions between pseudogapping and discontinuous constituency. Our comparison of the 'wrapping'-type analysis and the prosodic λ-binding-based analysis of discontinuous constituency revealed that the latter potentially allows for a much wider range of examples to be licensed by the grammar. This seems to allow for too much flexibility in the patterns exhibited by pseudogapping, and we have tentatively concluded that the 'wrapping'-type analysis seems more appropriate for the analysis of discontinuous pseudogapping. This of course does not mean that prosodic λ-binding in LCGs is an inappropriate tool for the analysis of natural language. It only means that care should be taken in applying such a powerful tool, and that, with any theoretical tool and any empirical phenomenon, one needs to weigh

---

[15] Levin (1979) provides several examples of (apparent) discontinuous pseudogapping. So far as we can tell, all of her examples belong to one of the following three classes: (i) antecedentless pseudogapping; (ii) pseudogapping combined with an independent nominal ellipsis or adjunct ellipsis; (iii) wrapping-type pseudogapping. For example, her (36) on p. 77 *Does it [writing a check at a grocery store] usually take this long? – No, it never did me before* can be analyzed as an instance of (i), where what's missing after *did* is simply the verb (plus preposition) *happen to*. We take such data to be analyzed along lines similar to antecedentless VP ellipsis discussed in Miller and Pullum (2012). Examples such as (1) on p. 75 *We'll share it–like we do ∅ the pink [blouse]* is an instance of (ii), where the ellipsis of *blouse* after *pink* is nominal ellipsis independent of pseudogapping.

the pros and cons of applying the former to the latter based on several criteria, including the issue of overgeneration (which was prominent in our discussion above) as well as the generality and simplicity of the analysis (which, in the case of other phenomena, such as quantifier scope and extraction, may argue in favor of employing a λ-binding-based technique over other types of techniques). In any event, we believe that it is only through such theory comparison based on careful empirical study (and one that seriously attempts to maintain the best balance between multiple, often conflicting theoretical desiderata) that we can ultimately arrive at a better understanding of what kinds of formal techniques are indispensable (or most optimal) for the analysis of natural language.

Acknowledgments. We thank three anonymous reviewers for LACL, whose pertinent observations and questions have helped us (re-)articulate the presentation of the paper substantially. Thanks are also due to Carl Pollard and Chris Worth. The first author acknowledges the financial support from the Japan Society for the Promotion of Science (Postdoctoral Fellowship for Research Abroad).

References

Bach, E.: Control in Montague grammar. Linguistic Inquiry 10, 515–531 (1979)

Bach, E.: Some generalizations of categorial grammars. In: Landman, F., Veltman, F. (eds.) Varieties of Formal Semantics, pp. 1–23. Foris Publications, Dordrecht (1984)

Barker, C.: Parasitic scope. Linguistics and Philosophy 30, 407–444 (2007)

Barker, C.: Scopability and sluicing. Linguistics and Philosophy 36, 187–223 (2013)

Barker, C., Shan, C.C.: Continuations and Natural Language. Oxford University Press, Oxford (to appear)

Bayer, S.: The coordination of unlike categories. Language 72, 579–616 (1996)

Bernardi, R.: Reasoning with Polarity in Categorial Type Logic. Ph.D. thesis, University of Utrecht (2002)

de Groote, P.: Towards abstract categorial grammars. ACL 39/EACL 10, 148–155 (2001)

Dowty, D.: Grammatical relations and Montague Grammar. In: Jacobson, P., Pullum, G.K. (eds.) The Nature of Syntactic Representation, pp. 79–130. Reidel, Dordrecht (1982)

Dowty, D.: Non-constituent coordination, wrapping, and multimodal categorial grammars (1996). Expanded draft of a paper published in Dalla Chiara, M. L., et al. (eds.) Structures and Norms in Science, pp. 347–368 (1997), ftp://ftp.ling.ohio-state.edu/pub/dowty/nccwmmcg.ps.gz

Gengel, K.: Pseudogapping and Ellipsis. Oxford University Press, Oxford (2013)

Hendriks, P.: Comparatives and Categorial Grammar. Ph.D. thesis, University of Groningen (1995)

Jacobson, P.: Antecedent contained deletion in a variable-free semantics. In: Barker, C., Dowty, D. (eds.) Proceedings of SALT 2, pp. 193–213. Department of Linguistics, Ohio State University (1992)

Jacobson, P.: Direct compositionality and variable-free semantics: the case of Antecedent Contained Deletion. In: Johnson, K. (ed.) Topics in Ellipsis, pp. 30–68. Cambridge University Press, Cambridge (2008)

Jäger, G.: Anaphora and Type-Logical Grammar. Springer, Berlin (2005)

Kubota, Y.: (In)flexibility of Constituency in Japanese in Multi-Modal Categorial Grammar with Structured Phonology. Ph.D. thesis, Ohio State University (2010)

Kubota, Y.: The logic of complex predicates: A deductive synthesis of 'argument sharing' and 'verb raising'. To appear in Natural Language and Linguistic Theory (2014)

Kubota, Y., Levine, R.: Gapping as like-category coordination. In: Béchet, D., Dikovsky, A. (eds.) LACL 2012. LNCS, vol. 7351, pp. 135–150. Springer, Heidelberg (2012)

Kubota, Y., Levine, R.: Against ellipsis: Arguments for the direct licensing of 'non-canonical' coordinations. ms. Ohio State University (2013a)

Kubota, Y., Levine, R.: Coordination in Hybrid Type-Logical Categorial Grammar. In: OSU Working Papers in Linguistics, vol. 60, 21–50. Department of Linguistics, Ohio State University (2013b)

Kubota, Y., Levine, R.: Gapping as hypothetical reasoning. To appear in Natural Language and Linguistic Theory (2014)

Kubota, Y., Pollard, C.: Phonological interpretation into preordered algebras. In: Ebert, C., Jäger, G., Michaelis, J. (eds.) MOL 10. LNCS, vol. 6149, pp. 200–209. Springer, Heidelberg (2010)

Kuno, S.: The syntax of comparative clauses. In: Hendrick, R., Masek, C., Frances, M.M. (eds.) CLS 17, pp. 136–155. University of Chicago, Chicago (1981)

Lambek, J.: The mathematics of sentence structure. American Mathematical Monthly 65, 154–170 (1958)

Levin, N.S.: Main Verb Ellipsis in Spoken English. Ph.D. thesis, Ohio State University (1979)

Mihaliček, V., Pollard, C.: Distinguishing phenogrammar from tectogrammar simplifies the analysis of interrogatives. In: de Groote, P., Nederhof, M.-J. (eds.) Formal Grammar 2010/2011. LNCS, vol. 7395, pp. 130–145. Springer, Heidelberg (2012)

Miller, P.: Pseudogapping and do so substitution. In: CLS 26, vol. 1, pp. 293–305. Chicago Linguistic Society, Chicago (1990)

Miller, P., Pullum, G.K.: Exophoric VP ellipsis. ms., Université Paris Diderot and University of Edinburgh (2012)

Moortgat, M.: Categorial Type Logics. In: van Benthem, J., ter Meulen, A. (eds.) Handbook of Logic and Language, pp. 93–177. Elsevier, Amsterdam (1997)

Moortgat, M., Oehrle, R.T.: Adjacency, dependence, and order. In: Dekker, P., Stokhof, M. (eds.) Proceedings of the Ninth Amsterdam Colloquium, pp. 447–466. Instituut voor Taal, Logica, en Informatica, Universiteit van Amsterdam (1994)

Morrill, G.: Type Logical Grammar. Kluwer, Dordrecht (1994)

Morrill, G.: Categorial Grammar: Logical Syntax, Semantics, and Processing. Oxford University Press, Oxford (2010)

Morrill, G., Merenciano, J.-M.: Generalizing discontinuity. Traitement Automatique des Langues 27(2), 119–143 (1996)

Morrill, G., Valentín, O., Fadda, M.: The displacement calculus. Journal of Logic, Language and Information 20, 1–48 (2011)

Muskens, R.: Language, lambdas, and logic. In: Kruijff, G.-J., Oehrle, R. (eds.) Resource Sensitivity in Binding and Anaphora, pp. 23–54. Kluwer, Dordrecht (2003)

Oehrle, R.T.: Term-labeled categorial type systems. Linguistics and Philosophy 17(6), 633–678 (1994)

Steedman, M.: The Syntactic Process. The MIT Press, Cambridge (2000)

Worth, C.: The phenogrammar of coordination. In: Proceedings of the EACL 2014 Workshop on Type Theory and Natural Language Semantics (TTNLS), pp. 28–36. Association for Computational Linguistics, Gothenburg (2014)

Monotonicity Reasoning in Formal Semantics Based on Modern Type Theories

Georgiana E. Lungu and Zhaohui Luo*

Royal Holloway, University of London
Egham, Surrey TW20 0EX, U.K.
Georgiana.Lungu.2013@live.rhul.ac.uk, zhaohui.luo@hotmail.co.uk

Abstract. Modern type theories (MTTs) have been developed as a powerful foundation for formal semantics. In particular, it provides a useful platform for natural language inference (NLI) where proof assistants can be used for inference on computers. In this paper, we consider how monotonicity reasoning can be dealt in MTTs, so that it can contribute to NLI based on the MTT-semantics. We show that subtyping is crucial in monotonicity reasoning in MTTs because CNs are interpreted as types and therefore the monotonicity relations between CNs should be represented by the subtyping relations. In the past, monotonicity reasoning has only been considered for the arrow-types in the Montagovian setting of simple type theory. In MTT-semantics, richer type constructors involving dependent types and inductive types are employed in semantic representations. We show how to consider monotonicity reasoning that involve such type constructors and how this offers new useful mechanisms in monotonicity reasoning in MTTs.

1 Introduction

Natural Logic arose from the observation that monotonicity plays an important role in natural language reasoning. Its early studies were conducted in different fields including, for example, Sommers [23] in philosophy, van Benthem [24,25] in logic, Purdy [20] in computer science and Dowty [8] in linguistics. In general, the studies have been based on the Montague semantics (and hence Church's simple type theory) and influenced by the research on generalised quantifiers.

Formal semantics in Modern Type Theories (MTTs), or MTT-semantics for short, was first studied by Ranta in Martin-Löf's type theory [22] and, more recently, developed by the second author and his colleagues in a series of papers such as [14,6]. It provides us with not only a viable alternative to the Montague Semantics, but potentially an attractive full-blown semantic tool with advantages in many respects. In particular, it provides a useful platform for natural language inference (NLI) where the proof technology provided by proof assistants can be used for inference on computers; for example, there has been work on NLI in the Coq proof assistant based on the MTT-semantics [5].

---

* This work is partially supported by the research grant F/07-537/AJ of the Leverhulme Trust in U.K.

N. Asher and S. Soloviev (Eds.): LACL 2014, LNCS 8535, pp. 138–148, 2014.

In this paper, we study monotonicity reasoning in MTTs and this will provide the basis for monotonicity reasoning in NLI based on MTT-semantics. Since CNs are interpreted as types (not as predicates) in MTT-semantics, the notion of monotonicity between CNs needs to be expressed by a relationship between types – here, the subtyping relation plays a crucial role. More precisely, the logical inclusion relationship between CNs N_1 and N_2 is represented by means of the subtyping judgement $N_1 \leq N_2$.[1] We spell out some of the rules with NLI examples for explanation.

In the past, monotonicity reasoning has only been considered for the arrow-types (non-dependent function types) in the Montagovian setting of simple type theory. In MTT-semantics, richer type constructors are employed in semantic representations, examples of which include various dependent types and inductive types such as dependent sum types, dependent product types, disjoint union types, among others. Some other type constructors not in the traditional type theories are also used – an example of this is the dot-types used to represent copredication [14,28]. We show how to consider monotonicity reasoning that involves such type constructors and how this offers new useful mechanisms in monotonicity reasoning in MTTs.

The main contribution of the current paper is two-fold: It shows how to deal with monotonicity reasoning in MTTs, on the one hand, and studies monotonicity reasoning for various type constructors in MTTs and shows that this brings new power of monotonicity reasoning, on the other. We shall start with the introduction of monotonicity reasoning in MTTs in the following section, showing how coercive subtyping is used essentially in monotonicity reasoning in MTTs. Then, in §3, based on a typing of generalised quantifiers in MTTs, we analyze the left (right) increasing (decreasing) monotonicity rules, as it is defined in Montague's grammar but from the perspective of MTTs. Monotonicity involving various type constructors are studied in §4, where we consider as examples Σ-types, Π-types, disjoint union types and vector-types, showing the corresponding rules and NLI reasoning examples involving them. In the concluding remarks, future and some related work is discussed.

2   Monotonicity Reasoning in MTTs: An Introduction

In order to conduct monotonicity reasoning in MTTs and the associated proof assistants, we need to spell out how monotonicity should be formulated in MTTs. The original idea of monotonicity reasoning (see, for example, [25]) is to generalise the notion of logical consequence to arbitrary types in the simple type theory to arrive at a partial order $\Longrightarrow$ for each type. Notationally, we write

$$X \Longrightarrow_A Y$$

---

[1] Note that, in MTTs, the subtyping relationship $N_1 \leq N_2$ is *not* a logical proposition (of type *Prop*). Rather $N_1 \leq N_2$ is a *judgement*, at the same level as typing judgements like $a : A$. Coercive subtyping [11,17], implemented in the proof assistants Coq [7], Lego [16], Matita [19] and Plastic [2], is an adequate subtyping mechanism for MTTs and is employed here for monotonicity reasoning as well.

to mean that $X \Longrightarrow Y$ for X and Y of type A. For instance, for arrow types, one can define that, for $e, e' : A \to B$, $e \Longrightarrow_{A \to B} e'$ if, and only if, $e(x) \Longrightarrow_B e'(x)$ for all $x : A$. We shall extend this to other types in MTTs and, in this paper, we shall work in the type theory UTT [10].

The basic laws for monotonicity reasoning are:

$$\frac{X \Longrightarrow_A Y \quad F : A \to B \quad F \uparrow}{F(X) \Longrightarrow_B F(Y)} \qquad \frac{X \Longrightarrow_A Y \quad F : A \to B \quad F \downarrow}{F(Y) \Longrightarrow_B F(X)}$$

where $F \uparrow$ and $F \downarrow$ mean that F is $\Longrightarrow$-preserving and $\Longrightarrow$-reversing, respectively.

For some types, the monotonicity order is specialised. For instance, monotonicity on propositions is identified with logical consequence/implication; in symbols,[2]

$$p \Longrightarrow_{Prop} q \quad \text{is defined to be} \quad p \supset q.$$

From this and based on the above rules, it is rather straightforward to derive the following:

– For predicates P and P' of the same domain type A (formally, $P, P' : A \to Prop$), $P \Longrightarrow_{A \to Prop} P'$ if, and only if, $P(a) \supset P'(a)$ for every $a : A$.

In an MTT with subtyping, monotonicity on types is identified with the subtyping relation: for types A and B,

$$A \Longrightarrow B \quad \text{if and only if} \quad A \leq B,$$

where $A \leq B$ means that $A \leq_c B$ for some functional operation from A to B. For instance, let CN be the type universe of (the interpretations of) common nouns.[3] Then, for N_1 and N_2 in CN, $N_1 \Longrightarrow_{CN} N_2$ if, and only if, $N_1 \leq N_2$.

The above has set up the basic framework for monotonicity reasoning in MTTs. Here are some examples, which are mostly taken from [26] with slight modifications. They are examples that can already be done in simple type theory, though we consider them in the MTT setting. Further examples about binary quantifiers and other MTT type constructors can be found in §3. (We ignore the syntax/semantics difference in the examples.)

– Adverbs as sentence modifiers. For example, when **gracefully** is considered as a sentence modifier, we have: (1) and (2) imply (3). (Such explanations are omitted below.)

(1) **Mary dances** $\Longrightarrow_{Prop}$ **Mary moves**

---

[2] In UTT, *Prop* is the impredicative universe of logical propositions. For those unfamiliar with MTTs, it may also be good to know that every proposition in *Prop* is a type and this fact is used, for example, to form the Σ-type $\Sigma([\![man]\!], [\![handsome]\!])$ where $[\![handsome]\!]$ is a predicate, i.e., a proposition-valued function and hence a type-valued function.

[3] In the MTT-semantics, CNs are interpreted as types. This is different from the Montague semantics, where CNs are interpreted as predicates. See [13] for more information about this.

(2) gracefully : $Prop \to Prop$ is $\Longrightarrow$-preserving.

(3) Mary dances gracefully $\Longrightarrow_{Prop}$ Mary moves gracefully

- Alternatively, one may say that gracefully actually modifies verbs such as dance and move. If analysed like this, we have:

(4) dance $\Longrightarrow_{Human \to Prop}$ move

(5) gracefully : $(A : \text{CN})(A \to Prop) \to (A \to Prop)$ and gracefully(A) is $\Longrightarrow$-preserving for each A.

(6) dance gracefully $\Longrightarrow_{Human \to Prop}$ move gracefully

Note that, from (6), we obtain (3) as a consequence as well.
- Sentence modifiers such as negation.

(7) Mary dances $\Longrightarrow_{Prop}$ Mary moves

(8) no : $Prop \to Prop$ is $\Longrightarrow$-reversing.

(9) Mary does not move $\Longrightarrow_{Prop}$ Mary does not dance

- Order-preserving quantifiers.

(10) dance $\Longrightarrow_{Human \to Prop}$ move

(11) everyone : $(Human \to Prop) \to Prop$ and is $\Longrightarrow$-preserving.

(12) Everyone dances $\Longrightarrow_{Prop}$ Everyone moves

- Order-reversing quantifiers.

(13) dance $\Longrightarrow_{Human \to Prop}$ move

(14) nobody : $(Human \to Prop) \to Prop$ and is $\Longrightarrow$-reversing.

(15) Nobody moves $\Longrightarrow_{Prop}$ Nobody dances

3 Binary Quantifiers in Monotonicity Reasoning

Generalised quantifiers have been studied extensively in the Montagovian setting (see, for example, [1,27]). In the MTT-semantics, similar considerations can be taken where, for example, a binary quantifier is of the following type:

$$\Pi A : \text{CN}. \ (A \to Prop) \to Prop.$$

In other words, a binary quantifier is an operator Q that takes a common noun N and a predicate P over N to form a proposition $Q(N, P)$. For instance, every is a binary quantifier whose semantics $[\![every]\!]$ is of the above type. Therefore, the following sentence (16) has its interpretation (17):

(16) Every student talks.

(17) $[\![every]\!]([\![student]\!], [\![talk]\!])$

where the formula in (17) is well-typed because $[\![student]\!]$ is of type CN and $[\![talk]\!]$ is of type $[\![human]\!] \to Prop$ which is a subtype of $[\![student]\!] \to Prop$.

In the Montagovian setting, a generalised quantifier Q of type $\langle 1,1 \rangle$ is said to be *right (left) monotone increasing* if $\forall B \subseteq B'$, $Q_M(A,B) \supset Q_M(A,B')$, respectively if $\forall A \subseteq A'$, $Q_M(A,B) \supset Q_M(A',B)$, where M is the universe we relate to. It is said to be *right (left) monotone decreasing* if $Q_M(A,B') \supset Q_M(A,B)$ (respectively $Q_M(A',B) \supset Q_M(A,B)$).

The binary quantifiers in MTTs can be studied similarly (see also the discussion in 5). A binary quantifier Q of type $\Pi A : \text{CN}. (A \to Prop) \to Prop$ takes a 'left' (first) argument A and a 'right' (second) argument B to form a proposition $Q(A,B)$. We can then consider:

- monotonicity (or the reverse monotonicity) in its first argument as expressed by the relation $\Longrightarrow_{CN}$, which is the subtyping relation $\leq$; and
- monotonicity (or the reverse monotonicity) in its second argument as expressed by the relation $\Longrightarrow_{A \to Prop}$, which is the predicate inclusion relation $\subseteq$ (i.e., $B \subseteq B' =_{\text{df}} \forall x : A. B(x) \supset B'(x)$).

Treated like this, we have the derived rules in Figure 1, which can be viewed as defining properties of the following notions, for any binary quantifier Q:

- Q is said to be *right increasing* if the rule (MON $\uparrow$) holds.
- Q is said to be *right decreasing* if the rule (MON $\downarrow$) holds.
- Q is said to be *left increasing* if the rule ($\uparrow$ MON) holds.
- Q is said to be *left decreasing* if the rule ($\downarrow$ MON) holds.

Here are some examples for the monotonicity rules (we only spell out the semantic interpretations in the first example):

- An example of left decreasing monotonicity i.e. $\Longrightarrow$-reversing in the first argument is $\forall$, which satisfies ($\downarrow$ MON); because of (18), we have (19) implies (20) (i.e., (19) $\Longrightarrow_{Prop}$ (20)).

(18) Scientists are human. (semantics: $[\![scientist]\!] \Longrightarrow_{CN} [\![human]\!]$)

(MON $\uparrow$)	$\dfrac{A : \text{CN} \quad B,\ B' : A \to Prop \quad B \Longrightarrow_{A \to Prop} B'}{Q(A,B) \Longrightarrow_{Prop} Q(A,B')}$	(Q *is MON* $\uparrow$)
(MON $\downarrow$)	$\dfrac{A : \text{CN} \quad B,\ B' : A \to Prop \quad B' \Longrightarrow_{A \to Prop} B}{Q(A,B) \Longrightarrow_{Prop} Q(A,B')}$	(Q *is MON* $\downarrow$)
($\uparrow$ MON)	$\dfrac{A,\ A' : \text{CN} \quad B' : A' \to Prop \quad A \Longrightarrow_{CN} A'}{Q(A,B') \Longrightarrow_{Prop} Q(A',B')}$	(Q *is* $\uparrow$ *MON*)
($\downarrow$ MON)	$\dfrac{A,\ A' : \text{CN} \quad B : A \to Prop \quad A' \Longrightarrow_{CN} A}{Q(A,B) \Longrightarrow_{Prop} Q(A',B)}$	(Q *is* $\downarrow$ *MON*)

Fig. 1. Derived reasoning rules for binary quantifiers

(19) Every human is mortal. (semantics: $[\![every]\!]([\![human]\!], [\![mortal]\!])$)

(20) Every scientist is mortal. (semantics: $[\![every]\!]([\![scientist]\!], [\![mortal]\!])$)

- Examples of right increasing binary quantifiers include $\forall$, $\exists$ and $Most$, which are $\Longrightarrow$-preserving w.r.t. its second argument and satisfy (MON $\uparrow$).

(21) Humans are mortal.

(22) Most scientists are human.

(23) Most scientists are mortal.

- Examples of left increasing binary quantifiers include $\exists$, which is $\Longrightarrow$-preserving w.r.t. its first argument and satisfy ($\uparrow$ MON).

(24) Scientists are human.

(25) Some scientists are mortal.

(26) Some humans are mortal.

- Examples of right decreasing binary quantifiers include **none**, which is $\Longrightarrow$-reversing w.r.t. its second argument and satisfy (MON $\downarrow$).

(27) Humans are mortal.

(28) No philosophers are mortal.

(29) No philosophers are human.

4   Monotonicity Reasoning with MTT Type Constructors

MTTs have a rich type structure and, in an MTT-semantics, these types are proved to be very useful in interpretations of various linguistic features. Here we study monotonicity in this rich type structure and consider some of the type constructors with respect to monotonicity reasoning.[4]

Dependent sums (Σ-types). An example of dependent types is *dependent sums* or Σ-*types* which have been employed in the MTT-semantics to interpret modified CNs. For example, "handsome men" can be interpreted as $\Sigma(Man, handsome)$ (or $\Sigma m{:}Man.\ handsome(m)$ in a more traditional notation), where $handsome :$ $Human \rightarrow Prop$. There are two natural subtyping relationships that can be considered.

- In the first place, $\Sigma(Man, handsome) \leq_{\pi_1} Man$ because a handsome man is a man. In general, we have

$$\Sigma(A, B) \leq_{\pi_1} A.$$

---

[4] Since the monotonicity relationship $\Longrightarrow$ over types is expressed by the subtyping relation $\leq$, the reader may be interested in the general study of the latter and, if so, please consult the papers [11,15].

In other words, when A interprets a CN and $\Sigma(A, B)$ a modified CN, we have

$$\Sigma(A, B) \Longrightarrow_{\text{CN}} A.$$

For example, we have that (30) implies (31).

(30) John is a handsome man.

(31) John is a man.

- Another subtyping relationship for Σ-types describes its structural relationships of its parameters. Informally, if A is a subtype of A' and B is a 'subtype' of B', then $\Sigma(A, B)$ is a subtype of $\Sigma(A', B')$. Formally, we have (for simplicity, we omit some premises), where we assume that A, $A' : \text{CN}$, $B : A \to Prop$ and $B' : A' \to Prop$:

$$(*) \qquad \frac{A \Longrightarrow_{\text{CN}} A' \quad B \Longrightarrow_{A \to Prop} B'}{\Sigma(A, B) \Longrightarrow_{\text{CN}} \Sigma(A', B')}$$

For example, we have that (32) implies (33):

(32) John is a smart and diligent student.

(33) John is a smart human.

When $[\![smart\ and\ diligent\ students]\!]$ and $[\![smart\ human]\!]$ are interpreted as $\Sigma(Student, S\&D)$ and $\Sigma(Human, S)$, respectively, the reasoning from (32) to (33) follows from the above rule. Note that, in this example, both premises involve strict monotonicity relations and are used essentially.

Disjoint union types. When A and B are types, we can form the disjoint union type $A + B$. This is employed in [4] to interpret privative adjectives like fake. Let us consider the type Car and the classification "fake cars" and "real cars". A car exclusively belongs to one of these two categories. In this case we say $Car = Car_{fake} + Car_{real}$. By disjoint union types are used to interpret privative adjectives, as the above example illustrates, both of the injections $inl : A \to A + B$ and $inr : B \to A + B$ are declared as coercions. For instance, we regard either a real car or a fake car as a car.

For disjoint union types, we can consider the following rule:

$$\frac{A \leq A' \quad B \leq B'}{A + A' \leq B + B'}$$

One may think that a real (fake) car is a real (fake) vehicle and hence, if we define $Vehicle = Vehicle_{fake} + Vehicle_{real}$, we have from the above rule that

$$Car = Car_{fake} + Car_{real} \leq Vehicle_{fake} + Vehicle_{real} = Vehicle.$$

Dependent products (Π-types). Dependent Π-types are a basic form of dependent types. In MTT-semantics, it is employed for many purposes and has proved very useful. For instance, it is used in [14] which models adverbs acting as verb modifiers. In general, in MTT-semantics, a verb-modifying adverb is of the following type:

$$\Pi A : \text{CN}. \; (A \to Prop) \to (A \to Prop).$$

For example, the adverb *gracefully* in the examples in §2 is interpreted as of the above type.

For Π-types, we can introduce the following monotonicity rule, where A, A' : CN, $B : A \to Type$ and $B' : A' \to Type$:[5]

$$\frac{A \Longrightarrow_{\text{CN}} A' \quad B \Longrightarrow_{A \to Type} B'}{\Pi(A, B) \Longrightarrow_{Type} \Pi(A', B')}$$

Vector types. For $A : CN$ and $n : Nat$, $Vec(A, n)$ is the inductive type of vectors whose lengths are n. Vector types may be used to deal with some linguistic features such as those involve collective predicates [3]. For instance, we may interpret *meet* as of the following type:

$$\llbracket meet \rrbracket : \Pi n : Nat. \; Vec(\llbracket human \rrbracket, n + 2) \to Prop.$$

The vector-types are monotone increasing for every n with the following rules:

$$\frac{A \Longrightarrow_{\text{CN}} A' \quad n : Nat}{Vec(A, n) \Longrightarrow_{Type} Vec(A', n)}$$

For instance, we have (34) implies (35).

(34) Three men met.

(35) Three humans met

Dot-types. These types are not inductive types found in traditional MTTs. They were introduced to model the linguistic feature of copredication [12]. If A and B are types do not share common components, then we can form a dot-type $A \bullet B$ for which we have two coercions from $A \bullet B$ to A and from $A \bullet B$ to B. For instance, in a sentence like

John picked up the book and mastered it,

book can be interpreted as of type $Phy \bullet Info$, where Phy and $Info$ are type of physical objects and informational objects, respectively. Indeed, this sentence implies both that 'John picked up the book (as a physical object) and 'John mastered the book (as an informational object)'. The monotonicity rule for dot-types is:

$$\frac{A \leq A' \quad B \leq B'}{A \bullet B \leq A' \bullet B'}$$

---

[5] Here, $Type$ is a type universe (and hence the formation of $A \to Type$ as a type is legal). This is a technicality that we may ignore here.

At the time of writing this paper, we have some rather artificial NL examples for this and it would be interesting to find some real NLI examples concerning dot-types.

5   Concluding Remarks

We have considered monotonicity reasoning in the MTT setting and developed the corresponding rules for the relevant type constructors. An obvious future work is to implement this, extending the NLI machinery in the Coq proof assistant developed by Chatzikyriakidis [5]. It is expected that this would improve the reasoning engine as a whole.

Reasoning in Natural Logic has been studied by several researchers, including MacCartney's work in implementing an NLI system based on monotonicity reasoning [18]. Embedding monotonicity reasoning in MTTs allows simpler ways of reasoning in many cases and its automation in proof assistants is expected. We can then compare this to MacCartney's work. In this respect, we should also mention the recent work of implementing natural logic in the Coq system [9], which is based on the Montagovian setting of simple type theory (without using Coq's MTT mechanisms in formal semantics).

In this paper, while analyzing monotonicity and the impact the coercive subtyping relation has, we touched a couple of points that could be the basis for further research. The work reported here is part of the development of a theory of generalised quantifiers in the MTT framework, hopefully to offer a richer alternative than that in the Montagovian setting. For instance, when considering a binary quantifier $Q(A, B)$ in an MTT, the domain of the second argument B needs to be a supertype of the first argument A (since $D_B \to Type \leq A \to Type$ if $A \leq D_B$). Furthermore, the quantifier properties such as conservativity and extensibility are also closed related to the situations in which these quantifiers are evaluated to see whether they are satisfied. This leads to the current work of the second author on representing (possibly infinite) situations or incomplete possible worlds by means of (finite) contexts in type theory. Some promising results have been obtained in this direction (and are to be reported elsewhere).

Another interesting direction is to study how to interpret mass nouns in MTTs. In [13], the second author has taken a set/type-theoretic view (instead of a mereological view as advocated by Quine [21] and others) and used the intuition of languages with classifiers like Chinese to motivate some uses of mass nouns: eg, in a bucket of water, the measure word (or classifier) is bucket, that provides the criterion of equality associated with CNs in general. It would be interesting to study this in connection with plurals and collective verbs, although further work is called for about their interpretations in MTTs.

For some topics such as the study of proof rules for monotonicity, a categorical framework may help to arrive at better understandings. For instance, it would be interesting to look at the relationships between $\Sigma(Human, handsome)$ and Man, for $Man \leq_c Human$, from a categorical perspective. Consider the following two derivations (due to transitivity of the coercive subtyping relations and the (∗) rule in §4):

$$\frac{\Sigma(Man, handsome) \leq_{\pi_1} Man \quad Man \leq_c Human}{\Sigma(Man, handsome) \leq_{c \, \circ \, \pi_1} Human}$$

$$\frac{\Sigma(Man, handsome) \leq_{c_\Sigma} \Sigma(Human, handsome) \quad \Sigma(Human, handsome) \leq_{\pi_1} Human}{\Sigma(Man, handsome) \leq_{\pi_1 \, \circ \, c_\Sigma} Human}$$

where $\circ$ is the composition operator and c_Σ is the coercion for the conclusion of the rule (∗) in §4, where this coercion is omitted. Coherence in coercive subtyping requires uniqueness of coercion and, in this example, we should have $\pi_1 \circ c_\Sigma = c \circ \pi_1$. This means that the following diagram should commute:

$$
\begin{array}{ccc}
\Sigma(Man, handsome) & \xrightarrow{\ \pi_1\ } & Man \\
c_\Sigma \downarrow & & \downarrow c \\
\Sigma(Human, handsome) & \xrightarrow[\ \pi_1\ ]{} & Human
\end{array}
$$

Note that there is also the interesting difference between the intensional equality in MTTs and the extensional equality in category theory, although the latter gives us interesting clues on some of the research challenges.

Acknowledgement. We'd like to thank Nicholas Asher, Stergios Chatzikyri-akidis and the anonymous LACL reviewers for helpful comments to an earlier version, which have helped a lot in improving the paper.

References

1. Barwise, J., Cooper, R.: Generalized quantifiers and natural language. Linguistics and Philosophy 4(2), 159–219 (1981)
2. Callaghan, P., Luo, Z.: An implementation of LF with coercive subtyping and universes. Journal of Automated Reasoning 27(1), 3–27 (2001)
3. Chatzikyriakidis, S., Luo, Z.: An account of natural language coordination in type theory with coercive subtyping. In: Duchier, D., Parmentier, Y. (eds.) CSLP 2012. LNCS, vol. 8114, pp. 31–51. Springer, Heidelberg (2013)
4. Chatzikyriakidis, S., Luo, Z.: Adjectives in a modern type-theoretical setting. In: Morrill, G., Nederhof, M.-J. (eds.) FG 2012/2013. LNCS, vol. 8036, pp. 159–174. Springer, Heidelberg (2013)
5. Chatzikyriakidis, S., Luo, Z.: Natural language inference in Coq. In: EACL Workshop on Type Theory and Natural Language Semantics, Goteborg (2013) (submitted manuscript)
6. Chatzikyriakidis, S., Luo, Z.: Natural language reasoning using proof assistant technology: Rich typing and beyond. In: EACL Workshop on Type Theory and Natural Language Semantics. Goteborg (2014)
7. The Coq Development Team. The Coq Proof Assistant Reference Manual (Version 8.1), INRIA (2007)

8. Dowty, D.: The role of negative polarity and concord marking in natural language reasoning. In: Proc of the 4th SALT Conference (1994)
9. Huijben, R.: A Coq module for natural logic. Master's thesis, Technische Universiteit Eindhoven (2013)
10. Luo, Z.: Computation and Reasoning: A Type Theory for Computer Science. Oxford University Press (1994)
11. Luo, Z.: Coercive subtyping. Journal of Logic and Computation 9(1), 105–130 (1999)
12. Luo, Z.: Type-theoretical semantics with coercive subtyping. In: Semantics and Linguistic Theory 20 (SALT20), Vancouver (2010)
13. Luo, Z.: Common nouns as types. In: Béchet, D., Dikovsky, A. (eds.) LACL 2012. LNCS, vol. 7351, pp. 173–185. Springer, Heidelberg (2012)
14. Luo, Z.: Formal semantics in modern type theories with coercive subtyping. Linguistics and Philosophy 35(6), 491–513 (2012)
15. Luo, Z., Adams, R.: Structural subtyping for inductive types with functorial equality rules. Mathematical Structures in Computer Science 18(5) (2008)
16. Luo, Z., Pollack, R.: LEGO Proof Development System: User's Manual. LFCS Report ECS-LFCS-92-211, Dept of Computer Science, Univ. of Edinburgh (1992)
17. Luo, Z., Soloviev, S., Xue, T.: Coercive subtyping: theory and implementation. Information and Computation 223 (2012)
18. MacCartney, B.: Natural Language Inference. PhD thesis, Stanford Universisty (2009)
19. The Matita proof assistant (2008), http://matita.cs.unibo.it/?
20. Purdy, W.C.: A logic for natural language. Notre Dame Journal of Formal Logic 32 (1991)
21. Quine, W.: Word & Object. MIT Press (1960)
22. Ranta, A.: Type-Theoretical Grammar. Oxford University Press (1994)
23. Sommers, F.: The Logic of Natural Language. Cambridge Univ. Press (1982)
24. van Benthem, J.: Essays in Logical Semantics. Reidel (1986)
25. van Benthem, J.: Language in Action: Categories, Lambdas and Dynamic Logic. Elsevier (1991)
26. van Eijck, J.: Natural logic for natural language. In: ten Cate, B.D., Zeevat, H.W. (eds.) TbiLLC 2005. LNCS (LNAI), vol. 4363, pp. 216–230. Springer, Heidelberg (2007)
27. Westerstahl, D., Peters, S.: Quantifiers in Language and Logic. Oxford University Press (2006)
28. Xue, T., Luo, Z.: Dot-types and their implementation. In: Béchet, D., Dikovsky, A. (eds.) LACL 2012. LNCS, vol. 7351, pp. 234–249. Springer, Heidelberg (2012)

Semantically Inactive Multiplicatives and Words as Types*

Glyn Morrill and Oriol Valentín

Universitat Politècnica
de Catalunya
morrill@lsi.upc.edu, oriol.valentin@gmail.com

Abstract. The literature on categorial type logic includes proposals for semantically inactive additives, quantifiers, and modalities (Morrill 1994[17]; Hepple 1990[2]; Moortgat 1997[9]), but to our knowledge there has been no proposal for semantically inactive multiplicatives. In this paper we formulate such a proposal (thus filling a gap in the typology of categorial connectives) in the context of the displacement calculus Morrill et al. (2011[16]), and we give a formulation of words as types whereby for every expression w there is a corresponding type $W(w)$. We show how this machinary can treat the syntax and semantics of collocations involving apparently contentless words such as expletives, particle verbs, and (discontinuous) idioms. In addition, we give an account in these terms of the only known examples treated by Hybrid Type Logical Grammar (HTLG henceforth; Kubota and Levine 2012[4]) beyond the scope of unaugmented displacement calculus: gapping of particle verbs and discontinuous idioms.

1 Introduction

Examples of collocations are as follows. Expletives:

(1) a. *It* rains.
     b. *There* came a man.

Discontinuous idiom:

(2) Mary *gives* Peter *the cold shoulder*.

Particle verb:

(3) a. Mary *calls* Peter *up*.
     b. Mary *calls up* Peter.

---

* Research partially supported by an ICREA Acadèmia 2012 to the alphabetically first author, and by BASMATI MICINN project (TIN2011-27479-C04-03) and SGR2009-1428 (LARCA). Many thanks to three anonymous LACL referees for valuable comments and suggestions.

N. Asher and S. Soloviev (Eds.): LACL 2014, LNCS 8535, pp. 149–162, 2014.

(Observe in (3) the non-determinism of the position of the object *Peter* with respect to the conjunct *calls up*.) We give an account of such collocations which respects the intuition that the constructions derive from content words (*rains, came, gives, calls*) which require certain other words without content in their grammatical context.[1] Furthermore we do this in such a way that it is possible to give an account of gapping as (almost) like type coordination which includes coverage of examples such as (4c, d), for which Kubota and Levine (2012[4]) invoke Hybrid Type Logical Grammar.

(4) a. Peter sees Mary and Robin, Clark.
   b. Peter calls up Mary and Robin, Clark.
   c. Peter calls Mary up and Robin, Clark.
   d. Peter gives Mary the cold shoulder and Robin, Clark.

Thus the technically and conceptually independently motivated machinery of semantically inactive multiplicatives and words as types accounts for the only known application of HTLG beyond the scope of displacement calculus.

In Section 2 we present the machinery. In Section 3 we give our empirical accounts. We conclude in Section 4.

2   Displacement Categorial Logic

The syntactic types of our categorial logic are sorted according to the number of points of discontinuity their expressions contain. Each *type predicate letter* will have a sort and an arity which are naturals, and a corresponding semantic type. Assuming ordinary terms to be already given, where P is a type predicate letter of sort i and arity n and $t_1, \ldots, t_n$ are terms, $Pt_1 \ldots t_n$ is an (atomic) type of sort i of the corresponding semantic type. Compound types are formed by connectives as indicated in Figure 1, and the homomorphic semantic type map T associates these with semantic types. Note the new semantically inactive concatenative (continuous) and intercalative (discontinuous) multiplicatives in the middle of the table.

The set O of *configurations* of (hyper)sequent calculus for our categorial logic is defined as follows, where Λ is the metalinguistic empty string and 1 is a metalinguistic placeholder:

(5) $O ::= \Lambda \mid 1 \mid \mathcal{F}_0 \mid \mathcal{F}_{i>0}\underbrace{\{O : \ldots : O\}}_{i\ O's} \mid O, O \mid [O]$

---

[1] As a referee points out, *gives . . . the cold shoulder* and *calls . . . up* are not completely frozen expressions: *Mary gives the same cold shoulder to Peter, Mary calls Peter right up.* Based on such observations Wasow, Sag and Nunberg (1983[20]) claim that the elements of such constructions should be assigned semantic interpretations. If this is the case the present paper presents a solution to a problem which does not exist, but we think that although the present paper is not the last word, such observations do not dissolve the reality of the qualitative difference between normal compositional semantics and idiomatic semantics with reduced content.

$$\mathcal{F}_0 ::= W(w) \qquad T(W(w)) = \top \qquad \text{words as types}$$
$$\mathcal{F}_j ::= \mathcal{F}_i \backslash \mathcal{F}_{i+j} \qquad T(A\backslash C) = T(A){\to}T(C) \qquad \text{suffix [7]}$$
$$\mathcal{F}_i ::= \mathcal{F}_{i+j} / \mathcal{F}_j \qquad T(C/B) = T(B){\to}T(C) \qquad \text{prefix [7]}$$
$$\mathcal{F}_{i+j} ::= \mathcal{F}_i {\bullet} \mathcal{F}_j \qquad T(A{\bullet}B) = T(A)\&T(B) \qquad \text{concatenation product [7]}$$
$$\mathcal{F}_0 ::= I \qquad T(I) = \top \qquad \text{concatenation product unit [6]}$$
$$\mathcal{F}_j ::= \mathcal{F}_{i+1}{\downarrow}_{\pm}\mathcal{F}_{i+j} \qquad T(A{\downarrow}_{\pm}C) = T(A){\to}T(C) \qquad \text{infix [16]}$$
$$\mathcal{F}_{i+1} ::= \mathcal{F}_{i+j}{\uparrow}_{\pm}\mathcal{F}_j \qquad T(C{\uparrow}_{\pm}B) = T(B){\to}T(C) \qquad \text{circumfix [16]}$$
$$\mathcal{F}_{i+j} ::= \mathcal{F}_{i+1}{\odot}_{\pm}\mathcal{F}_j \qquad T(A{\odot}_{\pm}B) = T(A)\&T(B) \qquad \text{intercalation product [16]}$$
$$\mathcal{F}_1 ::= J \qquad T(J) = \top \qquad \text{intercalation product unit [16]}$$
$$\mathcal{F}_i ::= \mathcal{F}_i \& \mathcal{F}_i \qquad T(A\&B) = T(A)\&T(B) \qquad \text{additive conjunction [5,10]}$$
$$\mathcal{F}_i ::= \mathcal{F}_i \oplus \mathcal{F}_i \qquad T(A \oplus B) = T(A)+T(B) \qquad \text{additive disjunction [5,10]}$$
$$\mathcal{F}_i ::= \bigwedge V\mathcal{F}_i \qquad T(\bigwedge vA) = F{\to}T(A) \qquad \text{1st order univ. qu. [17]}$$
$$\mathcal{F}_i ::= \bigvee V\mathcal{F}_i \qquad T(\bigvee vA) = F\&T(A) \qquad \text{1st order exist. qu. [17]}$$
$$\mathcal{F}_i ::= \Box\mathcal{F}_i \qquad T(\Box A) = \mathbf{L}T(A) \qquad \text{universal modality [11]}$$
$$\mathcal{F}_i ::= \Diamond\mathcal{F}_i \qquad T(\Diamond A) = \mathbf{M}T(A) \qquad \text{existential modality [9]}$$
$$\mathcal{F}_i ::= []^{-1}\mathcal{F}_i \qquad T([]^{-1}A) = T(A) \qquad \text{univ. bracket modality [12,8]}$$
$$\mathcal{F}_i ::= \langle\rangle\mathcal{F}_i \qquad T(\langle\rangle A) = T(A) \qquad \text{exist. bracket modality [12,8]}$$
$$\mathcal{F}_{i+j} ::= \mathcal{F}_{i+j} | \mathcal{F}_j \qquad T(B|A) = T(A){\to}T(B) \qquad \text{contr. for anaph. [3]}$$
$$\mathcal{F}_j := \mathcal{F}_i {\multimap} \mathcal{F}_{i+j} \qquad T(A{\multimap}C) = T(C) \text{ if } T(A) = \top \quad \text{left sem. inactive under}$$
$$\mathcal{F}_i := \mathcal{F}_{i+j} {\bullet\!\!-} \mathcal{F}_j \qquad T(C{\bullet\!\!-}B) = T(B) \text{ if } T(C) = \top \quad \text{left sem. inactive over}$$
$$\mathcal{F}_j := \mathcal{F}_i {-\!\!\bullet} \mathcal{F}_{i+j} \qquad T(A{-\!\!\bullet}C) = T(A) \text{ if } T(C) = \top \quad \text{right sem. inactive under}$$
$$\mathcal{F}_i := \mathcal{F}_{i+j} {\circ\!-} \mathcal{F}_j \qquad T(C{\circ\!-}B) = T(C) \text{ if } T(B) = \top \quad \text{right sem. inactive over}$$
$$\mathcal{F}_{i+j} ::= \mathcal{F}_i {\mathbf{O}} \mathcal{F}_j \qquad T(A{\mathbf{O}}B) = T(B) \text{ if } T(A) = \top \quad \text{right sem. inactive conc. product}$$
$$\mathcal{F}_{i+j} ::= \mathcal{F}_i {\mathbf{O}} \mathcal{F}_j \qquad T(A{\mathbf{O}}B) = T(A) \text{ if } T(B) = \top \quad \text{right sem. inactive conc. product}$$
$$\mathcal{F}_j := \mathcal{F}_i {\overset{\bullet}{\underset{\pm}{\,}}} \mathcal{F}_{i+j} \qquad T(A{\overset{\bullet}{\,}}C) = T(C) \text{ if } T(A) = \top \quad \text{lower sem. inactive infix}$$
$$\mathcal{F}_i := \mathcal{F}_{i+j} {\overset{\circ}{\underset{\pm}{\,}}} \mathcal{F}_j \qquad T(C{\overset{\circ}{\,}}B) = T(B) \text{ if } T(C) = \top \quad \text{lower sem. inactive circumfix}$$
$$\mathcal{F}_j := \mathcal{F}_i {\overset{\circ}{\underset{\pm}{\,}}} \mathcal{F}_{i+j} \qquad T(A{\overset{\circ}{\,}}C) = T(A) \text{ if } T(C) = \top \quad \text{upper sem. inactive infix}$$
$$\mathcal{F}_i := \mathcal{F}_{i+j} {\overset{\bullet}{\underset{\pm}{\,}}} \mathcal{F}_j \qquad T(C{\overset{\bullet}{\,}}B) = T(C) \text{ if } T(B) = \top \quad \text{upper sem. inactive circumfix}$$
$$\mathcal{F}_{i+j} ::= \mathcal{F}_i {\mathbf{\ominus}} \mathcal{F}_j \qquad T(A{\mathbf{\ominus}}B) = T(B) \text{ if } T(A) = \top \quad \text{lower sem. inactive interc. product}$$
$$\mathcal{F}_{i+j} ::= \mathcal{F}_i {\mathbf{\ominus}} \mathcal{F}_j \qquad T(A{\mathbf{\ominus}}B) = T(A) \text{ if } T(B) = \top \quad \text{upper sem. inactive interc. product}$$
$$\mathcal{F}_i ::= \mathcal{F}_i {\sqcap} \mathcal{F}_i \qquad T(A{\sqcap}B) = T(A) = T(B) \qquad \text{sem. inactive additive conjunction [17]}$$
$$\mathcal{F}_i ::= \mathcal{F}_i {\sqcup} \mathcal{F}_i \qquad T(A{\sqcup}B) = T(A) = T(B) \qquad \text{sem. inactive additive disjunction [17]}$$
$$\mathcal{F}_i ::= \forall V\mathcal{F}_i \qquad T(\forall vA) = T(A) \qquad \text{sem. inactive 1st order univ. qu. [17]}$$
$$\mathcal{F}_i ::= \exists V\mathcal{F}_i \qquad T(\exists vA) = T(A) \qquad \text{sem. inactive 1st order exist. qu. [17]}$$
$$\mathcal{F}_i ::= \blacksquare\mathcal{F}_i \qquad T(\blacksquare A) = T(A) \qquad \text{sem. inactive universal modality [2]}$$
$$\mathcal{F}_i ::= \blacklozenge\mathcal{F}_i \qquad T(\blacklozenge A) = T(A) \qquad \text{sem. inactive existential modality}$$
$$\mathcal{F}_i ::= {\triangleleft}^{-1}\mathcal{F}_i \qquad T({\triangleleft}^{-1}A) = T(A) \qquad \text{left projection [15]}$$
$$\mathcal{F}_i ::= {\triangleright}^{-1}\mathcal{F}_i \qquad T({\triangleright}^{-1}A) = T(A) \qquad \text{right projection [15]}$$
$$\mathcal{F}_i ::= {\triangleleft}\mathcal{F}_i \qquad T({\triangleleft}A) = T(A) \qquad \text{left injection [15]}$$
$$\mathcal{F}_i ::= {\triangleright}\mathcal{F}_i \qquad T({\triangleright}A) = T(A) \qquad \text{right injection [15]}$$
$$\mathcal{F}_{i+1} ::= {\overset{\vee}{\underset{\pm}{\,}}}\mathcal{F}_i \qquad T({\overset{\vee}{\,}}A) = T(A) \qquad \text{split [14]}$$
$$\mathcal{F}_i ::= {\overset{\wedge}{\underset{\pm}{\,}}}\mathcal{F}_{i+1} \qquad T({\overset{\wedge}{\,}}A) = T(A) \qquad \text{bridge [14]}$$
$$\mathcal{F}_i ::= \mathcal{F}_{i+j} \div \mathcal{F}_j^{\overline{p}} \qquad T(B \div A) = T(A){\to}T(B) \qquad \text{nondet. division [16]}$$
$$\mathcal{F}_{i+j} ::= \mathcal{F}_i \times \mathcal{F}_j \qquad T(A{\times}B) = T(A)\&T(B) \qquad \text{nondet. concatenation product [16]}$$
$$\mathcal{F}_j ::= \mathcal{F}_{i+1} {\Downarrow} \mathcal{F}_{i+j} \qquad T(A{\Downarrow}C) = T(A){\to}T(C) \qquad \text{nondet. infix [16]}$$
$$\mathcal{F}_{i+1} ::= \mathcal{F}_{i+j} {\Uparrow} \mathcal{F}_j \qquad T(C{\Uparrow}B) = T(B){\to}T(C) \qquad \text{nondet. circumfix [16]}$$
$$\mathcal{F}_{i+j} ::= \mathcal{F}_{i+1} {\circledcirc} \mathcal{F}_j \qquad T(A{\circledcirc}B) = T(A)\&T(B) \qquad \text{nondet. intercalation product [16]}$$

Fig. 1. Categorial logic types

The sort sA of a type A is the $i \in N$ such that $A \in \mathcal{F}_i$. The sort of a configuration Γ is the number of placeholders 1 that Γ contains.

Where Γ is a configuration of sort i and $\Delta_1, \ldots, \Delta_i$ are configurations, the *fold* $\Gamma \otimes \langle \Delta_1, \ldots, \Delta_i \rangle$ is the result of replacing the successive 1's in Γ by $\Delta_1, \ldots, \Delta_i$ respectively.

The usual configuration distinguished occurrence notation $\Delta(\Gamma)$ signifies a configuration Δ with a distinguished subconfiguration Γ, i.e. a configuration occurrence Γ with (external) context Δ. In the hypersequent calculus the distinguished *hyperoccurrence* notation $\Delta\langle\Gamma\rangle$ signifies a configuration *hyperoccurrence* Γ with external *and internal* context Δ as follows: the *distinguished hyperoccurrence* notation $\Delta\langle\Gamma\rangle$ abbreviates $\Delta_0(\Gamma \otimes \langle \Delta_1, \ldots, \Delta_i \rangle)$.

Where Δ is a configuration of sort $i > 0$ and Γ is a configuration, the *leftmost* metalinguistic wrap is given by

$$\Delta \underset{+}{\downarrow} \Gamma =_{df} \Delta \otimes \langle \underbrace{\Gamma, 1, \ldots, 1}_{i-1 \text{ 1's}} \rangle$$

i.e. the configuration resulting from replacing by Γ the leftmost placeholder in Δ; and the *rightmost* metalinguistic wrap is given by

$$\Delta \underset{-}{\downarrow} \Gamma =_{df} \Delta \otimes \langle \underbrace{1, \ldots, 1, \Gamma}_{i-1 \text{ 1's}} \rangle$$

i.e. the configuration resulting from replacing by Γ the rightmost placeholder in Δ.

The *figure* $\overrightarrow{A}$ of a type A is defined by:

$$(6) \quad \overrightarrow{A} = \begin{cases} A & \text{if } sA = 0 \\ A\{\underbrace{1 : \ldots : 1}_{sA \text{ 1's}}\} & \text{if } sA > 0 \end{cases}$$

A *sequent* $\Gamma \Rightarrow A$ comprises an antecedent configuration Γ of sort i and a succedent type A of sort i. The hypersequent calculus for the categorial logic has the following identity axiom and Cut rule:

$$(7) \quad \frac{}{\overrightarrow{A} : x \Rightarrow A : x} \, id \qquad \frac{\Gamma \Rightarrow A : \phi \qquad \Delta\langle \overrightarrow{A} : x \rangle \Rightarrow B : \psi}{\Delta\langle \Gamma \rangle \Rightarrow B : \psi\{\phi/x\}} \, Cut$$

The set $\mathcal{T}$ of *semantic types* of the semantic representation language is defined on the basis of a set δ of *basic semantic types* and includes:

$$(8) \quad \mathcal{T} ::= \delta \mid \top \mid \mathcal{T} \& \mathcal{T} \mid \mathcal{T} \to \mathcal{T}$$

A *semantic frame* comprises a family $\{D_\tau\}_{\tau \in \delta}$ of non-empty *basic type domains* and this induces a non-empty *type domain* D_τ for each type τ such that:

$$(9) \quad \begin{aligned} D_\top &= \{\emptyset\} \\ D_{\tau_1 \& \tau_2} &= D_{\tau_1} \times D_{\tau_2} \\ D_{\tau_1 \to \tau_2} &= D_{\tau_2}^{D_{\tau_1}} \end{aligned}$$

$$\frac{\Gamma \Rightarrow A{:}\phi \qquad \Delta\langle\vec{C}{:}z\rangle \Rightarrow D{:}\omega}{\Delta\langle\Gamma, \overrightarrow{A\backslash C}{:}y\rangle \Rightarrow D{:}\omega\{(y\,\phi)/z\}}\backslash L \qquad \frac{\vec{A}{:}x, \Gamma \Rightarrow C{:}\chi}{\Gamma \Rightarrow A\backslash C{:}\lambda x\chi}\backslash R$$

$$\frac{\Gamma \Rightarrow B{:}\psi \qquad \Delta\langle\vec{C}{:}z\rangle \Rightarrow D{:}\omega}{\Delta\langle\overrightarrow{C/B}{:}x, \Gamma\rangle \Rightarrow D{:}\omega\{(x\,\psi)/z\}}/L \qquad \frac{\Gamma, \vec{B}{:}y \Rightarrow C{:}\chi}{\Gamma \Rightarrow C/B{:}\lambda y\chi}/R$$

$$\frac{\Delta\langle\vec{A}{:}x, \vec{B}{:}y\rangle \Rightarrow D{:}\omega}{\Delta\langle\overrightarrow{A{\bullet}B}{:}z\rangle \Rightarrow D{:}\omega\{\pi_1 z/x, \pi_2 z/y\}}{\bullet}L$$

$$\frac{\Gamma_1 \Rightarrow A{:}\phi \qquad \Gamma_2 \Rightarrow B{:}\psi}{\Gamma_1, \Gamma_2 \Rightarrow A{\bullet}B{:}(\phi, \psi)}{\bullet}R$$

$$\frac{\Delta\langle\Lambda\rangle \Rightarrow A{:}\phi}{\Delta\langle\vec{I}{:}x\rangle \Rightarrow A{:}\phi}IL \qquad \frac{}{\Lambda \Rightarrow I{:}0}IR$$

$$\frac{\Gamma \Rightarrow A{:}\phi \qquad \Delta\langle\vec{C}{:}z\rangle \Rightarrow D{:}\omega}{\Delta\langle\Gamma \underset{d}{\downarrow} \overrightarrow{A{\downarrow}C}{:}y\rangle \Rightarrow D{:}\omega\{(y\,\phi)/z\}}{\underset{d}{\downarrow}}L \qquad \frac{\vec{A}{:}x \underset{d}{\downarrow} \Gamma \Rightarrow C{:}\chi}{\Gamma \Rightarrow A{\underset{d}{\downarrow}}C{:}\lambda x\chi}{\underset{d}{\downarrow}}R$$

$$\frac{\Gamma \Rightarrow B{:}\psi \qquad \Delta\langle\vec{C}{:}z\rangle \Rightarrow D{:}\omega}{\Delta\langle\overrightarrow{C{\uparrow}_d B}{:}x \underset{d}{\downarrow} \Gamma\rangle \Rightarrow D{:}\omega\{(x\,\psi)/z\}}{\uparrow}L \qquad \frac{\Gamma \underset{d}{\downarrow} \vec{B}{:}y \Rightarrow C{:}\chi}{\Gamma \Rightarrow C{\uparrow}_d B{:}\lambda y\chi}{\uparrow}R$$

$$\frac{\Delta\langle\vec{A}{:}x \underset{d}{\downarrow} \vec{B}{:}y\rangle \Rightarrow D{:}\omega}{\Delta\langle\overrightarrow{A{\odot}_d B}{:}z\rangle \Rightarrow D{:}\omega\{\pi_1 z/x, \pi_2 z/y\}}{\underset{d}{\odot}}L$$

$$\frac{\Gamma_1 \Rightarrow A{:}\phi \qquad \Gamma_2 \Rightarrow B{:}\psi}{\Gamma_1 \underset{d}{\downarrow} \Gamma_2 \Rightarrow A{\odot}_d B}{\underset{d}{\odot}}R$$

$$\frac{\Delta\langle 1\rangle \Rightarrow A{:}\phi}{\Delta\langle\vec{J}{:}x\rangle \Rightarrow A{:}\phi}JL \qquad \frac{}{1 \Rightarrow J{:}0}JR$$

Fig. 2. Semantically labelled multiplicative rules

Semantically labelled semantically active multiplicative rules are given in Figure 2. The term 0 is interpreted as the unique inhabitant of type $\top$.

2.1 Semantically Inactive Multiplicatives

Semantically labelled semantically inactive concatenative and intercalative multiplicative rules are given in Figures 3 and 4 respectively.

$$\frac{\Gamma \Rightarrow A:\phi \qquad \Delta\langle \overrightarrow{C}:z\rangle \Rightarrow D:\omega}{\Delta\langle \Gamma, \overrightarrow{A\multimap C}:y\rangle \Rightarrow D:\omega\{y/z\}} {-}\!\circ L \qquad \frac{\overrightarrow{A}:x, \Gamma \Rightarrow C:\chi}{\Gamma \Rightarrow A{\multimap}C:\chi} {-}\!\circ R$$

$$\frac{\Gamma \Rightarrow B:\psi \qquad \Delta\langle \overrightarrow{C}:z\rangle \Rightarrow D:\omega}{\Delta\langle \overrightarrow{C{\bullet}B}:x, \Gamma\rangle \Rightarrow D:\omega\{0/z\}} {\bullet}L \qquad \frac{\Gamma, \overrightarrow{B}:y \Rightarrow C:\chi}{\Gamma \Rightarrow C{\bullet}B:\lambda y0} {\bullet}R$$

$$\frac{\Delta\langle \overrightarrow{A}:x, \overrightarrow{B}:y\rangle \Rightarrow D:\omega}{\Delta\langle \overrightarrow{A{\odot}B}:z\rangle \Rightarrow D:\omega\{z/y\}} {\odot}L \qquad \frac{\Gamma_1 \Rightarrow A:\phi \qquad \Gamma_2 \Rightarrow B:\psi}{\Gamma_1, \Gamma_2 \Rightarrow A{\odot}B:\psi} {\odot}R$$

$$\frac{\Gamma \Rightarrow A:\phi \qquad \Delta\langle \overrightarrow{C}:z\rangle \Rightarrow D:\omega}{\Delta\langle \Gamma, \overrightarrow{A{-}\!\bullet C}:y\rangle \Rightarrow D:\omega\{0/z\}} {-}\!\bullet L \qquad \frac{\overrightarrow{A}:x, \Gamma \Rightarrow C:\chi}{\Gamma \Rightarrow A{-}\!\bullet C:\lambda x0} {-}\!\bullet R$$

$$\frac{\Gamma \Rightarrow B:\psi \qquad \Delta\langle \overrightarrow{C}:z\rangle \Rightarrow D:\omega}{\Delta\langle \overrightarrow{C{\circ}B}:x, \Gamma\rangle \Rightarrow D:\omega\{x/z\}} {\circ}L \qquad \frac{\Gamma, \overrightarrow{B}:y \Rightarrow C:\chi}{\Gamma \Rightarrow C{\circ}B:\chi} {\circ}R$$

$$\frac{\Delta\langle \overrightarrow{A}:x, \overrightarrow{B}:y\rangle \Rightarrow D:\omega}{\Delta\langle \overrightarrow{A{\odot}B}:z\rangle \Rightarrow D:\omega\{z/x\}} {\odot}L \qquad \frac{\Gamma_1 \Rightarrow A:\phi \qquad \Gamma_2 \Rightarrow B:\psi}{\Gamma_1, \Gamma_2 \Rightarrow A{\odot}B:\phi} {\odot}R$$

Fig. 3. Semantically labelled semantically inactive conc. multiplicative rules

2.2 Words as Types

Let Σ be the lexical vocabulary. The semantic type for types $W(w)$ where $w \in \Sigma^*$ is $\top$; the standard syntactical interpretation for types $W(w)$ is:

$$[[W(w)]] =_{\text{def}} \{w\}$$

Notice that in particular the interpretation of the continuous unit I coincides with the interpretation of $W(\epsilon)$, i.e.:

$$[[I]] = [[W(\epsilon)]] = \{\epsilon\}$$

Therefore we postulate the following logical rules related to $W(\epsilon)$:

$$\frac{\Delta\langle \Lambda\rangle \Rightarrow A:\phi}{\Delta\langle W(\epsilon):x\rangle \Rightarrow A:\phi} W(\epsilon)L \qquad \frac{}{\Lambda \Rightarrow W(\epsilon):0} W(\epsilon)R$$

In addition:

$$\frac{\Delta\langle W(w_1):x, W(w_2):y\rangle \Rightarrow A:\phi}{\Delta\langle W(w_1{+}w_2):z\rangle \Rightarrow A:\phi} W(w)L \qquad \frac{\Gamma_1 \Rightarrow W(w_1):\phi \qquad \Gamma_2 \Rightarrow W(w_2):\psi}{\Gamma_1, \Gamma_2 \Rightarrow W(w_1{+}w_2):0} W(w)R$$

This added machinary is clearly sound with respect to the syntactical interpretation given to displacement calculus (Morrill et al. 2011[16]). Cut-elimination applies as well.

$$\frac{\Gamma \Rightarrow A{:}\phi \qquad \Delta\langle \overrightarrow{C}{:}z\rangle \Rightarrow D{:}\omega}{\Delta\langle \overrightarrow{\Gamma \downarrow_\sigma A}\, \overset{\bullet}{\downarrow}\, C{:}y\rangle \Rightarrow D{:}\omega\{0/z\}}\ \overset{\bullet}{\downarrow} L \qquad\qquad \frac{\overrightarrow{A}{:}x \downarrow_\sigma \Gamma \Rightarrow C{:}\chi}{\Gamma \Rightarrow A\,\overset{\bullet}{\downarrow}_\sigma C{:}\lambda x0}\ \overset{\bullet}{\downarrow} R$$

$$\frac{\Gamma \Rightarrow B{:}\psi \qquad \Delta\langle \overrightarrow{C}{:}z\rangle \Rightarrow D{:}\omega}{\Delta\langle \overrightarrow{C\,\overset{\circ}{\downarrow}_\sigma B}{:}x \downarrow_\sigma \Gamma\rangle \Rightarrow D{:}\omega\{x/z\}}\ \overset{\circ}{\downarrow} L \qquad\qquad \frac{\Gamma \downarrow \overrightarrow{B}{:}y \Rightarrow C{:}\chi}{\Gamma \Rightarrow C\,\overset{\circ}{\downarrow}_\sigma B{:}\chi}\ \overset{\circ}{\downarrow} R$$

$$\frac{\Delta\langle \overrightarrow{A}{:}x \downarrow_\sigma \overrightarrow{B}{:}y\rangle \Rightarrow D{:}\omega}{\Delta\langle \overrightarrow{A\,\overset{\ominus}{}_\sigma B}{:}z\rangle \Rightarrow D{:}\omega\{z/y\}}\ \overset{\ominus}{} L \qquad\qquad \frac{\Gamma_1 \Rightarrow A{:}\phi \qquad \Gamma_2 \Rightarrow B{:}\psi}{\Gamma_1 \downarrow \Gamma_2 \Rightarrow A\,\overset{\ominus}{}B{:}\psi}\ \overset{\ominus}{} R$$

$$\frac{\Gamma \Rightarrow A{:}\phi \qquad \Delta\langle \overrightarrow{C}{:}z\rangle \Rightarrow D{:}\omega}{\Delta\langle \overrightarrow{\Gamma \downarrow_\sigma A}\,\overset{\bullet}{\downarrow}_\sigma C{:}y\rangle \Rightarrow D{:}\omega\{y/z\}}\ \overset{\bullet}{\downarrow} L \qquad\qquad \frac{\overrightarrow{A}{:}x \downarrow_\sigma \Gamma \Rightarrow C{:}\chi}{\Gamma \Rightarrow A\,\overset{\bullet}{\downarrow}_\sigma C{:}\chi}\ \overset{\bullet}{\downarrow} R$$

$$\frac{\Gamma \Rightarrow B{:}\psi \qquad \Delta\langle \overrightarrow{C}{:}z\rangle \Rightarrow D{:}\omega}{\Delta\langle \overrightarrow{C\,\overset{\bullet}{\downarrow}_\sigma B}{:}x \downarrow_\sigma \Gamma\rangle \Rightarrow D{:}\omega\{0/z\}}\ \overset{\bullet}{\downarrow} L \qquad\qquad \frac{\Gamma \downarrow \overrightarrow{B}{:}y \Rightarrow C{:}\chi}{\Gamma \Rightarrow C\,\overset{\bullet}{\downarrow}_\sigma B{:}\lambda y0}\ \overset{\bullet}{\downarrow} R$$

$$\frac{\Delta\langle \overrightarrow{A}{:}x \downarrow_\sigma \overrightarrow{B}{:}y\rangle \Rightarrow D{:}\omega}{\Delta\langle \overrightarrow{A\,\overset{\ominus}{}_\sigma B}{:}z\rangle \Rightarrow D{:}\omega\{z/y\}}\ \overset{\ominus}{} L \qquad\qquad \frac{\Gamma_1 \Rightarrow A{:}\phi \qquad \Gamma_2 \Rightarrow B{:}\psi}{\Gamma_1 \downarrow \Gamma_2 \Rightarrow A\,\overset{\ominus}{}B{:}\psi}\ \overset{\ominus}{} R$$

Fig. 4. Semantically labelled semantically inactive interc. multiplicative rules

3   Syntax and Semantics of Collocations

3.1   Expletives, Discontinuous Idioms and Particle Verbs

Expletives. Consider the following lexical entry for the verb *rains* in (1a) which needs the semantically dummy expletive pronoun *it*:

(10) *rains*: $W(it){-}\!\circ S$: **rain**

$$(11)\quad \frac{W(it){:}x \Rightarrow W(it){:}x \qquad S{:}z \Rightarrow S{:}z}{W(it){:}x,\ W(it){-}\!\circ S{:}y \Rightarrow S{:}y}\ {-}\!\circ L$$

The proof (11) gives the derivational semantics y, and then with the lexical semantics in (10), we get S: **rain**.[2]

---

[2] Two referees object that this treatment requires two types for *seems* to generate both *It seems to rain* and *John seems to smile* whereas if we assume a special N category $N(it)$ we can get by with a single type $\forall x((N(x)\backslash S)/(N(x)\backslash S_{inf}))$. However, this single syntactic category fails to reflect that the semantics must be treated differently in the two cases.

Discontinuous Idioms. The idiom *gives . . . the cold shoulder* in (2) can be generated with the following lexical assignment:

(12) *gives*: $(N\backslash S)/(N\mathbb{O}W(the+cold+shoulder))$: **shun**

We are able to generate example (2) in labelled ND format as follows:

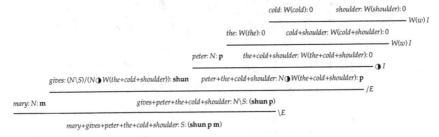

Particle Verbs. Particle verbs like *calls . . . up* can be accounted for with the following lexical assignment:

(13) *calls*: $(N\backslash S)/(N\mathbb{O}W(up))$: **phone**

The lexical assignment (13) generates (3a) as follows in labelled ND format:

(14)

$$\dfrac{mary: N: \mathbf{m} \quad \dfrac{calls: (N\backslash S)/(N\mathbb{O}W(up)): \mathbf{phone} \quad \dfrac{peter: N: \mathbf{p} \quad up: W(up): 0}{peter+up: N\mathbb{O}W(up): \mathbf{p}} \mathbb{O}I}{calls+peter+up: N\backslash S: (\mathbf{phone\,p})} /E}{mary+calls+peter+up: S: (\mathbf{phone\,p\,m})} \backslash E$$

If one wants to account for the non-determinism of examples (3a) and (3b), we need a more general assignment with a semantically inactive additive, for example:

(15) *calls*: $(N\backslash S)/((N\mathbb{O}W(up))\sqcup(W(up)\mathbb{O}N))$: **phone**

3.2 Interaction with Gapping

We turn now to gapping as like-category coordination. The standard type assignment for gapping (Morrill et al. 2011[16]) in the displacement calculus is the following:[3]

(16) *and*: $((S\uparrow_+TV)\backslash(S\uparrow_+TV))/\hat{}(S\uparrow_+TV)$: $\lambda P\lambda Q\lambda z[(Pz)\wedge(Qz)]$

However, as noted by Kubota and Levine (2012[4]), the lexical assignment (16) cannot generate cases with *complex* transitive verbs like discontinuous idiomatic transitive verbs or particle verbs.

---

[3] We use the defined connective bridge, $\hat{}A =_{df} A\mathbb{Q}I$, for which the derived Right rule is:

(i) $\dfrac{\Gamma \Rightarrow A: \phi}{\Gamma \downarrow \Lambda \Rightarrow \hat{}A: \phi} \hat{}R$

The HTLG Account. The set of types in HTLG is the smallest set which includes a denumerable set of atomic types closed by the standard Lambek divisions and the vertical slash |. This vertical slash allows HTLG to account for several complex phenomena of discontinuity. In particular, scoping interactions with gapping are elegantly and successfully explained.

HTLG's proof machinery is based on a labelled natural deduction system (LND) with the following constraints:

- Types the principal connective of which is Lambekian are inhabited by concatenations of syntactical (or prosodic) constants.
- Types the principal connective of which is the vertical slash | are inhabited by string lambda terms.

Despite the linguistic flexibility of the LND of HTLG, there are problems with the definition of types like $(CN\backslash CN)/(S|N)$ for a relative pronoun where the higher order argument subtype would be a string lambda term and therefore its concatenation is not defined. It follows that the algebra of types of HTLG is not free (M. Moortgat, p.c.) and requires a sorting discipline such as that "|" always outscopes "\" and "/". In HTLG a type for the relative pronoun would be then $(CN|CN)|(S|N)$.

The lexical entry proposed in HTLG for standard (simple transitive verb) gapping is the following:

(17) $\lambda\Phi\lambda\Psi\lambda v[(\Psi v)+and+(\Phi \epsilon)]: ((S|TV)|(S|TV))|(S|TV):\lambda P\lambda Q\lambda w.[(Q w)\wedge(P w)]$

For a complex transitive verb like a particle verb, the type entry proposed is:

(18) $((S|(TV|N))|(S|(TV|N)))|(S|(TV|N))$

The type assignment for standard gapping in the displacement calculus is:

(19) $((S{\uparrow}TV)\backslash(S{\uparrow}TV))/{\uparrow}(S{\uparrow}TV)$

If one assumes that in the displacement calculus the type of a complex transitive verb is $(N\backslash S){\uparrow}N$ (cf. [16]), there is no possibility to make an extraction of this type as in the case of standard gapping:

(20) $\dfrac{N, 1\{N\} \Rightarrow S{\uparrow}((N\backslash S){\uparrow}N)}{N, ((N\backslash S){\uparrow}N)\{N\} \Rightarrow S}$ *

Thus, provided it assumes two gapping lexical entries, HTLG is able to account for standard gapping and generalized gapping respectively whereas, apparently, displacement calculus can account for only the former. Here however, using the limited machinery which we have added to the displacement calculus, we will see that we are able to account for gapping with simple and complex transitive verbs, and furthermore do so with a single gapping lexical entry.

Generalized Gapping in D with Words as Types and Semantically Inactive Multiplicatives. Here we propose a new gapping coordinator lexical assignment which can generate both gapping with *simple* transitive verbs and gapping with *complex* transitive verbs. Let there be the following abbreviations for types:

(21) $GTV(w) := (N\backslash S)/(N\textbf{O}W(w))$

    $X(w) := (S\!\uparrow\!GTV(w))\overset{!}{\cdot} W(w)$

We propose the following generalized gapping lexical entry:

(22) *and*: $\forall u((X(u)\backslash X(u)/\mathord{\sim}X(u)): \lambda P\lambda Q\lambda z[(Pz) \wedge (Qz)]$

Notice the crucial use of both continuous and discontinuous semantically inactive connectives, as well as the use of the semantically inactive universal quantifier $\forall$. With this type for the coordinator we are able to generate the following instances of gapping:

(23) a. Peter sees Mary and Robin, Clark.
     b. Peter calls up Mary and Robin, Clark.
     c. Peter calls Mary up and Robin, Clark.
     d. Peter gives Mary the cold shoulder and Robin, Clark.

Notice the following important equivalence:

(24) $(N\backslash S)/(N\textbf{O}W(\epsilon)) \Leftrightarrow TV$

The proof of $TV \Rightarrow GTV(\epsilon)$ uses the Left rule for $W(\epsilon)$, while the proof of $GTV(\epsilon) \Rightarrow TV$ uses the Right rule for $W(\epsilon)$:

(25) a.
$$
\cfrac{
\cfrac{
\cfrac{
\cfrac{N, TV, N \Rightarrow S}{N, TV, N, W(\epsilon) \Rightarrow S}\ W(\epsilon)L
}{TV, N, W(\epsilon) \Rightarrow N\backslash S}\ \backslash R
}{TV, N\textbf{O}W(\epsilon) \Rightarrow N\backslash S}\ \textbf{O}L
}{TV \Rightarrow GTV(\epsilon) = (N\backslash S)/(N\textbf{O}W(\epsilon))}\ /R
$$

b.
$$
\cfrac{
\cfrac{
\cfrac{
\cfrac{\ }{N \Rightarrow N \wedge \Rightarrow W(\epsilon)}\ W(\epsilon)R
}{N \Rightarrow N\textbf{O}W(\epsilon)}\ \textbf{O}R \qquad N\backslash S \Rightarrow N\backslash S
}{GTV(\epsilon), N \Rightarrow N\backslash S}\ /L
}{GTV(\epsilon) \Rightarrow (N\backslash S)/N}\ /R
$$

Derivations of Generalized Gapping. Using the lexical entry for generalized gapping (22), we are able to account for standard gapping examples (simple transitives) like (23a) as well as gapping instances with for example a particle verb like (23c). For (23c) we have:

(26)
$$
\cfrac{
\cfrac{
\cfrac{
\cfrac{
\cfrac{N \Rightarrow N \quad W(up) \Rightarrow W(up)}{N, W(up) \Rightarrow N\textbf{O}W(up)}\ \textbf{O}R \qquad \cfrac{N \Rightarrow N \quad S \Rightarrow S}{N, N\backslash S \Rightarrow S}\ \backslash L
}{N, GTV(up), N, W(up) \Rightarrow S}\ /L
}{N, 1, N, W(up) \Rightarrow S\!\uparrow\!GTV(up)}\ \uparrow R
}{N, 1, N, 1 \Rightarrow X(up) = (S\!\uparrow\!GTV(up))\overset{!}{\cdot} W(up)}\ !R
}{\cfrac{N, N, 1 \Rightarrow \mathord{^\wedge}X(up)}{N, N \Rightarrow \mathord{\sim}X(up)}\ \mathord{\sim}R}\ \mathord{^\wedge}R
$$

$$\dfrac{\dfrac{N \Rightarrow N \qquad W(up) \Rightarrow W(up)}{N, W(up) \Rightarrow N \odot W(up)} \odot R \qquad \dfrac{N \Rightarrow N \qquad S \Rightarrow S}{\mid N, N \backslash S \Rightarrow S} \circ\text{-}L}{\dfrac{\dfrac{N, GTV(up), N, W(up) \Rightarrow S}{N, 1, N, W(up) \Rightarrow S\uparrow_+ GTV(up)} \uparrow R}{N, 1, N, 1 \Rightarrow (S\uparrow_+ GTV(up)) \downarrow_- W(up)} \uparrow R} /L}$$

(27)

$$\dfrac{GTV(up) \Rightarrow GTV(up) \qquad S \Rightarrow S}{(S\uparrow_+ GTV(up))\{GTV(up)\} \Rightarrow S} \uparrow L$$

$$\dfrac{W(up) \Rightarrow W(up) \qquad \dfrac{GTV(up) \Rightarrow GTV(up) \qquad S \Rightarrow S}{(S\uparrow_+ GTV(up))\{GTV(up)\} \Rightarrow S} \uparrow L}{(S\uparrow_+ GTV(up)) \downarrow_- W(up)\{GTV(up) : W(up)\} \Rightarrow S} \downarrow L}{N, GTV(up), N, X(up)\backslash X(up) \Rightarrow S} \backslash L$$

(26)   (27)

$\vdots$ $\vdots$

(28) $\dfrac{N, N \Rightarrow \,\widehat{}\,X(up) \qquad \dfrac{N, GTV(up), N, X(up)\backslash X(up) \Rightarrow S}{N, GTV(up), N, W(up), (X(up)\backslash X(up)/\,\widehat{}\,X(up)), N, N \Rightarrow S}}{N, GTV(up), N, W(up), \forall u((X(u)\backslash X(u))/\,\widehat{}\,X(u)), N, N \Rightarrow S} /L \quad \forall L, u := up$

Where lexical lookup gives $GTV(up)$ for *call*, (28) is a derivation of (23c). Using the lexical entry (22) for generalized gapping, one can account for gapping with simple transitive verbs like in sentence (23a), as derivation (29) shows:

(30)   (31)

$\vdots$ $\vdots$

(29) $\dfrac{N, N \Rightarrow \,\widehat{}\,X(\epsilon)) \qquad \dfrac{N, TV, N, X(\epsilon)\backslash X(\epsilon) \Rightarrow S}{N, TV, N, (X(\epsilon)\backslash X(\epsilon))/\,\widehat{}\,X(\epsilon)), N, N \Rightarrow S}}{N, TV, N, \forall u((X(u)\backslash X(u))/\,\widehat{}\,X(u)), N, N \Rightarrow S} /L \quad \forall L, u := \epsilon$

We show below the derivations (30) and (31) used in derivation (29):

(30)

$$\dfrac{\dfrac{\dfrac{\dfrac{N \Rightarrow N \qquad W(\epsilon) \Rightarrow W(\epsilon)}{N, W(\epsilon) \Rightarrow N \odot W(\epsilon)} \odot R \qquad \dfrac{N \Rightarrow N \qquad S \Rightarrow S}{N, N \backslash S \Rightarrow S} \backslash L}{N, GTV(\epsilon), N, W(\epsilon) \Rightarrow S} /L}{\dfrac{N, 1, N, W(\epsilon) \Rightarrow S\uparrow_+ GTV(\epsilon)}{N, 1, N, 1 \Rightarrow X(\epsilon) = (S\uparrow_+ GTV(\epsilon)) \downarrow_- W(\epsilon)} \uparrow R} \uparrow R}{\dfrac{N, N, 1 \Rightarrow \,\widehat{}\,X(\epsilon)}{N, N \Rightarrow \,\widehat{}\,X(\epsilon))} \,\widehat{}\,R} \,\widehat{}\,R$$

Notice in (31) the sub-derivation (25a) which gives a proof of $TV \Rightarrow GTV(\epsilon)$. Finally, in the appendix we give the derivation for (23d).

$$(31) \quad \cfrac{\cfrac{\cfrac{\cfrac{N \Rightarrow N \qquad W(\epsilon) \Rightarrow W(\epsilon)}{N, W(\epsilon) \Rightarrow N \mathbf{O} W(\epsilon)} \mathbf{O}R \qquad \cfrac{N \Rightarrow N \qquad S \Rightarrow S}{N, N\backslash S \Rightarrow S} \backslash L}{N, GTV(\epsilon), N, W(\epsilon) \Rightarrow S} /L}{\cfrac{N, 1, N, W(\epsilon) \Rightarrow S_+^{\uparrow} GTV(\epsilon)}{N, 1, N, 1 \Rightarrow (S_+^{\uparrow} GTV(\epsilon))_-^{\uparrow} W(\epsilon)} {\uparrow}R} {\uparrow}R}{N, TV, N, X(\epsilon)\backslash X(\epsilon) \Rightarrow S}$$

$$\cfrac{(25a)}{\cfrac{TV \Rightarrow GTV(\epsilon) \quad S \Rightarrow S}{\cfrac{W(\epsilon)R}{\cfrac{\Lambda \Rightarrow W(\epsilon) \qquad \cfrac{S_+^{\uparrow} GTV(\epsilon)\{TV\} \Rightarrow S}{S_+^{\uparrow} GTV(\epsilon)_-^{\uparrow} W(\epsilon)\{TV : \Lambda\} \Rightarrow S}}{} \backslash L}}{}}} {\uparrow}L$$

4   Conclusion

In this paper we have extended (displacement) categorial logic with semantically inactive multiplicatives and a proposal for words as types, innovations which fill existing technical and conceptual gaps in the type logical categorial architecture, while remaining within that architecture, and we have illustrated application to the syntax and semantics of collocations.

The semantically inactive multiplicatives are not indispensable, in that they can be simulated, for example by the usual multiplicatives with vacuous abstraction, just as the other semantically inactive connectives can be simulated by their semantically active counterparts. But the inactive variants provide for more economical grammatical specification. These proposals are implementable in the parser/theorem-prover CatLog (Morrill 2012[13]): the new sequent rules are of the same kind as existing ones and we only require by means of further addition lexical entries $v: W(v): 0$ for each contentless word v of collocations.

We have also shown how the only published examples of HTLG (Kubota and Levine 2012[4]) beyond the scope of the displacement calculus can be *simulated* by this enriched apparatus. HTLG is one of a family of categorial formalisms invoking higher-order syntactic abstraction (Oerhle 1994[19], de Groote 2002[1], Muskens 2003[18]). We think that such abstraction is problematic because parsing a formalism which uses syntactic beta-reduction apparently requires computing higher-order matching, which rapidly becomes intractable. This may explain why no parser yet exists for such formalisms. The displacement calculus with this little extra formal machinery seems to approximate the required expressivity given by HTLG, while maintaining implementability.

References

1. de Groote, P.: Towards Abstract Categorial Grammars. In: Proceedings of the 39th Annual Meeting of the Association for Computational Linguistics (ACL), Toulouse (2001)
2. Hepple, M.: The Grammar and Processing of Order and Dependency. PhD thesis, University of Edinburgh (1990)
3. Jäger, G.: Anaphora and Type Logical Grammar. Trends in Logic – Studia Logica Library, vol. 24. Springer, Heidelberg (2005)

4. Kubota, Y., Levine, R.: Gapping as like-category coordination. In: Béchet, D., Dikovsky, A. (eds.) LACL 2012. LNCS, vol. 7351, pp. 135–150. Springer, Heidelberg (2012)

5. Lambek, J.: On the Calculus of Syntactic Types. In: Jakobson, R. (ed.) Structure of Language and its Mathematical Aspects, Proceedings of the Symposia in Applied Mathematics XII, pp. 166–178. American Mathematical Society, Providence (1961)

6. Lambek, J.: Categorial and Categorical Grammars. In: Oehrle, R.T., Bach, E., Wheeler, D. (eds.) Categorial Grammars and Natural Language Structures. Studies in Linguistics and Philosophy, vol. 32, pp. 297–317. D. Reidel, Dordrecht (1988)

7. Lambek, J.: The mathematics of sentence structure. American Mathematical Monthly 65, 153–172 (1958), Reprinted in Buszkowski, W., Marciszewski, W., van Benthem, J. (eds.): Categorial Grammar. Linguistic & Literary Studies in Eastern Europe, vol. 25, pp. 153–172. John Benjamins, Amsterdam (1958)

8. Moortgat, M.: Multimodal linguistic inference. Journal of Logic, Language and Information 5(3,4), 349–385 (1996); Also in Bulletin of the IGPL 3(2,3), 371–401 (1995)

9. Moortgat, M.: Categorial Type Logics. In: van Benthem, J., ter Meulen, A. (eds.) Handbook of Logic and Language, pp. 93–177. Elsevier Science B.V. and the MIT Press, Amsterdam and Cambridge (1997)

10. Morrill, G.: Grammar and Logical Types. In: Stockhof, M., Torenvliet, L. (eds.) Proceedings of the Seventh Amsterdam Colloquium, pp. 429–450 (1990). Also in Barry, G., Morrill, G. (eds.): Studies in Categorial Grammar, Edinburgh Working Papers in Cognitive Science, vol. 5, pp. 127–148 (1990). Revised version published as Grammar and Logic. Theoria, LXII 3, 260–293 (1996)

11. Morrill, G.: Intensionality and Boundedness. Linguistics and Philosophy 13(6), 699–726 (1990)

12. Morrill, G.: Categorial Formalisation of Relativisation: Pied Piping, Islands, and Extraction Sites. Technical Report LSI-92-23-R, Departament de Llenguatges i Sistemes Informàtics, Universitat Politècnica de Catalunya (1992)

13. Morrill, G.: CatLog: A Categorial Parser/Theorem-Prover. In: LACL 2012 System Demonstrations, Logical Aspects of Computational Linguistics 2012, pp. 13–16, Nantes (2012)

14. Morrill, G., Merenciano, J.-M.: Generalising discontinuity. Traitement Automatique des Langues 37(2), 119–143 (1996)

15. Morrill, G., Valentín, O., Fadda, M.: Dutch Grammar and Processing: A Case Study in TLG. In: Bosch, P., Gabelaia, D., Lang, J. (eds.) TbiLLC 2007. LNCS, vol. 5422, pp. 272–286. Springer, Heidelberg (2009)

16. Morrill, G., Valentín, O., Fadda, M.: The Displacement Calculus. Journal of Logic, Language and Information 20(1), 1–48 (2011), doi:10.1007/s10849-010-9129-2

17. Morrill, G.V.: Type Logical Grammar: Categorial Logic of Signs. Kluwer Academic Publishers, Dordrecht (1994)

18. Muskens, R.: Language, lambdas, and logic. In: Kruijff, G.-J., Oehrle, R. (eds.) Resource-Sensitivity, Binding and Anaphora. Studies in Linguistics and Philosophy, vol. 80, pp. 23–54. Springer, Netherlands (2003)

19. Richard, T.: Oehrle. Term-labeled categorial type systems. Linguistics and Philosophy 17(6), 633–678 (1994)

20. Wasow, T., Sag, I.A., Nunberg, G.: Idioms: an interim report. In: Hattori, S., Inove, K. (eds.) Proceedings of the XIIIth International Congress of Linguists, Tokyo, pp. 102–115. CIPL (1983)

Appendix: Derivation of *Peter gives Mary the cold shoulder and Robin, Clark*

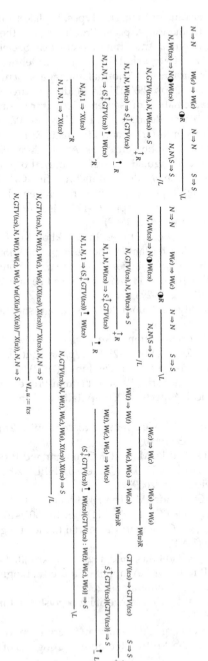

Generalising Predicate and Argument Invariance

Richard Zuber*

CNRS, Laboratoire de Linguistique Formelle, Paris, France
Richard.Zuber@linguist.univ-paris-diderot.fr

Abstract. Some constraints on higher order functions (maps from relations (or from sets and relations) to sets of type $\langle 1 \rangle$ quantifiers are studied. Such functions are denoted by "higher order" anaphors and comparatives. The constraints studied here are generalisations of similar constraints holding for "simple" functions from relations to sets denoted by "simple" anaphors and comparatives. Simple functions satisfy either predicate invariance or argument invariance. I propose a generalisation of these constraints. This generalisation makes it possible to spell out more formally differences and similarities between "simple" anaphors like *himself* and "higher order" anaphors like *each other* on the one hand, and between simple comparatives (like *the greatest number of books*) and "higher order" comparatives (like *the same books*) on the other.

1 Introduction

Invariance as discussed in this paper and used in formal (linguistic) semantics (Keenan and Westerståhl 1997), is a property of functions denoted by specific syntactic arguments of transitive verbs. These arguments, unlike "ordinary" noun phrases (NPs), cannot occur in all argumental positions; in particular they cannot occur in subject position. Occurring in oblique positions they form verb phrases (VPs) with transitive verb phrases (TVPs). Formally, the functions they denote take binary relations as arguments. Some of these functions have been investigated in connection with the study of type $\langle 1 \rangle$ quantifiers - ones like those denoted by *most cats* which map subsets of the domain of the model to truth values. Indeed, if type $\langle 1 \rangle$ quantifiers are typically denoted by NPs and if typical direct objects are NPs, then it is natural to allow type $\langle 1 \rangle$ quantifiers to apply also to binary relations in order to interpret VPs obtained by the application of the direct object NP to a TVP. Technically (see below), this is done by extending their domain of application. Extended in that way, type $\langle 1 \rangle$ quantifiers are arity reducers: they map binary relations to sets and sets to truth values (0-ary relations).

---

* Thanks to Ed Keenan and to reviewers for LACL 2014 for usually quite relevant remarks on the submitted version of the paper. Thanks also to a reviewer for *Journal of Logic, Language and Information* for important remarks on a previous very different version of this paper. Thanks to Ross Charnock for the usual help with English.

There are obviously other means that just the application of the "object" NPs to TVPs which make it possible to obtain syntactically complex VPs. The results presented here are related to the semantics and formal properties of sentences of the form given in (1):

(1)   NP TVP GNP

In this schema, GNP is a generalised noun phrase. GNPs are linguistic objects that can play the role of syntactic arguments of TVPs. Thus ordinary NPs (or DPs) are GNPs. However, there are GNPs which cannot play the role of the grammatical subject. I will be interested in the formal properties of some such GNPs.

Obviously GNPs can themselves be syntactically complex, and have the form GDet(CN), where GDet is a generalised determiner, that is an expression which takes CNs as arguments and gives a GNP as a result. Since CNs are assumed to denote sets and TVPs to denote binary relations GDets denote functions which take sets and (binary) relations as arguments.

Depending on the type of output two classes of functions interpreting GNPs can be distinguished: (1) *simple functions*, which give sets (of individuals) as output and (2) *higher order* functions, which have sets of type $\langle 1 \rangle$ quantifiers as output. Simple functions are needed to interpret sentences like (2):

(2)   Leo hates himself.

In (2) *himself* is a syntactic argument of *hates* with which it forms a VP. It is thus a GNP and it denotes the function $SELF$ defined as $SELF(R) = \{x : \langle x, x \rangle \in R\}$). It can be shown (Keenan 2007) that $SELF$ is not an extension of a type $\langle 1 \rangle$ quantifier and thus is not denoted by a "typical" NP. More formally this means that $SELF$ is a function from relations to sets which does not satisfy the extension condition which extended type $\langle 1 \rangle$ quantifiers satisfy. The extension condition and other, weaker conditions like the one satisfied by $SELF$ are formally defined in section 3. The following example illustrates the difference between extension condition and the condition satisfied by $SELF$. Suppose (3) is true. Then (4a) is also true but (4b) needs not be true:

(3)   Persons that Leo hates=persons that Lea admires.

(4)   a.   Leo hates two philosophers iff Lea admires two philosophers.

   b.   Leo hates himself iff Lea admires herself.

Thus the denotation of the ordinary NP in the object position does not have the same semantic properties as the denotation of the anaphor *himself/herself*.

The function $SELF$ satisfies a weaker condition, *predicate invariance*. Suppose (5a) is true. Then (5b) is also true:

(5)   a.   Persons that Leo hates=persons that Leo admires.

   b.   Leo hates himself iff Leo admires himself.

Consider now (6a), with the intended meaning given in (6b). The GNP *the greatest number of philosophers* is different from ordinary NPs since the function it denotes also does not satisfy the extension condition that type $\langle 1 \rangle$ quantifiers denoted by direct object NPs satisfy; (7) does not follow from (3):

(6)   a. Leo hates the greatest number of philosophers.

    b. Leo hates not less philosophers than anybody else.

(7)   Leo hates the greatest number of philosophers iff Lea admires the greatest number of philosophers.

The function denoted by the GNP *the greatest number of philosophers* satisfies a weaker condition, *argument invariance*. The entailment from (8a) to (8b) illustrates this condition:

(8)   a. Persons Leo hates=persons Lea hates.

    b. Leo hates the greatest number of philosophers iff Lea hates the greatest number of philosophers.

Simple functions satisfying argument or predicate invariance have been already studied to various degrees (Keenan and Westerståhl 1997, Keenan 2007, Zuber 2010, Zuber 2011b). As we will see, definitions of (simple) argument or predicate invariance do not apply to higher order functions, that is functions from relations to sets of type $\langle 1 \rangle$ quantifiers. Such functions are needed to interpret the GNPs one finds in (9) and (10):

(9)   Two philosophers hate each other.

(10)   Two philosophers read the same books.

Some properties of such higher order functions have been studied in Zuber 2013. The purpose of this paper is to generalise the notion of invariance so that it applies to higher order functions like those denoted by the GNPs in (9) and (10). As a consequence similarities and differences between anaphors in (2) and (9) and between comparisons in (6a) and (10) will be formally expressible.

Since I am basically interested in some abstract properties of functions denoted by GNPs, no attempt is made to provide an exhaustive semantic description of constructions given as examples. For the same reason syntactic considerations are very limited.

2   Formal Preliminaries

We will consider binary relations and functions over a universe E, assumed to be finite throughout this paper. If a function takes only a binary relation as argument, its type is noted $\langle 2 : \tau \rangle$, where τ is the type of the output; if a function takes a set and a binary relation as arguments, its type is noted $\langle 1, 2 : \tau \rangle$. If $\tau = 1$ then the output of the function is a set of individuals and thus the type of the function is $\langle 2 : 1 \rangle$ or $\langle 1, 2 : 1 \rangle$. For instance, the function $SELF$ is of type $\langle 2 : 1 \rangle$ and the function denoted by the anaphoric determiner *every...but himself* is of type $\langle 1, 2 : 1 \rangle$. The basic case we will consider here is when τ corresponds to a set of type $\langle 1 \rangle$ quantifiers and thus τ equals, in Montagovian notation, $\langle\langle\langle e, t \rangle t \rangle t \rangle$. In short, the type of such functions will be noted either $\langle 2 : \langle 1 \rangle \rangle$ (functions from binary relations to sets of type $\langle 1 \rangle$ quantifiers)) or $\langle 1, 2 : \langle 1 \rangle \rangle$ (functions from sets and binary relations to sets of type $\langle 1 \rangle$ quantifiers).

Basic type $\langle 1 \rangle$ quantifiers are functions from sets to truth-values. In this case they are denotations of subject NPs. However, NPs can also occur in oblique positions and in this case their denotations do not take sets (denotations of VPs) as arguments but rather denotations of TVPs (relations) as arguments. To account for this eventuality one extends the domain of application of basic type $\langle 1 \rangle$ quantifiers so that they apply to n-ary relations and have as output an (n–1)-ary relation (see Keenan 1987). Since we are basically interested in binary relations, the domain of application of basic type $\langle 1 \rangle$ quantifiers will be extended by adding to their domain the set of binary relations. In this case the quantifier Q can act as a "subject" quantifier or a "direct object" quantifier giving rise to the *nominative case extension* Q_{nom} and *accusative case extension* Q_{acc} respectively. They are defined as follows (Keenan and Westerstahl 1997):

Definition 1. *For each type* $\langle 1 \rangle$ *quantifier* Q, $Q_{nom}R = \{a : Q(Ra) = 1\}$, *where* $Ra = \{x : \langle x, a \rangle \in R\}$.

Definition 2. *For each type* $\langle 1 \rangle$ *quantifier* Q, $Q_{acc}R = \{a : Q(aR) = 1\}$, *where* $aR = \{y : \langle a, y \rangle \in R\}$.

From now on $Q_{nom}R$ will be noted QR.

Various motivations for the accusative case extension and some of its application are given in Keenan (2014). In what follows some applications of the nominal case extension will be given as well.

The standard definitions of post-negation, of dual, etc. of a basic type $\langle 1 \rangle$ quantifier also work for extended type $\langle 1 \rangle$ quantifiers. It easy to see for instance that $\neg(Q_{acc}) = (\neg Q)_{acc}$ and $(Q^d)_{acc} = (Q_{acc})^d$. A type $\langle 1 \rangle$ quantifier Q is *positive* iff $Q(\emptyset) = 0$ and Q is *atomic* iff it contains exactly one element, that is if $Q = \{A\}$ for some $A \subseteq E$. We will call a type $\langle 1 \rangle$ quantifier Q *natural* iff either Q is positive and $E \in Q$ or Q is not positive and $E \notin Q$. Two natural quantifiers have the same polarity iff either both are positive or neither of them is positive.

A special class of type $\langle 1 \rangle$ quantifiers is formed by *individuals*: I_a is an individual (generated by $a \in E$) iff $I_a = \{X : a \in X\}$. We will use more often a more general notion of a *(principal) filter generated by a set*. Thus $Ft(A)$, the (principal) filter generated by the set A, is defined as $Ft(A) = \{X : X \subseteq E \wedge A \subseteq X\}$. All proper principal filters are natural and have the same polarity.

We will use also the property of *living on* (cf. Barwise and Cooper 1981). The basic type $\langle 1 \rangle$ quantifier lives on a set A (where $A \subseteq E$) iff for all $X \subseteq E$, $Q(X) = Q(X \cap A)$. If E is finite then there is always a smallest set on which a quantifier Q lives. The fact that A is a set on which Q lives will be noted $Li(Q, A)$ and the fact that A is a smallest set on which Q lives will be noted $SLi(Q, A)$. If $Li(Q, A)$ and $B \subseteq A \wedge B \in Q$ then B is a *witness set* of Q. The fact that B is a witness set of the quantifier Q, which lives on A, will be noted

$B = Wt(Q, A)$. If $Li(Q, A)$ then $A \in Q$ iff $E \in Q$ and thus if $E \in Q$ and $Li(Q, A)$ then $A = Wt(Q, A)$.

Observe that any principal filter is a positive type $\langle 1 \rangle$ quantifier which lives on the set by which it is generated, and, moreover this set is its witness set. Atomic quantifiers live on the universe E only.

3 Invariance Principles

Let me start by recalling definitions of invariance for simple functions, that is type $\langle 2 : 1 \rangle$ and occasionally of type $\langle 1, 2 : 1 \rangle$ functions. Nominal and accusative extensions of type $\langle 1 \rangle$ quantifiers are such functions. Accusative extensions of type $\langle 1 \rangle$ quantifiers are specific type $\langle 2 : 1 \rangle$ functions. They are just those that satisfy the accusative extension condition **EC** (Keenan and Westerstahl 1997):

Definition 3. *A type $\langle 2 : 1 \rangle$ function F satisfies **EC** iff for R and S binary relations, and $a, b \in E$, if $aR = bS$ then $a \in F(R)$ iff $b \in F(S)$.*

Observe that if F satisfies **EC** then for all $X \subseteq E$ either $F(E \times X) = \emptyset$ or $F(E \times X) = E$. Given that $SELF(E \times A) = A$ the function $SELF$ does not satisfy **EC**. Similarly the type $\langle 2 : 1 \rangle$ function $F(R) = MORE_{l,Ph}(R) = \{x : |xR \cap Ph| > |lR \cap Ph|\}$ which is needed to interpret the verbal argument *more philosophers than Lea* in (11), does not satisfy **EC**:

(11)   Leo knows more philosophers than Lea.

The two functions above satisfy conditions weaker than **EC**. The function $SELF$ satisfies the following predicate invariance condition **PI**:

Definition 4. *A type $\langle 2 : 1 \rangle$ function F is predicate invariant (**PI**) iff for R and S binary relations, and $a \in E$, if $aR = aS$ then $a \in F(R)$ iff $a \in F(S)$.*

This condition is also satisfied for instance by the function $ONLY\text{-}SELF$ defined as follows: $ONLY\text{-}SELF(R) = \{x : xR = \{x\}\}$. Given that $ONLY\text{-}SELF(E \times \{a\}) = \{a\}$, the function $ONLY\text{-}SELF$ does not satisfy **EC**.

The **PI** condition is weaker than **EC**. The function $MORE_{l,Ph}$ above satisfies another weakening of **EC**, the so-called *argument invariance* condition **AI**:

Definition 5. *A type $\langle 2 : 1 \rangle$ function F is argument invariant iff for any binary relation R and $a, b \in E$, if $aR = bR$ then $a \in F(R)$ iff $b \in F(R)$.*

The conditions **EC**, **PI** and **AI** concern type $\langle 2 : 1 \rangle$ functions, considered here as being denoted by "full" verbal arguments or GNPs. Such verbal arguments can be syntactically complex in the sense that they are formed by the application of *generalised determiners* (GDets) to common nouns. For instance the GDet *every...except himself* can apply to the CN *student* to give a genuine GNP *every student except himself*. In this case GDets (when they take one common noun as the argument) denote type $\langle 1, 2 : 1 \rangle$ functions. Such functions also are constrained by invariance conditions. Thus:

Definition 6. *A type* $\langle 1, 2 : 1 \rangle$ *function* F *satisfies* **D1EC** *iff for* R *and* S *binary relations,* $X \subseteq E$ *and* $a, b \in E$*, if* $aR \cap X = bS \cap X$ *then* $a \in F(X, R)$ *iff* $b \in F(X, S)$.

Denotations of ordinary determiners occurring in determiner phrases which take direct object position satisfy **D1AE**. More precisely, if D is a type $\langle 1, 1 \rangle$ quantifier, then the function $F(X, R) = D(X)_{acc}(R)$ satisfies **D1EC**.

Functions denoted by properly anaphoric determiners (ones which form GNPs denoting functions satisfying **PI** but failing **EC**) do not satisfy **D1EC**. For instance the function $F(X, R) = \{y : X \cap yR = \{y\}\}$ denoted by the anaphoric determiner *no... except himself/herself* does not satisfy **D1EC**. Functions denoted by anaphoric determiners do satisfy the following condition (Zuber 2010):

Definition 7. *A type* $\langle 1, 2 : 1 \rangle$ *function* F *satisfies* **D1PI** *(predicate invariance for unary determiners) iff for* R *and* S *binary relations* $X \subseteq E$*, and* $a \in E$*, if* $aR \cap X = aS \cap X$ *then* $a \in F(X, R)$ *iff* $a \in F(X, S)$.

Functions denoted by determiners which form GNPs whose denotations satisfy **AI** have the following property:

Definition 8. *A type* $\langle 1, 2 : 1 \rangle$ *function* F *satisfies* **D1AI** *(argument invariance for unary determiners) iff for any binary relation* R*,* $X \subseteq E$ *and* $a, b \in E$*, if* $aR \cap X = bR \cap X$ *then* $a \in F(X, R)$ *iff* $b \in F(X, R)$.

The purpose of this paper is to generalise the definitions of the above constraints in such a way that they apply to higher order functions of type $\langle 2 : \langle 1 \rangle \rangle$. We will ignore here details of definitions of invariance applying to type $\langle 1, 2 : \langle 1 \rangle \rangle$ functions, except for argument invariance.

One can distinguish various kinds of type $\langle 2 : \langle 1 \rangle \rangle$ functions. For instance any type $\langle 2 : 1 \rangle$ function whose output is denoted by a VP can be lifted to the type $\langle 2 : \langle 1 \rangle \rangle$ (type $\langle \langle \langle e, t \rangle t \rangle t \rangle$ in Montague notation) function. This is in particular the case with the accusative and nominative extensions of a type $\langle 1 \rangle$ quantifier. For instance the accusative extension of a type $\langle 1 \rangle$ quantifier can be lifted to type $\langle 2 : \langle 1 \rangle \rangle$ function in the way indicated in (12). Such functions will be called *accusative lifts*. More generally, if F is a type $\langle 2 : 1 \rangle$ function, its lift F^L, a type $\langle 2 : \langle 1 \rangle \rangle$ function, is defined in (13):

(12) $Q_{acc}^L(R) = \{Z : Z(Q_{acc}(R)) = 1\}$.

(13) $F^L(R) = \{Z : Z(F(R)) = 1\}$.

The variable Z above runs over the set of type $\langle 1 \rangle$ quantifiers.

For type $\langle 2 : \langle 1 \rangle \rangle$ functions which are lifts of type $\langle 2 : 1 \rangle$ functions we have:

Proposition 1. *If a type* $\langle 2 : \langle 1 \rangle \rangle$ *function* F *is a lift of a type* $\langle 2 : 1 \rangle$ *function then for any type* $\langle 1 \rangle$ *quantifiers* Q_1 *and* Q_2 *and any binary relation* R*, if* $Q_1 \in F(R)$ *and* $Q_2 \in F(R)$ *then* $(Q_1 \wedge Q_2) \in F(R)$

For type $\langle 2 : \langle 1 \rangle \rangle$ functions which are accusative lifts we have:

Proposition 2. *Let F be a type $\langle 2 : \langle 1 \rangle \rangle$ function which is an accusative lift. Then for any $A, B \subseteq E$, any binary relation R, $Ft(A) \in F(R)$ and $Ft(B) \in F(R)$ iff $Ft(A \cup B) \in F(R)$.*

Propositions 1 and 2 need not hold for all type $\langle 2 : \langle 1 \rangle \rangle$ functions. As already mentioned there are GNPs which denote genuine higher order functions, that is functions which are not accusative lifts. Consider:

(14) a. Leo and Lea hug each other/read the same books.

      b. Bill and Sue hug each other/read the same books.

(15) Leo, Lea, Bill and Sue hug each other/read the same books.

Clearly (14a) in conjunction with (14b) does not entail (15). This means that the functions denoted by the subject NPs in (14a) and (14b) do not apply to the predicate denoted by the complex VPs in these sentences and thus the conjunction *and* is not understood pointwise. Hence, to avoid the type mismatch and get the right interpretations we will consider that the GNPs *each other* and *the same books* denote genuine higher order functions. However, since *each other* is an anaphor, that is an expression whose interpretation depends on the interpretation of its antecedent, the subject NP in this case, we want the function interpreting *each other* to have a property similar to the predicate invariance which is the property that functions interpreting anaphors like *himself* have. And, of course the **PI** as formulated above does not apply to higher order functions because in its definition the type of the output elements is essential.

There are many possible generalisations of **PI**, and for that matter, of **EC** and **AI** to higher order functions. One thing we require is that lifted higher order functions should satisfy them uniformly. Thus if **HPI** is a higher order generalisation of **PI** and F satisfies **PI** then F^L should satisfy **HPI**. Similarly with **HEC** and **HAI** generalisations of **EC** and **AI** respectively.

To begin, observe that any individual I_a is a type $\langle 1 \rangle$ quantifier which lives on $\{a\}$ and that (i) $aR = bS$ is equivalent to (ii) $\forall_{a \in \{a\}} \forall_{b \in \{b\}} (aR = bS)$. Given this and the definition of lifts we have the following equivalent "higher order" version of **EC**, for instance:

Proposition 3. *F satisfies **EC** iff for any $a, b \in E$ and any binary relations R, S, if $I_a R = I_b S$ then $I_a \in F^L(R)$ iff $I_b \in F^L(S)$.*

It is easy to formulate similar higher order versions of **PI** and **AI**. Of course these versions, lifted versions of **EC**, **PI** and **AI**, do not apply to the cases we are interested in, since the outputs of the higher order functions they characterise are individuals, which are denotations of singular NPs and in (9a) for instance, we have plural subjects. One way to avoid this difficulty is use generalisations proposed in the following definitions:

Definition 9. *A type $\langle 2 : \langle 1 \rangle \rangle$ function F satisfies **HEC** (higher order extension condition) iff for any natural type $\langle 1 \rangle$ quantifiers Q_1 and Q_2 with the same* *polarity, any $A, B \subseteq E$, any binary relations R, S, if $SLi(Q_1, A)$, $SLi(Q_2, B)$ and $\forall_{a \in A} \forall_{b \in B}(aR = bS)$ then $Q_1 \in F(R)$ iff $Q_2 \in F(S)$.*

Definition 10. *A type $\langle 2 : \langle 1 \rangle \rangle$ function F satisfies **HPI** (higher order predicate invariance) iff for any natural type $\langle 1 \rangle$ quantifier Q, any $A \subseteq E$, any binary relations R, S, if $SLi(Q, A)$ and $\forall_{a \in A}(aR = aS)$ then $Q \in F(R)$ iff $Q \in F(S)$.*

Definition 11. *A type $\langle 2 : \langle 1 \rangle \rangle$ function F satisfies **HAI** (higher order argument invariance) iff for any natural type $\langle 1 \rangle$ quantifiers Q_1 and Q_2 with the same polarity, any $A, B \subseteq E$, any binary relation R, if $SLi(Q_1, A)$, $SLi(Q_2, B)$ and $\forall_{a \in A} \forall_{b \in B}(aR = aS)$ then $Q_1 \in F(R)$ iff $Q_2 \in F(R)$.*

Obviously **HEC** entails both **HPI** and **HAI** in the same way that **EC** entails both **PI** and **AI**. More significantly, as we prove now, lifts of simple functions satisfying simple properties satisfy the corresponding higher order properties. More precisely we have:

Proposition 4. *If a type $\langle 2 : \langle 1 \rangle \rangle$ function F is an accusative lift then F satisfies **HEC**.*

Proof. Let $F = Z_{acc}^L$ for some type $\langle 1 \rangle$ quantifier Z. Suppose *a contrario* that there exist natural Q_1 and Q_2 with the same polarity such that $Li(Q_1, A)$, $Li(Q_2, B)$ and that (i), (ii) and (iii) hold: (i) $\forall_{a \in A} \forall_{b \in B}(aR = bS)$, (ii) $Q_1 \in Z_{acc}^L(R)$ and (iii) $Q_2 \notin Z_{acc}^L(S)$.

(a) Suppose first that both Q_1 and Q_2 are positive. In this case $E \in (Q_1 \cap Q_2)$ and thus $A \in Q_1$ and $B \in Q_2$. If (ii) holds then $Q_1(\{x : Z(xR) = 1\}) = 1$ and thus $A \cap \{x : Z(xR) = 1\} \neq \emptyset$ since Q_1 is positive and $A \in Q_1$. Hence $\exists_{a \in E}(a \in A \wedge Z(aR) = 1)$. If (iii) holds then $B \nsubseteq Z_{acc}(S)$. Hence $\exists_{b \in B} Z(bS) = 0$. But this is impossible since in this case it follows from (i) that $aR = bS$.

(b) Suppose now that neither Q_1 nor Q_2 is positive. Then we have: $A \notin Q_1$, $E \notin Q_1$, $B \notin Q_2$ and $E \notin Q_2$. If (ii) holds then $Q_1(Z_{acc}(R) = 1)$ and thus $A \nsubseteq Z_{acc}R$. Hence $\exists_{a \in E}(a \in A \wedge a \notin Z_{acc}R)$. Consequently $Z(aR) = 0$. If (iii) holds then $Q_2(Z_{acc}S = 0)$ and thus $B \cap Z_{acc}S \neq \emptyset$. Hence $\exists_{b \in B} b \in Z_{acc}S$ and thus $Z(aS) = 1$. But this is impossible because it follows from (i) that $aR = bS$. $\square$

Proposition 5. *If F is a type $\langle 2 : \langle 1 \rangle \rangle$ function which satisfies **PI** then F^L satisfies **HPI**.*

Proof. Let Q live on A and (i) and (ii) hold: (i) $Q \in F^L(R)$, (ii) $\forall_{a \in A}(aR = aS)$. It follows from (i) that $Q(F(R)) = 1$ and thus $Q(F(R) \cap A) = 1$. Given that F is predicate invariant we have $F(R) \cap A = F(S) \cap A$ (otherwise for some $a \in A$ such that $aR = aS$ one would have $a \in F(R)$ and $a \notin F(S)$, which is impossible since F is predicate invariant). Hence $Q(F(S) \cap A) = 1$ and thus $Q \in F^L(S)$. $\square$

Proposition 6. *If F satisfies **AI** then F^L satisfies **HAI***

Proof. Let (i) $\forall_{a \in A} \forall_{b \in B}(aR = bR)$.

(a) Suppose first that Q_1 lives on A, Q_2 lives on B and both are natural and positive. Suppose *a contrario* that $Q_1 \in F^L(R)$ and $Q_2 \notin F^L(R)$. This means that $Q_1(A \cap F(R)) = 1$ and $Q_2(B \cap F(R)) = 0$. Hence $A \cap F(R) \neq \emptyset$ and $B \not\subseteq F(R)$. But this is impossible given (i) and the fact that F is **AI**.

(b) Suppose now that both Q_1, which lives on A, and Q_2, which lives on B, are natural but neither of them is positive. Suppose *a contrario* that $Q_1 \in F^L(R)$ and $Q_2 \notin F^L(R)$. This means that $A \not\subseteq F(R)$ and $B \cap F(R) \neq \emptyset$. It follows from this that $\exists_{a \in A}(a \notin F(R))$ and $\exists_{b \in B}(b \in F(R))$. But this is impossible given (i) and the fact that F is argument invariant. □

Let me illustrate the above propositions. Though the functions which will be given are related to various natural language constructions they are given here just as an illustration of the properties discussed above and are not meant to fully characterise the semantics of these constructions. In particular, for reasons of formal simplicity and, I must confess, the difficulty of the problem, I will discuss only examples of functions which are "partial" in the sense that their range is purposely limited to a specific class of quantifiers. Possible implications of this move for compositionality will be ignored here.

Since there is a logical dependence between various invariance conditions it might be interesting to show not only that a given function satisfies the **HPI** but also that it does not satisfy other conditions. To show that a function does not satisfy the **HAI** the following obvious proposition will be used:

Proposition 7. *Let F satisfies **HAI** and let $R = E \times C$, for $C \subseteq E$ arbitrary. Then for any $X \subseteq E$ either $Ft(X) \in F(R)$ or for any X, $Ft(X) \notin F(R)$*

What proposition 7 states informally, is that a function satisfying **HAI** condition and whose argument is the cross-product relation of the form $E \times A$, has in its output either all principal filters or no principal filter.

Of course by showing that some function does not satisfy **HAI** we show that it does not satisfy **HEC** either.

To begin with consider a type $\langle 1 : \langle 1 \rangle \rangle$ function given in (16):

(16) $2\text{-}EA\text{-}ONLY(R) = \{Q : \exists_{a,b \in E}(a \neq b) \wedge aR = \{b\} \wedge bR = \{a\} \wedge Q = (I_a \wedge I_b)\}$

This function can be used to give the semantics of sentences like (17), that is sentences in which the GNP is *each other only* and its antecedent, the subject NP is a conjunction of two proper nouns:

(17)   Leo and Lea love each other only.

It is easy to show that $2\text{-}EA\text{-}ONLY$ satisfies **HPI**. Suppose that (i) $\forall_{x \in A}(xR = xS)$ and (ii) $I_a \wedge I_b \in 2\text{-}EA\text{-}ONLY(R)$, where $A = \{a, b\}$. It follows from (i) that $aR = aS$, $aR = bS$, $bR = aS$ and $bR = bS$. Hence, given (ii), $aS = \{b\}$ and $bS = \{a\}$ and thus $I_a \wedge I_b \in 2\text{-}EA\text{-}ONLY(S)$.

Furthermore, it follows from proposition 8 and from the fact that the filter $I_a \wedge I_b$ is in $2\text{-}EA\text{-}ONLY(E \times A)$ and no other filter is in $2\text{-}ONLY(E \times A)$, that function $2\text{-}EA\text{-}ONLY$ does not satisfy **HAI**.

As the next example consider (18):

(18) $Ft\text{-}RFL\text{-}RECIP(R) = \{Q : \exists_{A\subseteq E}(Ft(A)(Dom((A \times A) \cap (R \cap R^{-1})) = 1 \wedge Q = Ft(A)\}$

Informally, this function can be considered as the denotation of an anaphor like *each other or oneself or themselves* which has an NP denoting a principal filter generated by A as antecedent.

The following function excludes the "reflexive part" and interprets purely reciprocal anaphors (in their strong logical reading):

(19) $Ft\text{-}EA(R) = \{Q : \exists_{A\subseteq E}(|A| \geq 2 \wedge Ft(A)(Dom((A\times A)\cap(R\cap R^{-1})\cap I')) = 1 \wedge Q = Ft(A)\}$, where I' is the complement of the identity relation I.

In (20) a Boolean composition of two higher order functions is involved:

(20)   Leo and Lea admire each other and most teachers.

We want to give a function interpreting the complex "higher order" anaphor *each other and most teachers* with the antecedent NP denoting a principal filter. Obviously this function has to entail the function $Ft\text{-}EA$ above and be completed by the part corresponding to *most teachers*. It is given in (21):

(21) $Ft\text{-}EA_Q(R) = Ft\text{-}EA(R) \wedge Q_{acc}^L(R)$

All the above functions interpret "higher order" anaphors whose antecedent NPs denote principal filters. Interestingly they can be used to define denotations of anaphors with antecedents which do not denote principal filters. Consider (22):

(22)   Most philosophers hate each other.

The NP *most philosophers* does not denote a filter. Informally, (22) says, under its strong logical reading of reciprocity, that there is a group of philosophers which forms a majority of philosophers and such that all of its members hate each other. So this group is a witness set which generates a principal filter. Consequently we have the following function:

(23) $MOST\text{-}EA(R) = \{Q : \exists_{A,B\subseteq E}(B \subseteq A) \wedge B = Wt(MOST(A), A) \wedge Ft(B) \in Ft\text{-}EA(R) \wedge Q = MOST(A)\}$.

Among other NPs which do not denote filters and which can be antecedents of higher order anaphors are NPs formed with numerals as illustrated in (24). In (25) we have a function which can be used to give their semantics:

(24)   Five students kissed each other.

(25) $N\text{-}EA(R) = \{Q : \exists_{n\in N}\exists_{A\subseteq E}\exists_{B\subseteq A}(|B| \geq 2 \wedge Ft(B) \in Ft\text{-}EA(R) \wedge Q = n(A)\}$, where $n(A)$ is a type $\langle 1\rangle$ quantifier such that $n(A)(Y) = 1$ iff $|A \cap Y| \geq n$.

All the above functions have only positive quantifiers, denoted by the antecedents of anaphors, in their output. The example in (26) shows that this need always be the case. The reading of (26) given in (27) indicates how to obtain the corresponding function interpreting (26). This function is given in (28):

(26)   No three students kissed each other.

(27)   It is not true that three students kissed each other.

(28) $NEG\text{-}N\text{-}EA(R) = \{Q : \exists_{n \in N} \exists_{A \subseteq E}(n(A) \notin N\text{-}EA(R) \land Q = \neg n(A)\}$

We need also a function by which we can interpret higher order anaphors having a non-natural quantifier as antecedent. No atomic quantifier Q_A such that $Q_A(Y) = 1$ iff $Y = A$ and $E \neq A \neq \emptyset$ is normal. Some NPs denote, however, such quantifiers and can serve as antecedents of higher order anaphors. The NP *only Leo and Lea* in (29) denotes an atomic quantifier and the function given in (30) can be used to interpret the anaphor *each other* in (29):

(29)   Only Leo and Lea kissed each other.

(30) $AT\text{-}EA(R) = \{Q : \exists_{A \subseteq E}(|A| \geq 2 \land Ft(A) \in Ft\text{-}EA(R) \land \forall_{X \subseteq E}(X \neq A \land X \not\subseteq A) \rightarrow \neg 2(X) \in NEG\text{-}N\text{-}EA(R) \land Q = \{A\}\}$

Many, if not all of the above functions satisfy **HPI**. This has been shown above for 2-*EA-ONLY*. This is obvious for *AT-EA* since *AT-EA* has only non-normal quantifiers in its output. We show now here that *Ft-RFL-RECIP* satisfies **HPI**. Suppose that for some A we have $Ft(A) \in Ft\text{-}REF\text{-}RECIP(R)$. We have to show that if for some binary relation S (i) holds (i): $Ft(A)R = Ft(A)S$ then $Ft(A) \in Ft\text{-}RFL\text{-}RECIP(S)$. Given the definition of *Ft-RFL-RECIP* this happens when $Ft(A)(Dom((A \times A) \cap (S \cap S^{-1}) = 1$. But if (i) holds then $(A \times A) \cap (R \cap R^{-1}) = (A \times A) \cap (S \cap S^{-1})$. Hence $Ft(A) \in Ft\text{-}RFL\text{-}RECIP(S)$.

It is easy to show, using proposition 7, that functions *Ft-RFL-RECIP*, *Ft-EA*, *Ft-EA$_Q$*, *MOST-EA*, *N-EA(R)*, *NEG-N-EA* and *AT-EA* do not satisfy **HAI**. Concerning *AT-EA* observe that only $Ft(E)$ belongs to $AT\text{-}EA(E \times E)$ and thus, given proposition 7, *AT-EA* does not satisfy **HAI**. We prove now only that the function *Ft-RFL-RECIP* does not satisfy **HAI**. Given its definition in (20) we can see that for $C \subseteq E$ arbitrary, for any C_1 such that $C \subseteq C_1$ we have $Ft(C_1) \notin Ft\text{-}RFL\text{-}RECIP(E \times C)$ and for any $C_2 \subseteq C$ we have $Ft(C_2) \in Ft\text{-}RFL\text{-}RECIP(E \times C)$. Hence, given proposition 7, *Ft-RFL-RECIP* does not satisfy **HAI**.

Let us see now some examples of functions satisfying **HAI** and, possibly, not satisfying **HPI**. To show that a type $\langle 2 : \langle 1 \rangle \rangle$ function does not satisfy **HPI** the following proposition can be used:

Proposition 8. *Let F be a type $\langle 2 : \langle 1 \rangle \rangle$ function which satisfies **HPI** and let $C \cap A = \emptyset$, $C \cap B = \emptyset$, and Q be a natural quantifier such that $SLi(Q, C)$. Then $Q \in F(A \times X)$ iff $Q \in F(B \times Y)$, for any $X, Y \subseteq E$.*

Functions satisfying **HAI** are related to the semantics of GDets like *the same* or *different* (Zuber 2011a). Since such GDets denote type $\langle 1, 2 : \langle 1 \rangle \rangle$ functions, we need, strictly speaking a generalisation of **D1AI** (and not just **HAI**). It is given in the following definition:

Definition 12. *A type* $\langle 1, 2 : \langle 1 \rangle \rangle$ *function* F *satisfies* **D1HAI** *(higher order argument invariance for unary determiners) iff for any natural type* $\langle 1 \rangle$ *quantifiers* Q_1 *and* Q_2 *with the same polarity, any* $A, B \subseteq E$, *any binary relation* R, *if* $SLi(Q_1, A)$, $SLi(Q_2, B)$ *and* $\forall_{a \in A} \forall_{b \in B}(aR \cap X = bR \cap X)$ *then* $Q_1 \in F(X, R)$ *iff* $Q_2 \in F(X, R)$.

Given a type $\langle 1, 2 : \langle 1 \rangle \rangle$ function G we can obtain from it a class F_C of type $\langle 2 : \langle 1 \rangle \rangle$ functions $F_C(R) = G(C, R)$. Thus, for simplicity, in the examples to be discussed we fix the set argument and consider the denotation of GNPs like *the same CN* and not the denotation of just *the same*. The functions we will discuss will contain only a specific class of quantifiers in their input. Consider (31):

(31)   Leo and Lea/all students read the same books.

What (31) says is that there is a set of books such that all books from this set were read by Leo and Lea (or all students) and all remaining books are among the books not read by Leo or Lea (or any student). This leads to the function $Ft\text{-}SAME_C$ in (32a) and its equivalent definition in (32b):

(32)   a. $Ft\text{-}SAME_C(R) = \{Q : \exists_{C_1 \subseteq C} \exists_{A \subseteq E}(|A| \geq 2 \wedge C_1 \subseteq Ft(A)R) \wedge (C \cap C'_1) \subseteq Ft(A)R' \wedge Q = Ft(A)\}$

   b. $Ft\text{-}SAME_C(R) = \{Q : \exists_{A \subseteq E}(|A| \geq 2 \wedge Ft(A)R \cap C = Ft(A)^d R \cap C \wedge Q = Ft(A)\}$

To interpret sentences like (33) we may use the function in (34) and to interpret sentences like (35) we may use the function in (36):

(33)   Most students read the same books.

(34) $MOST\text{-}SAME_C(R) = \{Q : \exists_{A,B \subseteq E}(B \subseteq A) \wedge B = Wt(MOST(A), A) \wedge Ft(B) \in Ft\text{-}SAME_C(R) \wedge Q = MOST(A)\}$.

(35)   Seven students read the same books.

(36) $N\text{-}SAME_C(R) = \{Q : \exists_{n \in N} \exists_{A \subseteq E} \exists_{B \subseteq A}(|B| \geq 2 \wedge Ft(B) \in Ft\text{-}SAME_C(R) \wedge Q = n(A)\}$, where $n(A)$ is a type $\langle 1 \rangle$ quantifier such that $n(A)(Y) = 1$ iff $|A \cap Y| \geq n$.

In (37) we have a function whose output contains normal non positive quantifiers and which can be used to interpret sentences like (38):

(37) $NEG\text{-}N\text{-}SAME_C(R) = \{Q : \exists_{n \in N} \exists_{A \subseteq E}(n(A) \notin N\text{-}SAME_C(R) \wedge Q = \neg n(A)\}$

(38)   No three students read the same books.

It is easy, though tedious, to show that functions $Ft\text{-}SAME_C$, $MOST\text{-}SAME_C$, $N\text{-}SAME_C$ and $NEG\text{-}N\text{-}SAME_C$ satisfy **HAI**. Thus function $Ft\text{-}SAME_C$ satisfies **HAI** because if $\forall_{a \in A} \forall_{b \in B}(aR = bR)$ then $Ft(A)R = Ft(B)R$

and $Ft(A)^d R = Ft(B)^d R$. Concerning other functions we observe that they are defined with the help of $Ft\text{-}SAME_C$ in the way that satisfaction of **HAI** by $Ft\text{-}SAME_C$ is a sufficient condition for other functions to satisfy **HAI**.

Importantly, in addition, at least some of the above functions do not satisfy **HPI**. As an illustration I show, using proposition 8, that the type $\langle 2 : \langle 1 \rangle \rangle$ function $Ft\text{-}SAME_C$ does not satisfy **HPI**. Suppose that for some $A, D \subseteq E$, where $A \neq \emptyset$ and $D \neq E$ we have: $D \cap A = \emptyset$. One can check that $Ft(D) \in Ft\text{-}SAME_C(A \times D)$ and $Ft(D) \notin Ft\text{-}SAME_C(B \times E)$. But this means, given Proposition 8, that $Ft\text{-}SAME_C$ does not satisfy **HPI**.

Interestingly not all GNPs with *the same* are interpreted by "genuine" higher order argument invariant functions. Consider for instance (39). The GNP *the same five books* is interpreted by an instance of the function given in (40):

(39)   Leo and Lea read the same five books.

(40) $Ft\text{-}SAME_{n,C}(R) = \{Q : \exists_{A \subseteq E} \exists_{C_1 \subseteq C}(C_1 \subseteq Ft(A)R) \wedge |C_1| = n \wedge Q = Ft(A)\}$

The function $Ft\text{-}SAME_{n,C}$ is not a genuine higher order argument invariant function since it satisfies the stronger **HEC** condition. This observation leads to the question of what happens when two CNPs of different status are "mixed" (as in *each other and the same students*). This question deserves separate treatment.

4   Conclusion

The research presented in this paper concerns to general questions related to the problem of the expressive power of NLs. It is well-known (Keenan 2007, Zuber 2010) that the existence of anaphors and anaphoric determiners in NLs shows that the expressive power of natural languages would be less than it is if the only noun phrases we need were those interpretable as subjects of main clause intransitive verbs. The reason is that anaphors like *himself, herself* must be interpreted by functions from relations to sets which lie outside the class of generalised quantifiers as classically defined. Similarly some comparative constructions used in object positions cannot be interpreted by extended generalised quantifiers and their existence also extends the expressive power of natural languages (Zuber 2011b). The results presented in this paper provide a formal basis which can be used to show that the existence of higher order anaphors and comparatives even further extends the expressive power of NLs. However, functions denoted by such higher order anaphors and comparatives obey constraints similar to those interpreting simple anaphors and comparatives since the former are natural generalisations of the latter. These generalisations have been spelled out in some detail. They should be completed by additional empirical and, possibly, cross-linguistic research, which will make it possible to choose among proposals made here and provide more justification for them. In particular more research is required on the important problem of the plurality of subject NPs of sentences with GNPs, which has been left out of consideration here.

References

Barwise, J., Cooper, R.: Generalised quantifiers and natural language. Linguistics and Philosophy 4, 159–219 (1981)

Keenan, E.L.: Semantic Case Theory. In: Groenendijk, J., Stokhof, M. (eds.) Proc. of the Sixth Amsterdam Colloquium (1987)

Keenan, E.L.: On the denotations of anaphors. Research on Language and Computation, 5-1-5-17 (2007)

Keenan, E. L.: In Situ Interpretation without Type Mismatches. Forthcoming in A. Bianchi, (ed.) On Referring, OUP 2014 (2014)

Keenan, E.L., Westerståhl, D.: Generalized Quantifiers in Linguistics and Logic. In: van Benthem, J., ter Meulen, A. (eds.) Handbook of Logic and Language, pp. 837–893. Elsevier, Amsterdam (1997)

Zuber, R.: Semantic Constraints on Anaphoric Determiners. Research on Language and Computation 8, 255–271 (2010)

Zuber, R.: Generalised Quantifiers and the Semantics of the same. In: Ashton, N., et al. (eds.) Proceedings of SALT 21, e-Language, pp. 515–531 (2011a)

Zuber, R.: Some Generalised Comparative Determiners. In: Pogodalla, S., Prost, J.-P. (eds.) LACL 2011. LNCS, vol. 6736, pp. 267–281. Springer, Heidelberg (2011)

Zuber, R.: Some higher order functions on binary relations. In: Morrill, G., Nederhof, M.-J. (eds.) FG 2012/2013. LNCS, vol. 8036, pp. 277–291. Springer, Heidelberg (2013)

Formal Semantics in Modern Type Theories: Is It Model-Theoretic, Proof-Theoretic, or Both?

Zhaohui Luo*

Department of Computer Science
Royal Holloway, University of London
zhaohui.luo@hotmail.co.uk

Abstract. In this talk, we contend that, for NLs, the divide between model-theoretic semantics and proof-theoretic semantics has not been well-understood. In particular, the formal semantics based on modern type theories (MTTs) may be seen as *both* model-theoretic and proof-theoretic. To be more precise, it may be seen both ways in the sense that the NL semantics can first be *represented* in an MTT in a model-theoretic way and then the semantic representations can be understood *inferentially* in a proof-theoretic way. Considered in this way, MTTs arguably have unique advantages when employed for formal semantics.

1 Introduction

In logic, there are two well-developed traditions of semantic theories: model-theoretic semantics and proof-theoretic semantics. The former has been developed in Tarski's tradition while the latter by the logicians Gentzen and Prawitz and the philosopher Dummett among others (see, for example, [17]).

In formal semantics of NLs, the model-theoretic tradition has been dominant since the seminal work by Montague, a student of Tarski, who has used Church's simple type theory as an intermediate logical language for model-theoretic semantics [27]. The proof-theoretic semantics for NLs, however, has not been well developed, although there is recent work by Francez and colleagues in that direction (see, for example, [13,14]).[1]

We contend that, for formal semantics of NLs, the divide between model-theoretic semantics and proof-theoretic semantics has not been well-understood and may have been over-exaggerated. In fact, the formal semantics in modern type theories (MTT-semantics, for short) [32,22] may be seen as *both* model-theoretic and proof-theoretic. To be more precise, it may be seen both ways in

---

* This work is partially supported by the research grant F/07-537/AJ of the Leverhulme Trust in U.K.

[1] In philosophy, different kinds of philosophical semantics have been proposed, including the conceptual role semantics such as semantic inferentialism that has been advocated by Brandom [4,5] and others. Note that such philosophical semantic studies have rather different assumptions and more ambitious objectives as compared to formal semantics, although they have interesting influences on the latter.

N. Asher and S. Soloviev (Eds.): LACL 2014, LNCS 8535, pp. 177–188, 2014.
© Springer-Verlag Berlin Heidelberg 2014

the following sense: the NL semantics can first be *represented* in an MTT in a model-theoretic way and then the semantic representations can be understood *inferentially* in a proof-theoretic way.

The MTT-semantics is in the tradition of the Montague semantics [27] from which, however, it has a key difference which may be summarised as follows:

- In the Montague semantics, the meanings are given in the set-theoretical models of the simple type theory, which acts as the intermediate logical language for model-theoretic semantics.
- In the MTT-semantics, the meanings are given in the language MTT itself, not in the 'models' of the MTT.

Put in another way, in an MTT-semantics, the MTT is not acting as an intermediate language, but rather as the meaning-carrying language itself.[2] On the one hand, the MTT-semantics may be seen as model-theoretic because, in such semantics, an MTT is employed as a *representational* language and it can do so because of its rich representational structure[3] as well as its internal logic. On the other hand, the MTT-semantics may be seen as proof-theoretic because the meanings of MTT-judgements can be understood by means of their *inferential roles* according to the meaning theories such as that developed by Martin-Löf for his type theory [25,28].

Besides this main theme, some related technical developments are to be reported. We describe a method of representing situations (incomplete possible worlds), which may be infinite or involve more sophisticated phenomena, by means of finite contexts in type theory with manifest entries (c.f., the study of manifest fields in [20]) and/or subtyping entries (c.f., the study of coercion contexts and local coercions in [22,23]) as well as the usual membership entries. The extension with such contextual entries has nice meta-theoretic properties.

Extending a brief argument in §1.2.3 of [18], in agreement with Dummett [12], I shall argue that a proof-theoretic semantics of MTTs should take *both* aspects of inferential use (verification and consequential application) seriously and that this applies to the understanding of judgements and type constructors in MTTs.

In this talk, after giving a summary of the MTT-semantics,[4] I shall elaborate the above theme and point out that, if we accept such views, MTTs may have some unique advantages when employed for formal semantics of NLs.

---

[2] It could be possible for one to consider an MTT as an intermediate language for model-theoretic semantics, although this view is not usually taken and it might be difficult as well. See §4 for a brief discussion in this respect.

[3] To see that MTTs provide rich representational structures, one may compare the notion of type with that of set and the notion of an MTT context with that of situations or incomplete possible worlds. These will be elaborated below in §2.

[4] The summary is omitted in the current paper (but see §2.1). For its references, see [32,22,21,9] among others.

2   Model-Theoretic Characteristics of MTT-Semantics

A modern type theory (MTT) has a rich type structure, much richer than the simple arrow types as found in the Montagovian setting.[5] The richness of type structures in an MTT allows it to be used as a *representational* language for formal semantics. Besides logical propositions (i.e., types that are understood as propositions), it contains many *types* which are employed for various useful representational purposes in constructing a formal semantics. These types include those interpreting (to mention a few examples) logical operations, common nouns, adjectival modifications, adverbial modifications, coordination, and also more advanced features such as subtyping, copredication and linguistic coercions.

In an MTT, the notion of *judgement* is the most basic. A typical form of judgement is:

$$\Gamma \vdash a : A,$$

which intuitively says that 'object a is of type A in context Γ', where a context, in its traditional form,[6] is a finite sequence of variable-type pairs of the form

$$x_1 : A_1, \ x_2 : A[x_1], \ ..., \ x_n : A_n[x_1, ..., x_{n-1}],$$

by which we assume that x_i be of type $A_i[x_1, ..., x_{i-1}]$ in which the 'previous' $x_1, ..., x_{i-1}$ may occur $(i = 1, ..., n)$.

Employing MTTs for formal semantics, the following two points are worth being made explicit:

1. The types in MTTs can be used to represent collections of objects (or just called sets, informally) in a model-theoretic sense, although they are syntactic entities in MTTs.
2. The contexts in MTTs can be used to represent situations or (incomplete) possible worlds.

In this section, we shall illustrate these two points. First, in §2.1, we briefly describe how various type constructors in MTTs can be used in representing linguistic features in formal semantics. We then, in §2.2, give a simple example to explain how MTT contexts can be used to represent situations and, in §2.3, show how more sophisticated situations like infinite ones can be represented in

---

[5] Technically, MTTs may be classified into predicative type theories such as Martin-Löfs type theory [25,28] and impredicative type theories such as the calculus of constructions (CC) [11] and the unifying theory of dependent types (UTT) [18]. In computer science, MTTs have been implemented in the proof assistants such as Coq [10] which has been used to implement the MTT-semantics and conduct experiments in Natural Language Inference [9]. In this paper, the type theory UTT [18] is used when concrete examples are given.

[6] We shall later in the paper extend the notion of context with manifest entries and subtyping entries.

finite contexts by means of manifest entries (c.f., manifest fields in [20]) and subtyping entries (c.f., the study of coercion contexts and local coercions in [22,23]).[7]

2.1 Types as Sets: Examples

The rich type structure in MTTs provides adequate and useful tools for semanticists to construct formal semantics. Here, we only mention several examples without going into their details, because most of them have been explained in details in other places, and the appropriate references are given in each case.

1. Dependent sum types (Σ-types $\Sigma(A, B)$ which have product types $A \times B$ as special cases).
   - For example, Σ-types have been used to interpret adjectival modifications when the adjectives are intersective and subsective [32,8]. Note that subtyping is essential for such Σ-type interpretations to be adequate [22].[8]
2. Dependent product types (Π-types $\Pi(A, B)$, which have arrow-types $A \to B$ as special cases). These are basic dependent types that, together with universes (see below), provide polymorphism among other things.
   - For instance, verb modifying adverbs are typed by means of dependent Π-types (together with the universe CN of common nouns) [22,6].
3. Disjoint union types ($A + B$).
   - For instance, disjoint union types have been proposed to give interpretations of privative adjectives [8].
4. Universes. These are types of types, very useful since they make it possible to treat various collections of types as internal totalities. Typical examples of universes in MTT-semantics include, among others,
   - *Prop*, the universe of logical propositions, as found in impredicative type theories such as CC and UTT;
   - CN, the universe of (the interpretations of) common nouns [22]; and
   - *LType*, the universe of 'linguistic types', introduced in studying coordination [7].
5. Dot-types ($A \bullet B$). These are special types introduced to study the linguistic phenomena of copredication [22]. It is always worth mentioning that coercive subtyping is essentially employed in the formulation of the dot-types.

---

[7] It is worth remarking that, formally, the studies in [20] and [22,23] are technically more complex in both cases: we studied manifest fields (not just manifest contextual entries) in [20] and local coercions (not just subtyping contexts) in [22,23]. In this paper, when we only consider such entries in signatures (see the brief formal treatment of the extension at the end of §2.3), it is formally simpler.

[8] See §3.3 of [32] for a very interesting discussion of the problem of 'multiple categorisation of verbs'. A satisfactory solution is an adequate subtyping mechanism for MTTs, provided by the framework of coercive subtyping [19,24].

Besides the above, I should also emphasise that *subtyping* is crucial for an MTT to be a viable language for formal semantics. Furthermore, also very importantly, subtyping is needed when considering many linguistic features such as copredication [1,31]. However, introducing subtyping into a Montagovian semantics has proven difficult, if not impossible. Coercive subtyping in MTTs solves this problem – it not only provides a satisfactory solution to the copredication problem [22] but a useful way to formalise various linguistic coercions [2].

2.2 Situations Represented as Contexts: A Simple Example

Here, we present a small example to show that how an MTT can be used as a representational language. Situations,[9] or incomplete possible worlds, can be represented in MTTs as *contexts*. This was first studied by Ranta in [32]. Our example is simple; for instance, the domain of the situation in the example is finite. This will serve as a basis for our discussions on how more sophisticated situations such as those involving infinity or other special circumstances should be represented in §2.3, where we will show how manifest entries and subtyping entries can be used for such purposes.

Example 1. The example, taken from Chapter 10 of [33], is about an (imagined) situation in the Cavern Club at Liverpool in 1962 where the Beatles were rehearsing for a performance. This situation can be represented as follows.

1. The domain of the situation consists of several peoples including the Beatles (John, Paul, George and Ringo), their manager (Brian) and a fan (Bob). In type theory, this can be represented be means of the following context Γ_1:

   $$\Gamma_1 \equiv D : Type,$$
   $$John : D, \ Paul : D, \ George : D, \ Ringo : D, \ Brian : D, \ Bob : D$$

2. The assignment function which, for example, assigns predicate symbols such as B and G to the propositional functions expressing 'was a Beatle' and 'played guitar', respectively. We can introduce the following in our context to represent such an assignment function:

   $$\Gamma_2 \equiv B : D \rightarrow Prop, \ b_J : B(John), \ ..., \ b_B : \neg B(Brian), \ b'_B : \neg B(Bob),$$
   $$G : D \rightarrow Prop, \ g_J : G(John), \ ..., \ g_G : \neg G(Ringo), \ ...$$

   There are other predicate symbols as well: for example, there may be M being assigned the propositional function expressing 'was a manager', etc. We omit them here.

Eventually, we obtain a context $\Gamma \equiv \Gamma_1, \ \Gamma_2, \ ..., \ \Gamma_n$ that represents the situation. We shall then have, for instance,[10]

$$\Gamma \vdash G(John) \ true \ and \ \Gamma \vdash \neg B(Bob) \ true.$$

---

[9] Here, of course, we use the notion of situation informally, not in the formal sense in Situation Semantics [3].

[10] A judgement $\Gamma \vdash A \ true$ means that $\Gamma \vdash a : A$ for some a.

where $G(John)$ and $B(Bob)$ are the semantic interpretations of John played Guitar and Bob was a Beatle, respectively.

As we see from the above example, contexts in an MTT can be employed to represent situations model-theoretically and, in this endeavour, type theory is used as a meaning-carrying language (like set theory) rather than a language to be further interpreted.

2.3   Representing More Sophisticated Situations: Manifest and Subtyping Entries

The above example of situation is extremely simple: in particular, its domain D is finite. In general, one usually considers more sophisticated situations in which, for example, the domain is infinite or there are some other more sophisticated phenomena. In such cases, only using the traditional notion of context, which has only membership entries of the form $x : A$, is not enough. Here we consider two extensions to the notion of context:

1. *Manifest entries* of the form $x \sim a : A$, where $a : A$.[11]
2. *Subtyping entries* of the form $c : A < B$, where c is a functional operation from A to B.

They will provide extra powers in representing situations as contexts.

Manifest Entries in Contexts. A *manifest entry* in a context is of the form

$$x \sim a : A, \tag{1}$$

Informally, it assumes that x behave exactly the same as a of type A. Put in another way, in any place that we could use an object of type A, we could use x which actually plays the role of a. Formally, the above manifest entry (1) is an abbreviation of the following entry:

$$x : 1_A(a),$$

where $1_A(a)$ is the inductive unit type parameterised by $A : Type$ and $a : A$, whose only object is $*_A(a)$.[12] We have the following derivable formation rule for manifest contextual entries:

$$\frac{\Gamma \vdash a : A}{\Gamma, \, x \sim a : A \; valid} \quad (x \notin FV(\Gamma))$$

---

[11] Manifest entries are different from the definitional entries of the form $x = a : A$ in proof assistants – the former is just a notational abbreviation in the framework of coercive subtyping (see below), while the latter involves real extensions whose metatheory has proved to be not easy. For a study of the latter for Pure Type Systems, see [34].

[12] We omit the formal definition of $1_A(a)$ here; see, for example, [20] for its formal details.

Using manifest entries, we can not only simplify contextual representations (the following Example 2) but represent infinite or other sophisticated situations by means of the finite contexts in type theory.

Example 2. With manifest entries, the situation in Example 1 can be represented as the following context:

$$D \sim a_D : Type, \ B \sim a_B : D \rightarrow Prop, \ ... \tag{2}$$

where

- $a_D = \{John, \ Paul, \ George, \ Ringo, \ Brian, \ Bob\}$ is the finite type (not the finite set) consisting of *John* etc.
- $a_B : D \rightarrow Prop$, the predicate 'was a Beatle', is an inductively defined function such that $a_B(John) = a_B(Paul) = a_B(George) = a_B(Ringo) = True$ and $a_B(Brian) = a_B(Bob) = False$.

In other words, Γ_1 and Γ_2 in Example 1 are now expressed by the first two entries in (2), respectively.

Also, the domain in the situation in Example 1 is finite and, therefore, we can use the finitely many membership entries as in Example 1 to represent it. However, sometimes we have to deal with infinite domains. For instance, it is not difficult to imagine a situation where domain D consists of infinitely many things that we may represent by the natural numbers and some predicates are represented as propositional functions such as f over D. In such a case, we can use manifest entries like

$$D \sim Nat : Type, \ f \sim \text{f-defn} : D \rightarrow Prop$$

to introduce the infinite domain D and the infinite propositional function f, where f-defn can be defined inductively (in this case by inductive definition over the inductive type Nat).

Subtyping Entries in Contexts. Another useful form of contextual entries is the subtyping entries, for coercive subtyping, which are called coercion contexts in [22,23]. Formally, a subtyping entry is of the following form:

$$c : A < B,$$

where A and B are types and c is a functional operation from A to B. In a context with such an entry, A is a subtype of B via. coercion c.

Subtyping plays an essential role in MTT-semantics. It is not difficult to see that subtyping contextual entries are very useful in representing situations as contexts. As a simple example, one may introduce a subtyping entry to assume that everything in the domain D in Example 2 is a human: $D < Human$.

Subtyping entries are useful for some sophisticated circumstances as well. For instance,[13] one may imagine a situation (e.g., in the snake exhibition of a zoo) where every animal is a snake and such a situation may be represented by a context with a subtyping entry expressing $Animal < Snake$. One may regard this as a rather unusual contextual entry, although it describes the situation faithfully.[14]

Formal Treatment of the Contextual Extensions. The above extension of the notion of contexts with manifest and subtyping entries can formally be considered by introducing the notion of *signature*. Informally, signatures can be used to represent situations in formal semantics. Formally, we consider the following forms of judgements:

$$\Gamma \vdash_\Sigma J \tag{3}$$

where Γ is a context in the traditional sense (a sequence of membership entries of the form $x : A$), J is one of $a : A$, $a = b : A$, A *type* or $A = B$ *type*, and Σ is a signature, a sequence of entries of one of the following forms:

1. $x : A$ (usual membership entries)
2. $x \sim a : A$ (manifest entries)
3. $c : A < B$ (subtyping entries)

What is new here is signatures, which could formally be regarded just as initial contextual segments whose entries will never be abstracted to the right of the $\vdash$-sign. In other words, the judgement (3) could be treated as Σ, $\Gamma \vdash J$ except that the entries in Σ cannot be abstracted.[15]

Since manifest entries of the form $x \sim a : A$ are just abbreviations of membership entries of the form $x : 1_A(a)$, it is straightforward to see that the extended type theory preserves the nice properties of the original type system as long as the signatures concerned are coherent[16]. For instance, if Σ is coherent and $\Gamma \vdash_\Sigma a : A$, then all of the terms a, A, and those in Γ and Σ are strongly normalising (and, as a consequence among many others, the embedded logic is logically consistent).

3   Proof-Theoretic Characteristics of MTT-Semantics

Besides model-theoretic semantics, there is another kind of formal semantics: *proof-theoretic semantics*. Proof-theoretic semantics was pioneered by Gentzen [15], developed by Prawitz [29,30] and Martin-Löf [25,26] (among other logicians) to study meaning theories of logical systems, and studied by Dummett [12]

---

[13] Thanks to Nicholas Asher for this example (in a private communication).

[14] One may use a manifest entry to describe a similar situation. For instance, one may introduce a type Animal-at-Snake-Exhibition and use a manifest entry to define it to be *Snake*.

[15] This is similar to the treatment of signatures in Edinburgh LF [16].

[16] Let Σ be a well-formed signature. Then, Σ is *coherent* if $\Gamma \vdash_\Sigma A <_c B$ and $\Gamma \vdash_\Sigma A <_{c'} B$ imply $\Gamma \vdash_\Sigma c = c' : (A)B$. We do not get into the formal details here.

and Brandom [4,5] (among other philosophers) to study general philosophical theories of meaning of NLs. Proof-theoretic semantics is a form of inferential semantics in that it not only takes inference seriously but regards it as the central concept of meaning theories and such a direct link to inference is regarded as a key advantage of proof-theoretic semantics.[17]

3.1   Proof-Theoretic Semantics of MTTs

The MTT-semantics does not only have model-theoretic characteristics, as studied in the above section, but proof-theoretic characteristics. This is because that the meanings of judgements, which are the basic sentences in MTTs, can be understood in a proof-theoretic meaning theory. Martin-Löf has carried out a whole programme of proof-theoretic semantics, studying and developing it for his type theory [25,26].[18] Therefore, once MTT-semantics has been constructed, the statements in the semantics (i.e., judgement in the MTT) can be understood proof-theoretically.

Studying proof-theoretic meaning theories, people have considered two aspects of use: verification and consequential application. For MTTs, the first aspect is to consider how a judgement can be correctly asserted while the other (second) aspect is to consider what consequences it has to accept that a judgement is correct. The verificationist thinks that the first aspect of verification is the (possibly only) central conceptual focus in meaning theories while the pragmatist thinks that the second aspect of consequential application is instead central. For example, under the verificationist view on meaning explanations for type theory, one may consider such a meaning explanation of the judgement $a : A$ (I omit the context Γ here): it can correctly asserted if a computes to a canonical object of type A.

Personally, I take the view that *both* aspects of use are essential for a meaning theory of MTTs. This point of view is in agreement with Dummett [12] (if I read him correctly) and was briefly discussed in §1.2.3 of [18].[19] More concretely, this view says that the meanings of the type constructors are given by both of their introduction and elimination rules. Accordingly, the meanings of MTT-constructs and, in particular, the MTT-judgements, are given proof-theoretically (or inferentially, in more general terms). When the type constructors and judgements are employed in formal semantics, such proof-theoretic meanings can be taken as the basis of the semantics.

---

[17] There are philosophical arguments that conceptual role semantics (eg, proof-theoretic semantics) supports the view in cognitive science that something is meaningful just because that it plays a certain role (eg, inferential role) in a person's psychology. I ignore this because here proof-theoretic semantics is considered as an approach to formal semantics.

[18] But see Conclusion for the remarks on future work on meaning theories on MTTs in general and some existing problems (for example, about meaning explanations of hypothetical judgements).

[19] A reason for taking this view is that an MTT is much more sophisticated than first-order logical operators. However, I cannot detail its arguments in this paper.

$$
\begin{array}{ll}
(eI) & \dfrac{\Gamma,\ j\ \text{isa}\ X \vdash S[j]}{\Gamma \vdash S[\text{every}\ X]} \quad (j\ \textit{fresh}) \\[3ex]
(eE) & \dfrac{\Gamma \vdash S[\text{every}\ X] \quad \Gamma \vdash j\ \text{isa}\ X \quad \Gamma,\ S[j] \vdash S'}{\Gamma \vdash S'} \\[3ex]
(sI) & \dfrac{\Gamma \vdash j\ \text{isa}\ X \quad \Gamma \vdash S[j]}{\Gamma \vdash S[\text{some}\ X]} \\[3ex]
(sE) & \dfrac{\Gamma \vdash S[\text{some}\ X] \quad \Gamma,\ j\ \text{isa}\ X,\ S[j] \vdash S'}{\Gamma \vdash S'} \quad (j\ \textit{fresh})
\end{array}
$$

Fig. 1. The PTS-rules for a basic language in [13]

3.2 Francez's Proof-Theoretic Semantics

In the literature, there have been some, but not many, researches on proof-theoretic semantics of NLs. The most notable is the recent work by Francez and his colleagues in a series of papers (see [13,14] among others). What I shall do here is to embed the basic rules of Francez's proof-theoretic semantics in [13] into the MTT-semantics and show that they are actually derivable or admissible.[20]

For instance, consider the rules of Figure 1 in [13], repeated here in our Figure 1 (we omit the structural rules and its treatment of scope here, which is irrelevant to our point and can be restored if needed). Employing the following 'translation' $[\![\_]\!]$, it is easy to see that the rules in Figure 1 are all derivable or admissible in the MTT semantics:

- The syntactic isa corresponds to the colon sign (:) in type theory. Thus, for example, $[\![j\ \text{isa}\ X]\!] = j : [\![X]\!]$.
- $[\![\text{every}\ X]\!] = \forall([\![X]\!])$ of type $([\![X]\!])Prop$. For instance, the sentence (4) is interpreted as (5) after translation.

  (4) Every man walks.

  (5) $\forall([\![man]\!], [\![walk]\!])$

- $[\![\text{some}\ X]\!] = \exists([\![X]\!])$ of type $([\![X]\!])Prop$. (Example omitted.)

For instance, the rule (eI) becomes

$$
(eI') \qquad \dfrac{[\![\Gamma]\!],\ j : [\![X]\!] \vdash [\![S[j]]\!]}{[\![\Gamma]\!] \vdash [\![S[\forall(X)]]\!]}
$$

which is admissible according to $\forall$-introduction. (Note: the condition that j is fresh is now embodied in the well-formedness of $[\![\Gamma]\!],\ j : [\![X]\!]$.)

---

[20] I cannot make serious comparisons here and further work is needed to compare these two approaches in a more exact way.

4   Concluding Remarks

In this talk, I have argued that the MTT-semantics may be seen as both model-theoretic and proof-theoretic, with situations represented as contexts and judgements understood inferentially.

There are several interesting directions for future work, either proof theoretically or model theoretically. Proof theoretically, it is important to develop further the meaning theories of modern type theories in general. For instance, it is interesting to study and obtain a better meaning explanation of an impredicative universe like that found in UTT. Even just for predicative type theories like that of Martin-Löf, people may argue that it is still unclear how hypothetical judgements should be explained satisfactorily. Further studies are called for.

As remarked in Footnote 2, one might consider the model theory of MTTs, thinking of which as intermediate languages to be further interpreted when used for formal semantics. However, it is unclear whether such an approach can be successful, partly because that there is no such a general notion of models of MTTs as yet, although some initial work on models of generalised algebraic theories have been done. Substantial work is needed to get this clarified and developed.

References

1. Asher, N.: Lexical Meaning in Context: a Web of Words. Cambridge University Press (2012)
2. Asher, N., Luo, Z.: Formalisation of coercions in lexical semantics. Sinn und Bedeutung 17, Paris (2012)
3. Barwise, J., Perry, J.: Situations and Attitudes. MIT Press (1983)
4. Brandom, R.: Making It Explicit: Reasoning, Representing, and Discursive Commitment. Harvard University Press (1994)
5. Brandom, R.: Articulating Reasons: an Introduction to Inferentialism. Harvard University Press (2000)
6. Chatzikyriakidis, S.: Adverbs in a modern type theory. In: Asher, N., Soloviev, S. (eds.) LACL 2014. LNCS, vol. 8535, pp. 44–56. Springer, Heidelberg (2014)
7. Chatzikyriakidis, S., Luo, Z.: An account of natural language coordination in type theory with coercive subtyping. In: Duchier, D., Parmentier, Y. (eds.) CSLP 2012. LNCS, vol. 8114, pp. 31–51. Springer, Heidelberg (2013)
8. Chatzikyriakidis, S., Luo, Z.: Adjectives in a modern type-theoretical setting. In: Morrill, G., Nederhof, M.-J. (eds.) Formal Grammar 2012 and 2013. LNCS, vol. 8036, pp. 159–174. Springer, Heidelberg (2013)
9. Chatzikyriakidis, S., Luo, Z.: Natural language reasoning using proof-assistant technology: Rich typing and beyond. In: EACL Workshop on Type Theory and Natural Language Semantics, Goteborg (2014)
10. The Coq Development Team. The Coq Proof Assistant Reference Manual (Version 8.1), INRIA (2007)
11. Coquand, T., Huet, G.: The calculus of constructions. Information and Computation 76(2/3) (1988)
12. Dummett, M.: The Logical Basis of Metaphysics. Duckworth (1991)

13. Francez, N., Dyckhoff, R.: Proof-theoretic semantics for a natural language fragment. Linguistics and Philosophy 33(6) (2011)
14. Francez, N., Dyckhoff, R., Ben-Avi, G.: Proof-theoretic semantics for subsentential phrases. Studia Logica 94 (2010)
15. Gentzen, G.: Untersuchungen über das logische schliessen. Mathematische Zeitschrift 39 (1934)
16. Harper, R., Honsell, F., Plotkin, G.: A framework for defining logics. Journal of the Association for Computing Machinery 40(1), 143–184 (1993)
17. Kahle, R., Schroeder-Heister, P. (eds.): Proof-Theoretic Semantics. Special Issue of Synthese 148(3) (2006)
18. Luo, Z.: Computation and Reasoning: A Type Theory for Computer Science. Oxford University Press (1994)
19. Luo, Z.: Coercive subtyping. Journal of Logic and Computation 9(1), 105–130 (1999)
20. Luo, Z.: Manifest fields and module mechanisms in intensional type theory. In: Berardi, S., Damiani, F., de'Liguoro, U. (eds.) TYPES 2008. LNCS, vol. 5497, pp. 237–255. Springer, Heidelberg (2009)
21. Luo, Z.: Common nouns as types. In: Béchet, D., Dikovsky, A. (eds.) LACL 2012. LNCS, vol. 7351, pp. 173–185. Springer, Heidelberg (2012)
22. Luo, Z.: Formal semantics in modern type theories with coercive subtyping. Linguistics and Philosophy 35(6), 491–513 (2012)
23. Luo, Z., Part, F.: Subtyping in type theory: Coercion contexts and local coercions (extended abstract). In: TYPES 2013, Toulouse (2013)
24. Luo, Z., Soloviev, S., Xue, T.: Coercive subtyping: theory and implementation. Information and Computation 223, 18–42 (2012)
25. Martin-Löf, P.: Intuitionistic Type Theory. Bibliopolis (1984)
26. Martin-Löf, P.: On the meanings of the logical constants and the justifications of the logical laws. Nordic Journal of Philosophical Logic 1(1) (1996)
27. Montague, R.: Formal Philosophy. Yale University Press (1974); Collected papers Thomason, R (ed.)
28. Nordström, B., Petersson, K., Smith, J.: Programming in Martin-Löf's Type Theory: An Introduction. Oxford University Press (1990)
29. Prawitz, D.: Towards a foundation of a general proof theory. In: Suppes, P., et al. (eds.) Logic, Methodology, and Phylosophy of Science IV (1973)
30. Prawitz, D.: On the idea of a general proof theory. Synthese 27 (1974)
31. Pustejovsky, J.: The Generative Lexicon. MIT Press (1995)
32. Ranta, A.: Type-Theoretical Grammar. Oxford University Press (1994)
33. Saeed, J.: Semantics. Wiley-Blackwell (1997)
34. Severi, P., Poll, E.: Pure type systems with definitions. In: Matiyasevich, Y.V., Nerode, A. (eds.) LFCS 1994. LNCS, vol. 813, pp. 316–328. Springer, Heidelberg (1994)

Author Index